Intentional Revolutions

Intentional Revolutions

A Seven-Point Strategy for Transforming Organizations

Edwin C. Nevis
Joan Lancourt
Helen G. Vassallo

Jossey-Bass Publishers
San Francisco

A Gestalt Institute of Cleveland publication

Substantial discounts on bulk quantities of Jossey-Bass books are available to corporations, professional associations, and other organizations. For details and discount information, contact the special sales department at Jossey-Bass Inc., Publishers. (415) 433–1740; Fax (800) 605–2665.

For sales outside the United States, please contact your local Simon & Schuster International Office.

Jossey-Bass Web address: http://www.josseybass.com

Library of Congress Cataloging-in-Publication Data

Nevis, Edwin C.
    Intentional revolutions : a seven-point strategy for transforming organizations / Edwin C. Nevis, Joan Lancourt, Helen G. Vassallo.
        p. cm. — (Jossey-Bass business & management series)
    Includes bibliographical references and index.
    ISBN 0-7879-0240-3
        1. Organizational change—Management.   2. Strategic planning.
I. Lancourt, Joan   II. Vassallo, Helen G.   III. Title.
IV. Series.
HD58.8.N48   1996
658.4'063—dc20   96-525

FIRST EDITION
HB Printing   10 9 8 7 6 5 4 3 2

Contents

Preface

Intentional Revolutions is about organizational change that requires people to examine and alter the basic assumptions driving and supporting the present state of their organizational life. It is about change that asks people to do things in dramatically new and different ways, as opposed to making small improvements in current practices. In the latter approach, the underlying behavioral model remains basically the same. In the former, a transformation occurs in the organization's fundamental external form and inner nature, calling for a set of entirely new, interdependent behaviors.

The book begins with the realization that there is a growing need in today's world for organizations of all kinds to make multiple discontinuous changes in significant aspects of their being. The requirements for remaining competitive often include sharp breaks with past beliefs and practices. This kind of change is very difficult to bring about.

For one thing, established entities do not easily support internal revolutions against themselves. To make a revolution is to attack values and practices that are valued or cherished or accepted within the prevailing culture. People in leadership positions who sincerely seek change are often the most successful products of the culture they are trying to change. It is not easy for them to see how radical thinking can be helpful, nor can they grasp counterintuitive solutions when their intuitive powers have been an important part of the organization's success in the past. In addition, on a systemic level the factors that have led to success in the past are now embodied in powerful forces that work against significant change. Research into organizational learning has revealed that firms that experience an extended period of good performance are neither prone to question the assumptions under which they have been operating nor good at sensing and assimilating early signs of disconfirming feedback. Their assumptions have become institutionalized and have a tenacious life of their own. Socialization is as powerful as sociologists have been saying it is.

For reasons such as these, we do not think it useful or illuminating to lay blame for the problems of companies such as Digital Equipment and IBM at the feet of their displaced CEOs, Ken Olsen and John Akers. As prisoners in the fortress of their success, they can be seen as fallen heroes in an industrial Greek tragedy rather than as leaders who are simply out of touch with the times. This does not absolve them of responsibility, but it may be more functional to focus on why they were unable to lead their problem-ridden organizations through a successful transformation. This focus leads to the realization that the practice of transformational change is enormously complex and difficult, and that most of us have a lot to learn about it.

Intended Audience

This book is designed to help those who work at the business of change to be more effective in bringing about transformational change. We address senior executives, managers, and others at all organizational levels who take on the role of agent of change. Our perspective is especially directed to professionals who earn a living as interveners or facilitators in programs aimed at achieving new ways of doing things.

Underlying Assumptions

Several critical assumptions underlie our approach. The first is that traditional managerial efforts to implement change that are based on a rational-mechanical model are not adequate to today's task. The implication has been that there is one best way to do things and that management's task is first to find this way and then to get it accepted by others. We propose that a better approach is to think about organizational reality as made up of a range of experiences and meanings, and that there are a number of realities and a number of ways of arriving at workable solutions.

A second major assumption we make is that no single method of influence is sufficient to do the job of transformational change. The typical approach has been to use one or two methods or tools, such as persuasion, coercion, or reengineering, as though these were magic bullets that would solve the problem. In our experience, the enormously difficult and complex task of transformational change is more likely to be successful if it involves simultaneous use of multiple methods of influence.

We have identified seven such methods—persuasive communication, participation, expectancy, role modeling, structural rearrangement, extrinsic rewards, and coercion—each of which is based on a different but complementary theory of human motivation that has been tested over many years. Each method addresses a different aspect of individual, group, or organizational-level behavior. Each assumes a different view of human existence and thus addresses different conceptions of reality. When applied to the problem of transformation in an integrated way, as opposed to being used as single interventions, these methods provide a means for creating what is essentially a new organizational reality. We argue that the success or failure of transformational change can be determined by how well these methods are applied in an integrated, systematic way.

Our approach is supported by Lewinian field theory (1951), by the social constructionist views of Alfred Schutz (1967) and Berger and Luckman (1966), and by the principles of Gestalt psychology, Gestalt therapy, and cognitive psychology. It is philosophically aligned with a phenomenological perspective. Conversely, we also draw from theories of selective reinforcement (the Skinnerian model), social learning theory (à la Bandura and other advocates of behavior modeling), and other behavioral theories. We attempt to integrate these approaches into what we believe is a powerful model for understanding organizational reality and for developing and implementing transformational change.

Background of the Book

The idea for *Intentional Revolutions* grew out of a course on theories of change that was developed by Nevis and taught for some years at the Massachusetts Institute of Technology's Sloan School of Management in the mid 1980s. As a student in this course, Vassallo became intrigued with the utility of the approach and has been using it in her teaching at Worcester Polytechnic Institute and in her consulting work. Lancourt, as part of her work as a member of Digital Equipment Corporation's Organizational Consulting Group, was involved in expanding their understanding of the pragmatic requirements of implementing multiple discontinuous changes. As a sociologist by training, she is versed in the social constructionist perspective and has also published on the use of collective power in bringing about significant change. Nevis and Lancourt became acquainted through consulting work the former was doing at Digital Equipment. The book evolved as the authors collaborated to focus on the problem of how to implement and sustain the multiple levels of complex, interdependent, discontinuous changes that are inherent in the concept of transformation.

Overview of the Contents

Part One begins by discussing the need to create organizations that are continuously and fundamentally adaptive and self-renewing. In our opinion, creating organizations that are capable of this requires a change so significant that one could rightly say that one had created a "new" organization. We have therefore defined the problems of transformation as those involved with the creation of a new organizational reality. We use this definition in an attempt to clarify the important differences between transformation and large-scale change that is not discontinuous or discontinuous change that is not large-scale, neither of which require the creation of a new organizational reality.

In Part One we also identify the phases of transformation and the essential task of resocializing the organizational members so that the new behaviors and structures become internalized as *the* new shared reality. As a crucial first step in the creation of a new reality and as a means of facilitating resocialization, we have reframed resistance to change as the need to manage the multiple realities that already exist in an organization. Failure to focus on multiple realities and on the resocialization process results in the all-too-familiar gradual erosion of the hard-won change.

Part Two deals with the seven methods of influence, which taken together constitute our strategy for resocialization. Each of the first seven chapters in the section explores one of the methods and elaborates its basic assumptions, identifies the skills and conditions for its successful application, and provides examples of its use as well as the problems faced in applying it. The final chapter assesses several successful cases that have used all seven methods in an integrated fashion.

We realize that our agenda is very ambitious and that we cannot have succeeded fully in reaching our objectives. In addition, we have given little attention to the nuts and bolts of managing, and we have not addressed the issues that pertain to developing an effective business strategy. These topics have been covered in detail in many other works. Nevertheless, we hope that we have presented a picture of a powerful intervention model that will expand the perspective and the competence of those who would attempt genuinely transformational change.

Acknowledgments

The concept of a seven-point strategy owes its genesis to my association with Elliott R. Danzig and builds on his "Five Factors of Change" theory, first elaborated in 1968. I will always be grateful for the years of our stimulating exchanges. The perspective of resistance as the existence of multiple realities stems from the Gestalt theory of resistance and techniques for dealing with these realities. I am indebted to my colleagues at the Gestalt Institute of Cleveland, with whom these ideas were developed over a thirty-five-year period of collective study and teaching of others. Finally, I owe much to Richard Beckhard and Edgar Schein, who made it possible for me to become part of the MIT Sloan School of Management. They provided me with a priceless opportunity to develop and test the seven-point strategy for implementing transformational change.

—E. C. N.

I would like to acknowledge three people who held up new lenses through which I could more clearly see the world around me: the late Warren Haggstrom, who introduced me to the sociology of knowledge and the idea that it is possible to change reality; to Charles Savage, who earlier than most understood the need for a paradigm shift in the nature and shape of our organizations; and to Margaret Wheatley, whose application of the "new sciences" to organizational life opened a new world of liberating, empowering possibilities. I am also indebted to my colleagues at the Ernst &

Young LLP Center for Business Innovation for their support and encouragement as I worked to finish my share of the manuscript.

—J. L.

In the early 1980s, after twenty-two years in the pharmaceutical industry, I had the pleasure of being a visiting fellow at the MIT Sloan School of Management, where I had the great delight of having Ed Nevis for a sequence of two classes in managing change. Not only did we students become well grounded in the vast "change" literature, but I also found the seven-point strategy such a valuable tool that I have used it extensively in my courses and in my speeches over the past fourteen years as a professor of management. I would like to acknowledge Ed and his impact on my thinking and on my career. I am also indebted to my colleagues at Worcester Polytechnic Institute and to my ten children, both for their understanding during a transitional year and for having provided for me a living laboratory for many of the principles contained within this book.

—H. G. V.

Collectively, we wish to acknowledge the help and support of our editor at Jossey-Bass, Sarah Polster, particularly for an early intervention that refocused our work in a very fruitful way. In addition, we wish to thank the anonymous reviewers who provided us with some of the most useful feedback authors can ever hope to receive.

February 1996   Edwin C. Nevis
                                         Brookline, Massachusetts

                                            Joan Lancourt
                                         Boston, Massachusetts

                                          Helen G. Vassallo
                                       Worcester, Massachusetts

The Authors

. . . .

Edwin C. Nevis just completed seventeen years at the Massachusetts Institute of Technology (MIT) Sloan School of Management, where he served first as a member of the Organization Studies Group, then became director of the Program for Senior Executives. More recently, he has served as director of special studies of the MIT Organizational Learning Center, in which capacity he has conducted research in organizational learning.

In addition to his work in executive education, Nevis has practiced organizational consulting for forty years. Since 1973 he has trained consultants in advanced programs, more recently concentrating on working with international consultants engaged in cross-cultural and global change efforts. His book *Organizational Consulting: A Gestalt Approach* (1987) has been widely used as a model for this work. He has been a founder or officer of several successful consulting firms, including Personnel Research & Development Corporation in Cleveland, Ohio. From 1960 to 1972 he was president of the Gestalt Institute of Cleveland, during which time it became a major center for advanced studies by helping professionals.

Nevis holds an M.A. degree in counseling from Columbia University and a Ph.D. degree in industrial and organizational psychology from Case Western Reserve University.

Joan Lancourt is a principal at Innovation Associates, an Arthur D. Little Company, where she consults on organizational transformation, change management, and organizational learning. Previously she was a senior organizational development consultant at Digital Equipment Corporation, director of human resources at New England Electric System, and manager of organizational and management development at several Boston-based companies.

Lancourt has managed and consulted for almost twenty years in the areas of large-scale organizational change, implementation strategies, total quality management, business process reengineering, learning organizations, and human resource management. A previous book, *Confront or Concede* (1979), is an assessment of the Alinsky model of community development. In addition, she has written articles on organizational transformation, the changing nature of human resource management, and the role of the consultant. She received an M.S.W. degree from the University of California, Los Angeles, and a Ph.D. degree in social policy from the Florence Heller Graduate School at Brandeis University.

Helen G. Vassallo is the former department head and Harry Stoddard Professor of Management at Worcester Polytechnic Institute. She holds a B.S. degree in biology from Tufts University, an M.S. degree in pharmacology from Tufts University School of Medicine, a Ph.D. degree in physiology from Clark University, and an M.B.A. degree from Worcester Polytechnic Institute. She was associated for many years with Astra Pharmaceutical Products, where she was head of data evaluation and associate director and then director of clinical research. She has been named National Woman of the Year by the American Business Women's Association. She has published extensively in the field of local anesthesia, where she holds two patents, and continues to give expert witness testimony. She presently teaches and consults in the fields of organizational behavior, project management, and the management of planned change.

Intentional Revolutions

Part I

The Challenge of
Transformational Change

1

Discontinuous Thinking

The Challenge of Transformational Change

Whether we look across industries or continents, the environments in which corporate organizations must now operate have one characteristic in common: turbulence. Markets, competitors, and suppliers have become more global; new markets appear overnight and old ones shift with little warning; and every opportunity brings a host of new competitors and the need for new and shifting sets of relationships. Continual advances in the information and telecommunication revolutions are irreversibly changing the nature of work itself and the speed with which companies must now respond to the problems and challenges of a complex and interdependent environment. Upheavals and shifts in the political arena have also dramatically altered the business landscape. The world of the three decades following World War II no longer exists.

Fueled by rapid and unpredictable changes in their environments, more and more firms are finding that the traditional response modes, such as downsizing and piecemeal structural and process rearrangements, no longer provide sufficient competitive advantage. Incremental change, as well as other time-honored management values and methods of the industrial era (for example, command-and-control-style leadership and hierarchical structure), is proving to be inadequate in solving today's business problems. In the late 1970s, Xerox discovered that the fine-tuning of its traditional management systems and its massive downsizing would not be sufficient to ensure the company's competitiveness against the Japanese. In the words of then-CEO David Kearns, Xerox had to "get a hundred thousand people to act and think differently toward the product, the customer, and each other, every hour of the day" (Kearns and Nadler, 1992, p. 147).

As it has turned out, the process of getting people to *think* and *behave* differently is proving to be far more difficult and complex than Kearns initially imagined—and in this unhappy discovery, Xerox has not been unique. More of or better than what we did yesterday will no longer suffice. Instead, there is a growing recognition that to remain viable, corporations must change in ways that are *discontinuous* with what has gone before.

However, there is not yet a great deal of clarity as to what such change really means. Phrases such as large-scale change, breakthrough thinking, continuous innovation, discontinuous change, and organizational transformation are applied as if they were interchangeable; but in significant ways they refer to different games—a fact that frequently leads to actions akin to trying to score a basket with a tennis racquet, or to playing rugby, tennis, and basketball at the same time on the same playing field. Eliminating several layers of middle managers or shifting from geographic business units to an industry focus may be a large-scale change, but it is not a transformation. A process focus may be discontinuous with a functional focus, but it is not, a priori, a transformation. Outsourcing may be a discontinuous change, but it is not necessarily a large-scale change. Adding a 360-degree perspective to an otherwise unchanged performance appraisal system and work structure may be large-scale change, but it is not a discontinuous change. Experimenting with self-managed teams may be discontinuous change, but if such teams exist in the context of management command and control, that change is not transformational.

Simultaneously, and ironically, a number of potentially transformative management philosophies, such as Total Quality Management (TQM) and Socio-Technical Work Redesign, have more often than not been reduced to a set of fragmented flavor-of-the-month programs and tools. Even Business Process Reengineering, once heralded as *the* method of discontinuous change and business transformation, has often resulted in simply making existing processes more efficient, or in turning vertical functional stovepipes into horizontal process stovepipes.

The need to bring clarity to this confusion is of more than academic importance. Unless management knows which game needs to be played and whether a baseball bat or a tennis racquet is needed, a great many efforts will continue to be halfway measures that produce halfway results. To achieve this clarity, however, takes more than the willingness to take the time to do it. To paraphrase Einstein, one cannot solve a problem from the same consciousness that created it. To redefine the game and to decipher the new rules requires stepping back and finding a new vantage point. The literature dealing with this issue is growing: Beckhard (1992) and Nadler, Shaw, Walton, and Associates (1995) elaborate well the challenges involved in this endeavor.

While the business environment has changed dramatically, the mental models that guide management's search for solutions have not yet become discontinuous. In his work on mental models, Senge (1990) makes it clear that if management wants to achieve discontinuous thinking, it must make explicit the individual and collective assumptions that underlie prevailing business and organizational models. If it does not, organizations will remain trapped, like flies in amber, in old modes of thinking and dysfunctional ways of organizing their work.

Unfortunately, by their very nature mental models, or *paradigms*, are self-perpetuating and therefore resistant to change. Failure to understand this has caused management to seriously underestimate the task at hand. Furthermore, as greater insight is gained into the complexity of the change required, it becomes apparent that more than one or two self-contained changes are needed; rather, multiple, interrelated discontinuous changes must be made. In other words, whole systems must be changed, not simply a piece here and there.

What is needed are organizational and individual changes that are far deeper and more fundamental than has heretofore been anticipated. At an individual level, for example, management frequently treads on highly emotional ground: people frequently are asked to let go of behaviors that are part of their sense of self or psychological identity, often the very behaviors that have made them successful. To make matters worse, a crisp set of new behaviors does not yet exist to replace the old ones, nor is there much experience on which to draw in making changes of this magnitude.

The Dilemma of Changing Paradigms

As already noted, the turbulent business environment requires a complex series of interlocking, overlapping, and interdependent paradigm shifts. Following is a list of some of these major shifts:

From	To
Stability	Continuous change
Change as disruption	Change as normal
Local, point solutions	Integrated, systemic solutions
Focus on technology	Focus on customer needs
National focus	Global focus
One right solution	Multiple possible solutions
Individuality and competition	Cooperation and collaboration
Hierarchical control	Flatter, flexible networks
Managers and controllers	Coaches, servants, and catalysts
White-male-dominated power structures	Racial, ethnic, gender, and stylistic diversity
Leaders as generals	Leaders as servants

Even a cursory examination of this list makes several things apparent. First, to some extent most of these shifts are already taking place, but the degree of progress at any given company or in any given individual on any specific shift varies greatly. Second, the items in each column are in multiple ways inextricably *interconnected* with the other items in that column. For example, if change is viewed as normal, it is easier to undertake continuous change; systemic solutions are enhanced by collaborative relationships and activities; coaches, servants, and catalysts support collaborative interactions, as do flexible, flatter networks; and multiple levels of diversity and collaboration are necessary for both global success and the generation of multiple possible scenarios.

Third, both individually and collectively these paradigm shifts have multiple *behavioral* implications. At the individual level, cooperation and collaboration require people to be open to new ideas, to have the ability to relate to and respect others whose knowledge and points of view differ from their own, to value these differences, and to refrain from trying to eliminate them. They also require probing and questioning for deeper understanding, listening actively, suspending judgment, looking for synergy and connection, actively building on the ideas of others, looking for the strengths in others, contributing to the success of others, knowing how to engage in constructive conflict, being comfortable with creative tensions, and taking the time to create shared understandings.

Organizations must also create the infrastructure necessary to support the new paradigms. At the organizational level, flatter, flexible networks not only require people to network in order to get their work done, but it also requires the organization to provide the rewards for doing so. In other words, networking must be made easy, which might include instituting various forms of job rotations or job sharing, using whole-systems change methodologies, creating knowledge directories, defining the managerial role as resource finder, and providing training in teaming skills as an essential core competency for organizational success.

Even this brief treatment makes it clear that what we are describing is a whole organizational environment or culture that not only differs in fundamental ways from what exists today in most organizations but also is antithetical to or discontinuous with it. Is it any wonder that most leaders and managers are experiencing confusion, frustration, and anxiety? To deal with so much at once is an enormous task.

Some companies, such as General Electric, Xerox, and Motorola, have managed to achieve shifts in some of the above paradigms, but they have repeatedly admitted that the changes were more problematic and took far longer than they ever imagined; and despite enormous expenditures of energy by large numbers of very bright people, most organizations have repeatedly run into roadblocks. One reason for these difficulties is becoming clear: the methods used by organizations and individuals to bring about these changes is part and parcel of the problem. As Pogo, the cartoon character, said: "We have met the enemy, and he is us!"

Some examples help drive home this point. First, despite pervasive lip service to the concept of employee participation and empowerment, most change is still initiated and planned at the top, announced, and expected to be executed by the rest of the organization. This happened repeatedly in TQM programs in which senior managers saw TQM as applying to their subordinates. That the managers also were part of the equation and needed to change how they thought and acted was slow to dawn. By contrast, one reason Motorola has been successful in its TQM endeavor is that its earliest efforts focused heavily on education and attitude changes at the highest levels of the firm (Nevis, DiBella, and Gould, 1995).

Another example of how organizations are constrained by traditional management paradigms is found in the application of Socio-Technical Design methods. This approach requires that *social* and *technical* aspects of work design be addressed together as an integrated whole; yet the power of the prevailing technical mind-set is such that many sociotechnical efforts continue to address the social and organizational factors only as an afterthought. While it is not hard to grasp the sociotechnical concept at an intellectual level, assumptions about the primacy of the technical realm are so deep-seated that they continue to shape actual behaviors in ways that short-circuit the intent of the model.

A third example is found in efforts to develop high-performance work teams. A high-performing team is every manager's dream. Initially, this concept was widely embraced; however, the romance quickly soured as it became apparent that creating a high-performance team involved a radical redefinition of the role of manager. In place of planning, organizing, scheduling, and controlling, managers of high-performance (or self-managed) teams found themselves shorn of the familiar duties of hiring, firing, performance review, and day-to-day problem solving. Instead, they were expected to focus on boundary management, resource development and allocation, long-range planning, and providing the kind of leadership that creates an environment supportive of integrated team activities. For many managers, these changes represented a loss of control and required skills they did not possess.

Finally, most change has traditionally been thought of as having a beginning, a middle, and an end. In other words, it has been thought that once a change was made, a new equilibrium would develop and a new norm would be established. However, when innovation and breakthrough thinking become the norm—in other words, when discontinuous change becomes continuous—organizations have no choice but to reevaluate the way they *think* about the process of change itself. Thus, in addition to everything else, a paradigm shift is needed in how change is managed.

The experience of a number of senior executives underscores this need. They are finding that when change becomes continuous, organizing around specific products or core competencies may be less the real issue than preparing and enabling their organizations to meet the challenge of perpetual discontinuous change. One vice president of a global corporation went so far as to say that the real business they were in was the change business.

A deeper understanding of the interconnectedness and behavioral implications of the paradigm shifts listed earlier reveals that inherent in the new paradigm is the need to build into the way work is organized a capacity for flexibility and continuous change. Building this capacity requires changes in the processes, structures, infrastructures, and day-to-day behaviors needed to accomplish the work, as well as changes in management's expectations of and relationship to employees, customers, suppliers, partners, competitors, and the community at large. To achieve change of this magnitude, management must better understand why paradigmatic change is so difficult, and what needs to be done to facilitate it.

Thomas Kuhn (1970) identifies several of the invisible restraints that prevent organizations from moving forward. First he defines *paradigm* as a framework of presuppositions that serves as a lens or intellectual gestalt that determines what people perceive *and what they do not perceive.* By repeatedly directing a person's attention to one set of inputs rather than another, a paradigm is inherently self-perpetuating and resistant to change. This is one of the reasons successful organizations have difficulty reading the signs of growing environmental shifts.

Second, people become *emotionally* as well as intellectually attached to paradigms. Human needs for certainty, identification, and security are not matters to be settled simply by reason and reflection; they require involvement of the heart as well as the mind.

Third, prevailing paradigms are frameworks or models to which a relevant *community* has given its stamp of approval. They can only be sustained and promulgated through dialogue among members of that community. Thus, Einstein's theory of relativity only supplanted the previous paradigm after prolonged, controversial consideration by many physicists and others who ultimately accepted his assumptions, thereby forming a new community.

Both the emotional attachment to a given set of assumptions and the social nature of those assumptions result from the way paradigms are acquired and sustained. In a complex and highly emotion-laden dialectic between the inner, private world and the external world (a dialectic known to sociologists as the process of socialization), each person develops the values, assumptions, concepts, and meanings appropriate to a particular paradigm, and learns the roles, relationships, norms, and behaviors that support these values, assumptions, concepts, and meanings. These roles, relationships, norms, and behaviors are embedded in an intricate web of shared understandings that becomes institutionalized, thereby reinforcing and maintaining the particular set of assumptions and its prescribed behaviors. They constitute one's perception of what is real.

By identifying these three important characteristics of paradigms—they are *inherently* self-perpetuating; they are *emotional* as well as intellectual constructs; they are *shared* constructs and hence communally reinforced—Kuhn helps clarify why it is so difficult to change them. A paradigm shift does not simply represent a modification of a prevailing framework; rather, it is the acceptance of a contradictory framework. Thus, the process of changing from one paradigm to another is inherently wrenching and difficult.

It is our contention, however, that it is possible for organizations to significantly increase their ability to make complex paradigmatic change if they do two things. First, management needs to understand that in calling for transformational change they are in essence involved in the creation of a new organizational reality. Second, to create and maintain this new reality, management must view the implementation process as one of resocialization (in other words, helping organizational members to internalize the new assumptions, frameworks, values, norms, roles, and behaviors).

Reframing Transformational Change

To transform something is to change its fundamental external form or inner nature. Physicists refer to transformation as the conversion of one form of energy to another. When water is boiled, it is transformed into steam. Its chemical formula is the same, but its form and properties are qualitatively different. In the world of nature, a caterpillar is transformed into a butterfly; its DNA remains unchanged, but its form and properties are fundamentally different. *A butterfly is not a caterpillar with wings strapped to its back.*

Similarly, in an organizational context transformation is not simply a shifting of vertical functional stovepipes to horizontal process stovepipes. It is not a grafting of teams onto the lower layers of an essentially hierarchical organization, nor is it the pushing, selling, or cascading of an executive vision through the layers of a command-and-control organization. While there is no denying that some of these changes represent significant large-scale organizational change, and while some of them are even discontinuous with what went before, from our perspective they do not constitute transformations.

What, then, is organizational transformation? In the context of the growing need for multiple and interconnected paradigm shifts, we define organizational transformation as the commitment to *fundamentally changing the whole*, not just some of its parts. In essence, organizational transformation is the *creation of a new organizational reality*. As such, it requires changing not only the practices, policies, behaviors, and structures but also the underlying mental models, meanings, and consciousness of the people involved. To do this requires that management engage organizational members in a process of resocialization.

We hasten to add that in defining transformation in this way we are not suggesting that one can or should change the whole all at once. In fact, considerable experience indicates that the actual process of transformation takes place in successive phases that are a nonlinear combination of vision and emerging possibility.

Inherent in thinking of transformation as the creation of a new social or organizational reality are four basic assumptions that affect the ability to create a new reality and effectively resocialize organizational members:

1. Social or organizational "reality" is not a given; it is
   constructed through the *interactions* of people, creating
   common, shared understandings. Reality is what people
   make it at a given time; it is not permanent or immutable
   and it *can* be changed in response to new experience.

2. Social reality is created out of the interplay between the
   external world and the *subjective* world of the participants
   as they interact to construct common understandings.
   There is no one right way of seeing the world; rather, "truth"
   is the outcome of the interaction of the multiple realities
   of the various organizational members.

3. A new social reality alters in significant and fundamental
   ways not only how people do their work but how they *experience* themselves. Transformation is the destruction of existing
   understandings and meanings and their replacement by a significantly different set of *shared understandings and meanings*.

4. The creation of a new social reality is as much a complex
   influence process as it is an analytical process, and no single
   method of influence is powerful enough to transform an
   organizational reality.

Defining organizational transformation as the creation of a new
social and organizational reality clearly requires a dramatic shift in
thinking, from organizational reality as objective, immutable phenomenon to organizational reality as that which exists and changes
in the consciousness of people. Also, as we noted earlier, part and
parcel of this shift is a new approach to the process of change itself.

Transforming the Paradigm for Change

Faced with the need to create a new organizational reality, management can no longer afford to think of making the required changes
as a series of independent pieces or programs, decided at the top and

pushed as rapidly as possible through the organization. The creation of a new reality requires shifting the emphasis to the orchestration of a process that will result not only in the creation of a new organizational reality but in the resocialization of organizational members. Without resocialization, the new reality will not be able to sustain itself. Unfortunately, the current model of change is not only unhelpful in the undertaking of this task; it also prevents management from seeing many of the crucial elements they must address.

Historically, the *observable* physical world has been the primary mental model for managers, and they have come to regard organizations as giant machines with tangible parts that have to be controlled and arranged in ways that enhance the ability to control them. This paradigm (derived from Newtonian physics) has tended to focus the organizational world on objective, sensory, behavioral reality as *the* reality. Subjective, intangible phenomena are considered nuisances that cloud our ability to see what is real (in other words, tangible). This attitude manifests in organizations in the almost exclusive emphasis on rational problem solving, and on getting people to accept the one "right" way of doing things. Similarly, it has caused management to see the informal organization as an obstacle to the development of an ideal *formal* organization that governs all behavior. Further, in this model change is achieved through the manipulation of parts, the application of external force to those parts, and a drive toward the achievement of a stable state.

As management grapples with the problems of existing in a world of continuous change, facing the need to create a flexible, highly adaptive organizational reality and engage in effective and ongoing processes of resocialization, *the change paradigm must shift from a focus on the observable physical world to the observation of the invisible*. Management needs to see organizations as sets of possibilities, tendencies, interconnections, and interactions, all aimed at increasing the organization's ability to adapt.

The "new science" paradigms (Wheatley, 1992) offer useful

models for "seeing" organizations as complex, dynamic, emergent systems of continuously shifting patterns of tangible and intangible (invisible) things. Quantum physicists work all the time with things they cannot see (for example, magnetic and electrical energy fields). They know such fields exist because of the effects they have on things they can see. Similarly, while we cannot see an expectation, a culture, or a possibility, we know they exist because of the effect they have on people's behavior.

Shifting our attention from the tangible thing to the dynamic interaction among things is a crucial lesson we can learn from quantum physics. In the quantum world, for example, nothing exists independent of its relationship to something else. Whether something is a particle or wave depends on its relationship to the things around it—including the physicist doing the observing. If his or her interest is in particles, that is what will be seen; if waves, that is what will be seen.

This dynamic can be of great help to us in rethinking our approaches to organizational change. By focusing on interactions rather than on separate objects, one is able to see, for example, that no response (such as resistance to change) is independent of the interactive dynamics that produce it. Thus, what has long been attributed to human nature—namely, resistance to change—may be, in large measure, a result of our failure to develop a different way of managing the relationships and interactions between the resisters and the message to which the resistance is a response. By focusing on changing the interaction rather than on the "truth" of the message or on the resisters themselves, it becomes possible to devise a more effective approach to catalyzing and managing the transformation process.

Methods of Influencing Behavior

This focus on the inseparable nature of the network of shifting interactions and interrelationships is particularly relevant to the relationship among the seven methods of influence that we have identified as necessary to reshape organizational and individual behaviors:

1. *Persuasive communication:* The introduction of a message in an attempt to create a change in belief, value, or behavior in another person or group who have some degree of freedom to accept or reject the message.

2. *Participation:* The involvement of people in decision making, organizational design, or the formulation of policies and procedures in an attempt to increase the quality of the decisions through the use of all possible resources.

3. *Expectancy:* The inducement of self-fulfilling prophecies by behaving as though the expectation were a reality. This behavior assumes that the expectation held by one person about others will be realized through the actions of the person making the prediction.

4. *Role modeling:* Learning that takes place through the observation of the behaviors of others who are seen as attractive or admirable in some way.

5. *Extrinsic rewards:* The reinforcement of desired behaviors based on the assumption that the behavior will not be maintained without the reward.

6. *Structural rearrangement:* The creation of behavioral change by altering work design, organizational structure, or core processes. This action assumes that behavior will change if the environment is changed.

7. *Coercion:* The attempt to influence and control the behavior of others based on the assumption that people will comply because they see themselves as unable to leave the field in which the power is applied.

We propose that, like an energy field, these methods of behavioral influence all give out "messages" that combine and interact to shape organizational and individual behaviors *whether the messages are consciously sent or not.* Therefore, to the extent that the transformation effort ignores any of the seven behavioral change methods, management is putting mixed messages into the organizational system, thereby retarding the process of resocialization and ultimately of transformation.

The simultaneous and coordinated use of these seven methods to create a new organizational reality and the behaviors necessary for its maintenance forms the primary focus of this book. However, before we explore each of the methods and its contribution to the transformation and resocialization process, it is important to understand how a social reality is created in the first place and how the socialization process operates to sustain the tangible and intangible roles, relationships, structures, values, assumptions, and so forth that form that reality. Since the *processes that must be used to change the current reality are the same ones used to create it,* organizations have at their disposal the means for changing it.

In Chapter Two we develop a definition of social reality and explore how it is created and maintained, the role socialization plays in the process, and how the seven influence methods together constitute a strategy for resocialization.

2

Building a New Consciousness
The Creation of Organizational Reality

How do we come to perceive something as real, as a part of our existence? If we touch a table, we experience its reality, but how can we say that an organization or a city or a government is real even though we cannot touch it? From the beginning of recorded history, human beings have grappled with this question, but there has never been one commonly accepted answer. Among psychologists, for example, traditional behaviorists claim that everything can be understood solely in terms of directly observable behavior. A related perspective states that what we sense through touch, sight, smell, and so forth is what is real. These perspectives emphasize physical reality and focus on environmental forces as the major source of influence on human behavior. Traditional science and business are based on this way of seeing the world.

While this approach has led to important understandings about human nature, for many people it fails to grasp the importance of the so-called subjective or intangible experiences such as thoughts, feelings, dreams and fantasies, intentions and free will. Multiple schools of thought have argued that not every aspect of an individual's reality is directly observable; rather, reality is that which is experienced by an individual in his or her consciousness. Thus, everyone can look at the same table and experience it differently. One person sees the texture or beauty of the wood; another, its potential utility.

Is it possible, then, to view the table as having only one reality? The answer is yes and no. On one level, everyone sees a table, but the *meaning* of the table is not the same for everyone. Some scholars refer to one aspect of the experience as "objective reality" and the other aspect as "subjective reality." Others think in terms of "alternate" or "multiple realities" to signify the *legitimacy* of different perceptions and to avoid the pejorative implication of "objective" as somehow more desirable than "subjective." We prefer the term "multiple realities" to connote the *simultaneous* existence of different worldviews or realities.

As we noted in Chapter One, the new paradigm for organizations and organizational change increases management's ability to go beyond the definition of reality as merely what is tangible. While the table in the above example is tangible, the meanings given to it are not. There are many facets of organizational life that are neither visible nor tangible, yet they are absolutely real in that they exert an extremely powerful influence on individual and collective behavior. Examples are the organization's culture, norms, understandings, judgments, and meanings. The seven behavioral influence methods listed in Chapter One are also intangibles. Influence is impossible to touch, as are the interactions and interrelationships among the seven methods as they operate collectively to shape behavior. Nevertheless, their effect is very real.

For the purposes of the discussion that follows, therefore, we define organizational reality as the *combination of tangible and intangible factors that make up members' experience of an organization and in one way or another shape or reshape their behavior.* These factors include the various aspects of organizational culture, the roles and relationships defined by how the work tasks are divided, and the various infrastructures (budgeting systems, technologies, decision-making and recruiting processes, and so forth) that support the work, as well as people's perceptions of and feelings about the organization, the unfolding change, their roles, and their degree of commitment to organizational goals and visions.

This definition is important because it shapes people's view of the organization and determines what data or "facts" they take in. Having defined reality in this way, we now examine how a reality is created.

Creating Social and Organizational Reality

Social reality arises from the social relationships or social context of human activity. It develops through the interaction of people *over time* and through the efforts of the individual to comprehend his or her world. What emerges is a *shared understanding* of what matters.

To illustrate how a social or organizational reality begins, we can consider the situation of three people who decide to form a business. Typically, there is a great deal of discussion among them as they define the business and plan how to get started. Issues of markets to be served require attention, as do questions of product or service design and the tasks and responsibilities of each member of the group. Through repeated interaction, a host of *reciprocal expectations* emerge. For example, it may be agreed that two members will work on product design while the third devotes time to raising capital and developing the market. Having decided on this division of labor, the members carry on their work with the assumption that common understandings have been reached. Other critical understandings will develop around the appropriate and acceptable ways each member should behave in carrying out his or her tasks and around how they will relate to each other. These understandings will grow out of the language the individuals use while sharing their personal, subjective perceptions and meanings in their attempt to create common awareness and understanding of who is doing what to whom.

Over time, reciprocal expectations and the actions or behaviors that arise from them in a given situation become *habitual* and *predictable*. This predictability is desirable in that it decreases the uncertainty and anxiety that accompany any interaction in which people do not know what to expect. One probably could not live in a world that did not have some level of the order and predictability that comes from common understandings. The anxiety would be too great and the diffusion of energy required to make sense of every interaction would prevent us from accomplishing very much. Predictable and habitual behavioral interactions enable people to focus their energy on selected problems as opposed to constantly reinventing the wheel.

(Parenthetically, this is one major reason why transitions are so difficult: there is, as yet, no predictability of behavior. It is also why there is an increased need for more two-way communication: such communication is the primary means for creating the shared understandings that engender order and a sufficient level of predictability to enable action.)

As common understandings and behavioral expectations are sustained, they become full-fledged *roles* that people play vis-à-vis one another. In this context, a role is a set of reciprocal expectations of a series of behavioral routines that are more or less predictable within generally know parameters. At a societal level, spouses learn to expect certain things from each other, parents behave in certain ways toward their children, and children are expected to act in certain ways toward their parents. At an organizational level, managers behave in certain ways toward their subordinates, and employees act in particular ways toward their bosses. Customers have roles to play, as do suppliers. Individual development is the continual expansion and refinement of the multiple roles people play throughout their lives.

Thus, it is possible to begin to appreciate the importance of having a set of common understandings in organizations, not only about each role but about how those roles will be played in relation to one another. Over time, and with the multiplication of the number of people and job functions, there is a need to ensure that all the roles will be played and coordinated appropriately, and that there will be broad acceptance of role definitions. To achieve sufficient predictability on a large scale and ensure some measure of stability in the increasingly complex series of social interactions, these roles and relationships must become embedded in the organizational infrastructures. We refer to this state of affairs as the *organizational reality*.

We now turn to a brief examination of how these roles and relationships become embedded, maintained, and reinforced.

Maintaining and Reinforcing Organizational Reality

Following is a list, drawn from Schein's (1983) studies of leadership and culture, of the mechanisms by which organizational reality (in Schein's terminology, "culture") is transmitted by founders and key leaders and embedded in an organizational infrastructure to ensure sustainability:

1. Formal statements of organizational philosophy, charters, creeds, materials used for recruitment and socialization

2. Design of physical spaces, facades, and buildings

3. Deliberate role modeling, teaching, and coaching by leaders

4. Explicit reward and status systems, and promotion criteria

5. Stories, legends, myths, and parables about key people and events

6. What leaders pay attention to, measure, and control

7. Leader reactions to critical incidents and organizational crises (when organizational survival is threatened, norms are unclear or challenged, insubordination occurs, threatening or meaningless events occur, and so forth)

8. How the organization is designed and structured (design of work, who reports to whom, degree of decentralization, functional or other criteria for differentiation, and mechanisms used for integration, all of which carry implicit messages of what leaders assume and value)

9. Organizational systems and procedures (types of information, control, and decision support systems in terms of categories of information, time cycles, who gets what information, and when and how performance appraisal and other review processes are conducted, which carry implicit messages of what leaders assume and value)

10. Criteria used for recruitment, selection, promotion, leveling off, retirement, and "excommunication" (the implicit and possibly unconscious criteria that leaders use to determine who "fits" membership roles and key slots in the organization and who does not)

This list is interesting in several respects. First, it includes both explicit/tangible and implicit/intangible mechanisms. Some messages are presented in explicit, unambiguous terms, such as formal statements of philosophy and the design of physical spaces. Others are implicit, such as the implications of how the founders respond to problems and key incidents.

Second, and most important for our argument in favor of the need for multiple methods of influence in the transformation process, the mechanisms are based on numerous strategies. Schein finds in his observations of founders and their organizations clear evidence of all seven of the behavioral change methods we develop in this book.

Taken in concert, these mechanisms serve not only to transmit and reinforce the organizational reality to both existing and new organizational members, but they do so in a way that creates a widely shared understanding and acceptance of the reality.

While Schein's list of the multiple mechanisms through which an organizational reality is created, embedded, and sustained is of key importance, it does not address the dynamic, interactive process that is necessary to ensure that each organizational member (and each organizational subgroup) internalizes and accepts the organizational reality as the way things are.

The Role of Socialization

Generally speaking, socialization may be understood as the intimate dialectic between the inner reality of the individual and the reality that exists outside. When successful, the result of socialization is an internalization of that external world. In essence, the individual and the external world become one. People learn who they are in relation to that external world and they take on the objectives of the culture in which they live. When the process of socialization is successful, there is relatively little difference between individual goals and behaviors and organization or community objectives and the behaviors needed to achieve them.

Early socialization generally takes place through the intermediation of the family, by which children come to understand the complex system of expectations, behaviors, roles, relationships, and institutional arrangements of the social world into which they are born. Through role modeling, cognitive and emotional persuasion, coercion, expectations, rewards, and structures provided by significant others such as parents, siblings, and grandparents, children participate in learning who they are in relation to those around them, and they learn how they are expected to behave. They learn to play different roles, to participate in appropriate ways, to control many of their inner impulses and to give meaning to their personal experiences. The deepest sense of self, of who one is, is a magical and elusive combination of messages given during the early years of socialization and the unique meaning the individual ascribes to those messages.

The process of early socialization is not just a cognitive one in which ideas are presented for reasoned consideration. The atmosphere of the family is always emotionally charged and the external world is not simply presented as a series of choices the individual is free to make based on personal tastes or desires. Notions of good and bad, right and wrong, attitudes toward authority, toward work, love, success, failure, gender roles, God, and so forth, are presented as givens that carry a heavy emotional valence. Because of this emotional aspect, once socialization at the early stages of life has been accomplished, what has been assimilated retains a degree of power that later refinements seldom match.

As the individual develops and ventures into the world, socialization focuses on acquiring a multiplicity of roles, knowledge, and standards of performance. Largely guided by teachers operating in institutional settings such as schools and churches and by the community setting in general, socialization continues. *The sum total of this socialization process is what makes up a person's social reality.* Psychologically and socially, the more successful the socialization process, the more people find themselves firmly anchored and invested in the existing social reality. Is there any reason, then, that we should expect transformational change to be anything but difficult?

There may be some truth to the sayings, "Once a marine, always a marine" and "You can't teach an old dog new tricks," but the issue in organizational transformation is not inherent inability or resistance. In fact, the new science paradigms indicate that not only is continuous, significant change possible, it is also a normal, inherent part of life. In some ways, it is our systems and our mental models that hold us back—not human nature.

The poor success rate of organizational transformation is less the result of human nature than of *failure to understand and therefore to recreate the complex forces that can produce a change in our more deeply embedded attitudes, assumptions, and mental models.* It is for this reason that we have taken the time to review the early socialization process and to emphasize its uniquely emotional character. Attitudes toward authority, control, social status, and gender—to name but a few of the assumptions that must change in order to create a new organizational reality based on the paradigm shifts identified in Chapter One—are not created de novo in an organizational context; they are inculcated quite literally at the parental knee. Therefore, if aspects of the new organizational reality require a significant rethinking of such attitudes, this cannot be done successfully unless management acknowledges and recreates some version of the emotional conditions under which they were formed.

Organizational Socialization

In an organizational context, socialization is an interactive learning process in which the individual is encouraged or pressured to assimilate the organization's objectives and to accept the organization's definition of reality.

Organizational socialization takes place through many mechanisms, most of which are encompassed by the seven influence methods listed in Chapter One. Organizational socialization begins with the criteria for selecting organization members. Then, as orientation, new members are provided with educational programs that teach the norms, roles, and values of the organization. Organizational policy and procedure manuals are also used for this purpose.

Of more importance, however, in terms of impact is the nature of the interpersonal relationships to which members are exposed. Supervisors, "big brothers/sisters," more experienced peers, and managers and senior executives set forth the expectations that are held for the newcomer. They do this through *persuasive communication, role modeling* of the desired behaviors, manipulation of *extrinsic rewards,* and provision of opportunities for *participation* and interaction. By stating what is important and by setting examples in their own behavior, they show newcomers how to succeed in the organization. The newcomer learns how things work, the acceptable range of behaviors that do not follow the letter of the organization's rules, and so forth.

Organizational socialization is also a process of *persuasive communication,* in which the goal is to change attitudes and inculcate a new mental model in members. In this process, information and arguments are presented that attack the existing belief structure of the individual. The success of this approach depends on the source and content of the message and on the creditability of the persuader.

Perhaps even more important, though less obvious, is what is communicated by example. The observation of desired behavior is one of the more powerful forms of learning. For centuries, the customary way of developing skilled tradespeople has been through apprenticeship, in which learners spend a good deal of time watching the masters do their work. In some Japanese companies, it has long been the custom to provide newcomers with a kind of "benevolent uncle," a creditable older person who gives informal advice and feedback outside the chain of command. Role modeling of desired behaviors is essential, yet most organizations give little thought to how newcomers are assigned to work groups, supervisors, or mentors, or to what opportunities they have to interact with those from other parts of the organization.

The use of *extrinsic rewards* in the socialization process is also important. Similar to the granting of gold stars to good students, newcomers are rewarded through recognition and increased status and by additional benefits or "perks" as they show evidence of becoming socialized.

In addition, we cannot overlook the possible need for *coercion* as a means of getting the process started, and of keeping the image of transformation in the forefront of everyone's consciousness. Almost by definition, socialization itself is not a process of free choice: it is something in which people participate, with varying degrees of willingness.

Participation is essential for effective socialization. People have to be actively engaged for the process to happen, and as we have noted in our discussion of early, familial socialization processes, the more fully engaged one is, emotionally as well as rationally, the more one will internalized the desired behaviors. Finally, socialization is also carried out through a series of *structural arrangements* (for example, functional or cross-functional teams, work processes, or professional groups) that give essential messages about the roles and behaviors members must learn.

We have described how socialization occurs in large measure through the simultaneous use of these multiple methods for influencing behavior. Although we have focused primarily on the initial stages of organizational socialization, we hasten to add that socialization is an ongoing and, almost always, incomplete process. Day-to-day changes and developments in organization life make it necessary to engage in continuous "relearning." However, when the number of relearnings are multiplied, and the new attitudes, skills, and behaviors are discontinuous with the old, management is then faced not simply with a continuation of the socialization process but with the additional issues of resocialization.

Recreating Organizational Reality

Like paradigms, organizational realities are hard to change—and for many of the same reasons: they are self-perpetuating, members become emotionally invested in the status quo, and the prevailing reality is sustained by a community of agreement as to the way things should be.

One useful analogy for creating a new organizational reality is the difference between remodeling an old house and building a new house. In a new house, one does not have to concern oneself with dismantling the old plumbing and wiring or with the eccentricities of old building methods and outmoded patterns of use. One may be missing a great deal in terms of ambiance, gracious proportions, and a sense of connection with history, but starting with a clean slate has advantages.

In remodeling, one can retain the charm, but one must deal with pulling out or refurbishing the old utilities. In this sense, organizational transformation is more like remodeling. Management is seldom dealing with a clean slate. Everyone brings with them their old wiring and plumbing, and resocialization must take into account the need to deconstruct the old as well as construct the new. Further, the deconstruction must be done in ways that do not create hidden fissures and weaknesses in the new house. On the whole, a new organizational house is constructed by the inhabitants of the old house who, like immigrants arriving on a foreign shore, cannot help but bring the old ways with them. The problem faced by the architects of the new house is how to help the immigrants let go of the old ways, learn the new ways, and accept the new house as their home.

The unlearning of old behaviors and ways of thinking is not an insignificant task for an organization. Behaviors have been inbred through a lifetime of reinforcement. Managers may be renamed "coaches," but it is not easy to eschew the old command-and-control behaviors; it also is not easy for "subordinates" to let go of their old expectations of their managers.

Even the language organizations use works against them. If you are not a manager, you are an "individual contributor," and the experience of individual contributors makes it difficult to behave as a team. Typically, teams act as beads on a string, with each member's input added to but distinct from that of the other members, rather than as the blended ingredients of a cake mix, in which one can no longer identify the flour and sugar and vanilla as separate contributions.

Clearly, to unlearn old ways is no easy task, especially when much of what has to be unlearned is part and parcel of people's sense of self—and self-esteem—as well as their definitions of success and status and their notions of good and bad. Also, *it is no more possible for people to unlearn these things on their own than it was to learn them on their own.* Socialization is by definition a social process, and the importance of group support becomes even more important during resocialization. Thus, socialization requires the coordinated use of all seven behavioral influence methods—and one thing more: the acknowledgment that it is an emotional as well as a rational process. Letting go of deeply embedded behaviors can involve a tremendous sense of loss, and loss is nothing if not an emotional experience.

To facilitate this process, managers and supervisors must become skillful in guiding rather than suppressing the necessary emotional conversations, and informal social support networks must be encouraged rather than merely tolerated.

As important as it is to address the emotional component of resocialization and transformation, there are several other components that are also essential to success. In Chapter Three we identify the phases and activities of transformational change, discuss how the seven behavioral influence methods facilitate moving through those phases, and explore how the acknowledgment of the legitimacy of multiple realities contributes to the creation of a new organizational reality.

. . . .

3

Practical Dimensions of Transformational Change

Phases and Methods

A major challenge of transformational change is to influence people to develop or accept a new reality or worldview and then to motivate them to undertake the work required to turn that worldview into a new way of organizational functioning. In this chapter we offer a three-dimensional model for managing this process (see Figure 3.1). The first dimension deals with the *major phases* involved in the endeavor. The second dimension addresses the *methods of influence* we have identified as useful in motivating people to accept a need for change and to carry out the work necessary to achieve it. The third dimension handles the *management of resistance*, which we define as the management of multiple realities. A basic premise of the model is that all three dimensions operate in an interactive, holistic fashion. For transformation to be successful, managing the interplay between and among the dimensions is critical.

Douglas McGregor (1960) was among the first management theorists to point out the complexity of managing change and the fact that reliance mainly on the use of authority (in other words, coercive power) would not suffice to bring about lasting change. We have come a long way since then in recognizing and accepting this view, but a full understanding of the range of options, how they may be applied effectively, and how they can be combined to achieve maximum leverage for change has not yet been achieved. A better

Figure 3.1. A Three-Dimensional Model of Transformational Change.

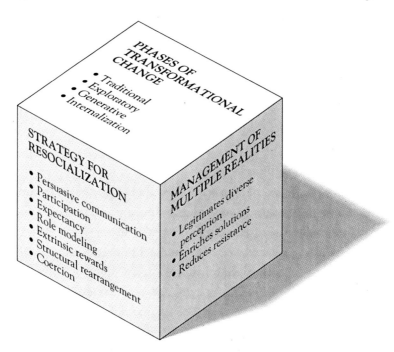

understanding is needed of how various methods of influencing behavior can facilitate moving through the phases of transformational change, but before this can be accomplished, managers must first become familiar with the four phases companies go through in the course of creating a new reality and resocializing its members.

Dimension 1: The Phases of Transformational Change

By definition, transformational change is an attempt to alter significantly the fundamental customs, values, and basic assumptions of the paradigm under which an organization has been functioning. A transformation attacks the tried and true mechanisms that have been largely responsible for producing the "comfort zone" within which the organization has functioned in the past, often highly successfully. Moreover, it asks members of the organization to embark on a difficult and ambitious journey for which the road maps and destinations are often not clear at the outset of the trip.

Kotter (1995) suggests that many transformational efforts fail because of errors made during one or another of what he identifies as a series of essential steps; Kilmann (1989) proposes an integrated program for change that includes five simultaneous paths of action. From our perspective, however, two key elements are missing from the various frameworks.

First, while the change models they propose are designed to ensure effective implementation of large-scale or even discontinuous change, the creation of a new organizational reality requires the recognition of the resocialization process as central to transformational change. It is this process that keeps management focused on behavioral change and on the urgent need to help the organization's members internalize the new ways of thinking and behaving as quickly as possible. Internalization is important to ultimate success because it is internalization of the new that enables people to let go of the old. The question, How can this task be done in a way that facilitates the resocialization of organizational members? becomes a guide in the planning and execution of the activities associated with transformation; and the question, To what extent did this approach facilitate and maximize the resocialization of the organizational members? becomes one of the key measures for determining progress.

We have come to a second insight based on years of experience with organizations that have focused a great deal of effort and significant resources on designing and implementing major changes in an attempt to renew and revitalize themselves, only to find that they have been unable to sustain the change. An analysis of these efforts and of others that have succeeded has led us to a deeper appreciation of the ability of an organization's existing reality or culture to sustain itself in the face of multiple efforts to change it. We find that unless there is a strong focus on internalization of the new ways of thinking and behaving, the old organizational reality will inevitably prevail. If, however, resocialization becomes the "energy field" within which the other tasks and processes unfold and interact, then the stronger, original reality can be prevented from over-powering the initially more fragile new reality.

Acknowledgment of the centrality of the need for resocialization and of the need to internalize the new behaviors raises the second key element: that transformation is a process with a number of generally identifiable phases, the "final" one of which is the internalization of the new behaviors. Identification of phases and of activities that occur during each phase is useful for several reasons. First, it helps an organization acknowledge that transformation is a developmental process; second, it enables an organization to chart its progress; and third, it helps maintain a focus on the ultimate goal: internalization of the new ways.

Figure 3.2 identifies four major phases of the transformation process and the key characteristics of each phase, and illustrates the cyclical, nonlinear nature of creating an organization capable of continuous adaptation to discontinuous change. Our identification of these phases and their characteristics is based on what we have observed in companies that have successfully transformed themselves.

We have labeled the first phase the *Traditional Phase*. We have chosen this term to acknowledge the fact that the emphasis in this phase is still on rational problem solving, one right answer, and formal control mechanisms. At this stage, there is an increasing awareness of the gap between the performance needed to meet competitive business demands and the organization's actual performance, and an increased sense of urgency on the part of senior leadership. However, there is still a reliance on traditional problem-solving approaches, adaptive and reactive behaviors, and the hope that some quick-fix program will solve the problems. As a result of conscious attempts to better understand what is going on, one or more senior executives begin to educate themselves about

Figure 3.2. Phases of Organizational Transformation.

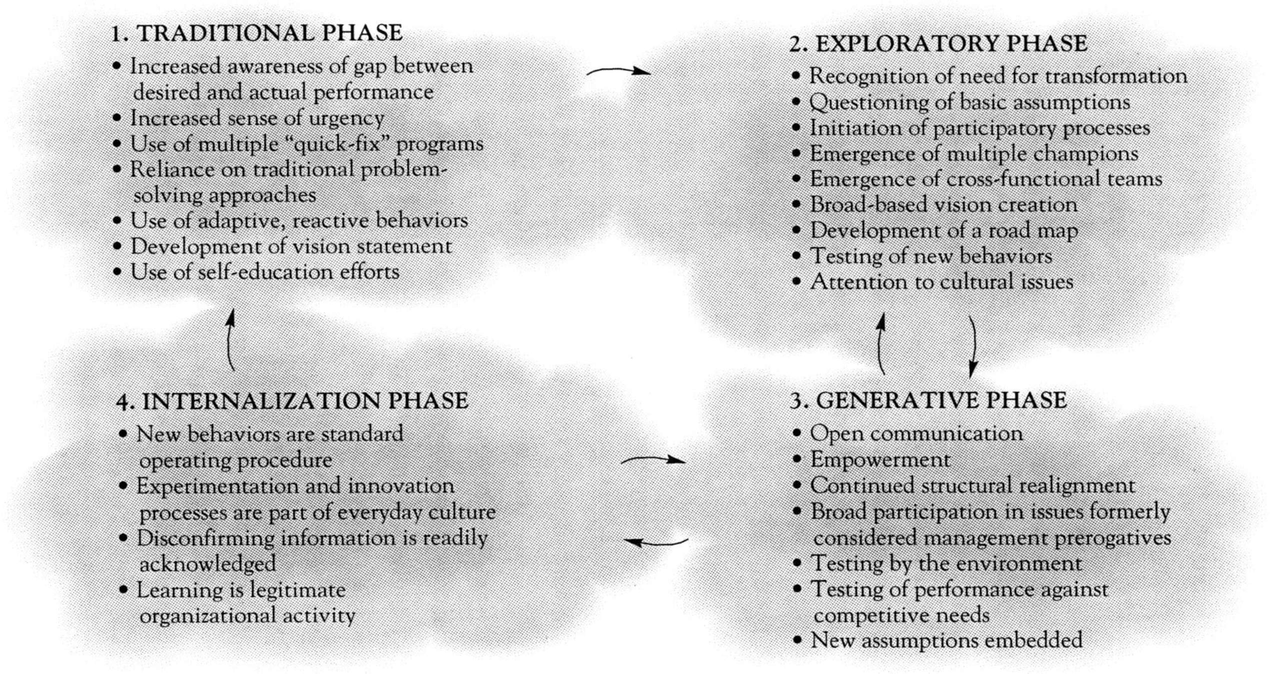

1. TRADITIONAL PHASE
- Increased awareness of gap between desired and actual performance
- Increased sense of urgency
- Use of multiple "quick-fix" programs
- Reliance on traditional problem-solving approaches
- Use of adaptive, reactive behaviors
- Development of vision statement
- Use of self-education efforts

2. EXPLORATORY PHASE
- Recognition of need for transformation
- Questioning of basic assumptions
- Initiation of participatory processes
- Emergence of multiple champions
- Emergence of cross-functional teams
- Broad-based vision creation
- Development of a road map
- Testing of new behaviors
- Attention to cultural issues

3. GENERATIVE PHASE
- Open communication
- Empowerment
- Continued structural realignment
- Broad participation in issues formerly considered management prerogatives
- Testing by the environment
- Testing of performance against competitive needs
- New assumptions embedded

4. INTERNALIZATION PHASE
- New behaviors are standard operating procedure
- Experimentation and innovation processes are part of everyday culture
- Disconfirming information is readily acknowledged
- Learning is legitimate organizational activity

alternatives, and at some point an intellectual veil lifts. There follows a recognition that the old paradigms are preventing the organization from moving forward.

At this point, the organization shifts into the *Exploratory Phase*. Here, there is a realization that a transformation is needed, but neither the scope nor the specific dimensions are clear as yet. There is a lot of sincere talk about the new behaviors, but implementation is still somewhat clumsy. It is during this phase that a new understanding of the change process itself begins to develop. More and more, basic assumptions are questioned, and as aspects of the new organizational paradigm are put into practice, a more open, trusting environment emerges. Participative processes are initiated, and cross-functional teams begin to emerge; structures and processes are rearranged, some form of road map is developed, and multiple champions serve to push the organization forward into new territory.

As the exploration continues, some parts of the organization move into the *Generative Phase*. Here, the environment is one of open communication and empowerment, and new approaches develop with far more spontaneity. Participation begins to occur in areas that were formerly considered to be management prerogatives, and the new environment, behaviors, and underlying assumptions are able to withstand even some severe tests. Leaders and organizational members are emboldened, and there is a willingness to experiment with radically new ways of doing things. Different parts of the organization may move into this phase at different times, and some parts of the organization may slip back into the Exploratory Phase on particular issues, but more and more, the organization thinks as a system, digs deeper into issues, and is increasingly able to cycle the learnings back into the organization. This phase can appear chaotic, but by now the shared vision of the future becomes a kind of DNA that keeps things focused. External controls have been loosened, structures are tested and refined, and extrinsic rewards are brought into alignment, while fixed, formal boundaries are either made more permeable or are eliminated altogether.

Collaboration is now standard operating procedure, and as the new processes become "the way we do things here," the organization moves into the *Internalization Phase*. Here, experimentation and innovation are part of the very fiber of the organizational processes, disconfirming information is routinely folded into the plans for moving forward, and organizational learning has become a fully legitimate activity. On the whole, people have become more comfortable with ambiguity and change, and at this point the focus on learning, on taking in disconfirming information, and on experimentation creates a new gap between the desired and actual performance, and the cycle begins again—with a reliance on existing methods, until an acknowledgment of the need for a more paradigmatic shift emerges and once again propels the organization into the Exploratory Phase.

As we have indicated, the boundaries between these phases are not rigid, and the time frames for moving through them vary significantly. One to three years seems to be the range for the Traditional Phase, with two to four years for each of the remaining three phases. Clearly, creating a new organizational reality and resocializing people into it is not a short-term undertaking.

How quickly and how well an organization moves through the four phases depends on a number of variables, but it is our contention that the process can be greatly facilitated if the resocialization strategy is based on the use of all seven methods of influence.

Dimension 2: Transformational Change as a Process of Influence

Successful resocialization is a complex process of influencing people in ways that make them willing to think and act differently. By influence we do not mean simply the use of personal, positional, or coercive authority to get people to behave differently. Rather, we define influence as the ability to successfully

- Create a new awareness and *consciousness* about problems
- Support the development of *energy* to actualize the vision
- Provide a *context* in which effective actions can emerge
- *Manifest* the new behavioral skills
- Help people articulate the *new meanings* that arise from a new way of doing things
- *Internalize* the new ways of thinking and behaving

To achieve these outcomes, as we have indicated previously and as experience has repeatedly demonstrated, no one method of influence is sufficient. Instead, multiple methods must be used, and there is a considerable body of evidence that shows greater success when several methods are used simultaneously. One study of more than fifty change programs showed that use of participation with structural rearrangement produced results superior to the use of either method alone (Nicolas, 1982). Another study makes the case for using participation and coercive power to manage different barriers in a large-scale change effort (Dunphy and Stace, 1988). Furthermore, extensive studies of individual change through counseling and psychotherapy show that successful therapeutic influence relies on all seven methods (Strupp, 1976; Marmor, 1976).

Both research and our experience, then, support our view that the concurrent use of the seven methods for influencing behavior will increase success in organizational transformation. Taken together, these methods form a resocialization strategy that effectively recreates the socialization process. Each of the methods are derived from a number of tested theories of behavioral change that have been applied in the fields of individual, organizational, and social change. Case data accumulated over many years show the application of these theories in change efforts at different levels of the organizational systems. While there may be other valuable theories, we have selected these because of the substantial body of mainstream research in the behavioral and social sciences that supports their effectiveness.

In choosing these seven methods, we were cognizant of the fact that their application has historically been used to support two seemingly opposite points of view. The first view is based on an individual perspective: to change organizations, it is first necessary to change the behavior of the individual. The second view is based on an environmental perspective: to change the behavior of individuals, it is first necessary to alter the physical and social conditions that define their existence. Table 3.1 illustrates which theories have supported each of these perspectives.

Researchers who have preferred the individual perspective have developed and tested theories emphasizing strategies of persuasion and learning. They have emphasized findings that support the development of individual awareness and of both cognitive and emotional insights. They have also highly valued the development of individual behavioral skills. The use of persuasion, face-to-face dialogue, and educational interventions are strongly supported by those who hold this perspective.

Table 3.1. Behavioral Influence Theories Supporting Individual and Environmental Change Perspectives.

Perspective	Behavioral Influence Theory
Individual	Persuasive communication
	Participation
	Expectancy
	Role modeling
Environmental	Extrinsic rewards
	Structural rearrangement
	Coercion

Those who prefer the environmental perspective have provided data that indicate that all the education and persuasion in the world will not change people if they continue to live in an environment that reinforces old behaviors. This group of researchers holds a pessimistic view of people's ability to make and sustain change to themselves without use of powerful external forces. They have strongly valued the importance of reinforcement strategies (variations on the Skinnerian model) and organizational and social restructuring. They have also tended to be more comfortable with the uses of external power that take advantage of differential levels of influence between the advocates of change and those whose behavior they wish to change.

This binary thinking is not helpful if our task is transformation and resocialization. These perspectives are, in fact, not mutually exclusive positions. Some of the influence methods may be more critical than others at different stages of the change process, but it is the use of all of them in an integrated way that recreates the socialization process. Table 3.2 provides a matrix of the relationship between each of the behavioral influence methods and the phases of transformation.

To expedite the resocialization of organizational members and the internalization of a new set of behaviors, *all* the behavioral influence methods in use must send a coherent set of messages at all times. Nothing retards the progress of internalization as much as when organizational members are bombarded by conflicting sets of messages from the various behavioral influence methods. However, we do not mean to imply that all the methods must be used equally during all phases of transformation. As Table 3.2 illustrates, each of the methods is more or less important at different stages of the transformation. Of particular interest is the heavy use of persuasive communication and coercion during the Traditional Phase, and of participation, role modeling, and structural rearrangement during the Generative Phase. In later chapters, we discuss why this appears to be so.

Table 3.2. Relationship of Behavioral Influence Methods to the Phases of Transformational Change.

Resocialization Strategy	Phases of Transformational Change			
Methods of Influence	Traditional	Exploratory	Generative	Internalization
Persuasive communication	xxx	xx	x	x
Participation	x	xx	xxx	xx
Expectancy		x	xx	x
Role modeling		xx	xxx	x
Extrinsic rewards		x	x	xx
Structural rearrangement		x	xxx	xx
Coercion	xx	x		

Legend: x = More than routinely useful
   xx = Highly essential
   xxx = Absolutely critical

At this time it is also useful to point out that just as each of the methods may be more or less important during each of the four phases, the methods are also useful when differentially applied to various barriers to change. Table 3.3 provides a few examples that help to illustrate this point.

Having identified both the phases and activities of transformation and the use of the seven behavioral influence methods to create a new organizational reality and resocialize organizational members, an example of how this dynamic approach plays out in practice would be helpful. In succeeding chapters, we offer additional case material, but for now, we focus on a Brazilian company, Semco (Semler, 1993, 1994).

Semco manufactures marine pumps, commercial dishwashers, industrial cooling units, mixers, slicers, and turnkey biscuit factories. Recently, it entered the environmental waste disposal consulting business, and with its emphasis on creativity, innovation, and flexibility there is no telling what it may do next.

Table 3.3. Differential Application of Behavioral Influence Methods to Barriers to Change.

Barrier:	People do not believe the change makes sense for the organization.
Method:	Persuasive communication, participation
Barrier:	People are asked to achieve new/different levels of performance, but work structures do not facilitate this achievement.
Method:	Structural rearrangement, participation
Barrier:	"What's in it for us if we behave the new way?"
Method:	Persuasive communication, extrinsic rewards
Barrier:	People are anxious, confused and hesitant to act.
Method:	Participation, persuasive communication
Barrier:	People are expected to behave in ways that did not exist before.
Method:	Role modeling, expectancy, extrinsic rewards
Barrier:	After repeated attempts to do so, organization members have not embraced the need to change.
Method:	Coercion

Semco's transformation began in the early 1980s when Ricardo Semler replaced his father as CEO. Semco had been a traditional company, and at first the young CEO was primarily interested in diversifying. He brought on a new executive team that put in place many new procedures, an elaborate new budgeting process, a number of new license agreements, and made several acquisitions.

But the new processes did not seem to help. The company was still unable to make on-time deliveries, and employees "just did not seem to care" (Semler, 1993, p. 52). Workers had to be pushed to produce, but Semler dreamed of having a "self-propelled work force" (p. 52). This is a good example of what happens during the Traditional Phase. There is a sense that something must be done, a path is decisively embarked upon, only to be found wanting. Xerox,

too, experienced this in its pursuit of total quality, and many reengineering projects are making the same discovery.

The issues began to crystalize for Semler when conflict surfaced
in his management team. During a series of exploratory meetings, he
realized that complicated numbers-driven budgeting systems would
never get them where they needed to go. His decision to reduce the
number of cost centers from four hundred to five and to sever
Semco's relationship with the manager who had advocated that system is an example of structural rearrangement as well as the use of
coercion. In an effort to get people to care, Semler and his team tried
one quick-fix program after another. Each program worked for a
while, but the old ways soon reasserted themselves.

Frustrated, Semler began to think about the company's underlying values: employees were not trusted, dress codes whispered subtle messages about conformity, the physical layout separated people
from one another, and people had little control over their work lives.
At this point, the change effort began to move into the Exploratory
Phase. Semler recognized that before he could get anyone else to
change, he would have to change his own behavior. He began to delegate more, worked at home, and began to lead a more balanced
life as a way of demonstrating both his trust in others and his belief
in creating an environment in which the whole person could flourish.
He even stopped wearing a watch so as to escape from its tyranny.

Concurrently, workers' committees were formed. These committees included union representatives, and the committee charters were
negotiated with the unions—an example of how positive expectations
can create positive outcomes. Starting with small issues such as
modernizing the locker rooms, the committees soon broadened their
scope, and when the Brazilian economy took a dive, the committees
took on the arduous tasks of lowering salaries, increasing hours, and
cutting costs to save jobs; and when layoffs became inevitable, they
participated in the decision as to who would go and who would stay.

Little by little, participation became spontaneous: teams were
formed to improve everything from the quality of the cafeteria food to

changing the casings of a meat grinder to make it easier to clean to coming up with a new way to put a matte finish on stainless steel slicers. The groups were diverse, with no formal leaders, and the problems they tackled were of their own choosing. One night, when some needed parts arrived at the last minute, employees returned on their own time and worked until the wee hours to make their production goal—a clear indication that empowerment was becoming internalized.

As the transformation continued, employees became involved in doing salary surveys, and a strike generated by several misperceptions concerning the ensuing raises served as a test of senior management's commitment. Semler refused to fire anyone; there was no retribution, benefits continued during the strike, and Semco learned that participation by itself was not enough. Communications would have to be significantly improved because it was misperception, not fact, that had been a main cause of the strike. These events signaled a clear move into the Generative Phase. The last bastions of management prerogatives—salaries and adversarial union relationships—were being scaled and the new environment was being tested. It was not found wanting, and open information became one of the cornerstones of Semco's transformation. All financial information, salary information, and performance appraisal information are available to anyone who asks to see it.

Structures and systems continued to be revised as Semco employees studied other companies and ultimately decided that small business units were the best way to ensure the flow of relevant information, to give each employee a sense of belonging and the ability to influence what was going on, and to adapt to the economic swings that continued to plague the Brazilian economy. Within these units, employees performed multiple jobs, job descriptions became unnecessary, and salary decisions were altered to incorporate the multiple skill and task combinations—all indications that flexibility and adaptability were being built into the organizational processes. To bring extrinsic rewards into alignment with the emergence of the adaptive culture, profit sharing became a natural next step. Employees were involved in deciding the percentage of profits to be shared, and the process for sharing them.

Participative approaches had clearly become internalized, and as Semco moved into the Internalization Phase, a flowering of other innovative changes indicated that the new culture had become a way of life. Job rotations in which 20 to 25 percent of the managers shift jobs each year became part of management's expectation of themselves and others. The Family Silverware program gave preference to internal candidates for promotion (Semler, 1993, p. 171), and the establishment of Hepatitis Leave, a sabbatical to enable people to think and refocus personal and professional priorities (p. 159), indicated that the search for new forms of extrinsic rewards were being discovered and incorporated into "the way we do things here." Twenty-five percent of the work force set its own salaries, and a voluntary program of "risk salary" (pp. 202–203) indicated that participation had permeated the organization's thinking. New mental models had been created.

Structural rearrangement continued to evolve through all four phases. Based on a rejection of the hierarchy, there are only four job categories at Semco: *counselors,* who act as catalysts; *partners,* who oversee the business operations; *coordinators,* who lead departments or activities and who guide teams of five to twenty *associates.* To emphasize collective responsibility, the six counselors rotate the CEOship. The institution of this practice and the development of a group called the Nucleus of Technological Innovation that focuses on improving existing processes or devising new products and services indicated a decisive shift into the Generative Phase.

Flexible as Semco had become, they still were not flexible enough for the Brazilian economy and it became clear that no amount of participation and cost control would ever be enough. Semco's response was to push its circular organization a step further and to become a "satellite" organization. This was a form of "outsourcing," but outsourcing to companies formed by Semco employees. Semco helped these employees start their own businesses, provided training in writing business plans, managing inventories, and so forth, and even leased or sold them Semco machinery. Satellites could contract with other companies as well as Semco, and Semco did not have to contract with the satellites. But to date, two dozen satellites have been started and none have failed. That disconfirming information is readily taken in and that experiments and risk taking have become a way of life are all indications of Semco's having moved into the Internalization Phase.

Today, Semco has no information systems, quality control, or training departments. It has dozens of different salary arrangements, and the role of human resources is to "foster change and nurture daring initiatives" (Semler, 1993, p. 149). Employees manage the benefits, self-organizing teams are common, and the company is willing to tolerate a "touch of civil disobedience . . . to alert the organization that all is not right" (p. 167). Change has become the norm, but nevertheless, employees feel a strong sense of purpose. Despite repeated recessions, Semco has grown, productivity and products have increased, and they are number one or number two in all their markets. But Semler has even transformed his definition of success. "Success means not making . . . [decisions] myself" (p. 3).

Semco embodies the shift in thinking that is necessary for genuine transformation. Implicitly and explicitly, Semco thinks of itself as a dynamic system in which the relationship between the parts is as important as the parts themselves. The sense of urgency about the need to change was periodically provided by the Brazilian economy, but even in good times the steady stream of innovative programs indicates a continuous focus on the gap between actual and desired performance. While there was no road map for the transformation as a whole, the key executives were guided by a powerful belief in the abilities of the employees, and the role of these executives became that of catalyst and removers of barriers to change. Champions and role models emerged at all levels, and Semler set the tone in his willingness to change his own behaviors first. Over time, managers whose behavior served as role models were hired and rotated, and there was a consistent and continuing emphasis on bringing all policies, processes, and structures into alignment with the vision of a company whose employees were entrepreneurial, creative, and trusted.

Semco's transformation evolved with no linear master plan but with a deep sense of overall direction and the ability to take advantage of every opportunity or crisis to move forward, a sure sign of the internalization of the new ways of thinking and behaving. The transformation tasks and the behavioral influence methods were used repeatedly, creating the kind of powerful energy field that resulted in resocialization. As Semler proudly admits, Semco is no longer a reflection of him. Semco is a reflection of Semco.

One of the hallmarks of Semler's ability to catalyze the transformation was his ability to reframe the phenomenon of resistance to change. His view of "a touch of civil disobedience" as not only tolerable but desirable is an example of his attitude, and there are other examples of his acknowledging, valuing, and accepting others' points of view. This brings us to the third dimension in our transformational change model.

Dimension 3: The Reframing of Resistance

Since the beginning of modern planned change, the concept and centrality of resistance has been important. From the early work of Freud, the strength of resistance has been recognized as making the difference between staying the same and changing. While the seven methods of influence are all ways of dealing with resistance, special considerations need to be made if the methods are to be applied effectively in support of transformation.

Traditionally, in the organizational world resistance has been an evaluative term and has been used to describe the failure of some organizational members to see or accept what others have decided is good for them and/or the organization. When proponents of change experience resistance to their efforts, they see the resisters as nonconforming or deviant in their behavior. Not only are the behaviors or attitudes of those who resist seen as being different from that of the advocates of change, but the advocates often assume that there is something bad, wrong, or inferior about those who continue to manifest those behaviors or attitudes. This definition of resistance as a value judgment has dominated the organizational world.

As long as the experience of the resister is disparaged and not seen as legitimate, even when it is not necessarily useful to the attempted change, the effectiveness of the methods of behavioral influence and the possibilities for resocialization will be limited. Maintaining a disrespectful response to resistance leads to increasing use of force by the change advocates or, at best, more exhortation to "get with it." Both of these responses merely serve to increase the force with which the resisters object.

As an alternative to this approach, we suggest reframing the response to resistance as *the need to manage the multiple realities,* including those of both the advocates and the organizational members. This perspective assumes that all parties have a stake in the level of organizational performance and that they all have legitimate viewpoints; but it also assumes that different individuals or groups see problems with different worldviews or constructions of reality. In our three-dimensional model, the surfacing and managing of these differing views acts as the glue that binds together the other two factors. Because of the importance of this perspective and because of the frequent lack of understanding of it by advocates of change, the next chapter is devoted to the management of multiple realities.

4

The Path of Least Resistance
Working with Multiple Realities

Individuals living in an apparently common organizational reality often construct different versions of this reality, influenced by the differential forces that create their subunit, referent group, or individual role. The accounting manager who reviews reports of expenditures for customer entertainment may see the matter as one of needing to control *expenses*, while the sales manager who incurred the expenditures may see it as *investing* in future income. The optimist sees a partially filled glass of water as half full; the pessimist sees it as half empty. Following a field-theory/phenomenological perspective, it can be said that although people may be in the same physical space at a given moment, the nature of their consciousness and the meaning of their current experience may vary significantly.

Most of the time, these differences are background factors as people relate to each other in more or less routine ways. People do not state their worldviews or their nonnegotiable values every time they engage in social interaction. Yet, if they become aware of forces acting to change their customary routines, their values exert a strong influence on how they perceive these forces. What they then experience as reality is their construction of events and the meaning of those events, and frequently one person's construction will be different from the next person's. Whenever people try to change a system, these differences bring forth strong feelings from everyone involved, including people with apparently similar goals. It is as though it only takes a small taste or smell of the winds of change to arouse awareness in the parties involved as to what their hard-won and deeply assimilated version of reality is, and that it is about to be challenged.

There are many ways in which differences in construction of reality can be categorized. The most obvious of these have to do with the meaning and use of language that stem from particular cultural backgrounds, such as ethnic, geographical, race, or gender differences; with differences in mental models that derive from varying perceptual styles; or with different learning styles. Educational, work group and professional group memberships produce other differing sets of reality-images, such as college-trained engineers versus high-school graduate factory workers, engineers versus scientists, or hardware versus software specialists; other groupings can easily be defined.

Much has been written about the ways in which various individuals or groups construct their reality, about the problems that arise from clashes of these different worlds, and about methods to resolve them. Yet, despite widespread discussion, the advocates of organizational change usually fail to grasp fully the significance of multiple realities when attempting transformational change. Typically, there is a lack of attention to understanding how the people involved perceive and create their worlds and how they make meaning out of their experiences. The advocates of change assume that their own reality, or their analysis of the multiple realities of other organization members, is the "correct" reality; but it is more likely that *what the advocates of change take to be reality will not be the same as the realities experienced by other organizational members.* This discrepancy helps to explain why people sometimes seem unwilling to embrace suggestions or programs that appear to be in their best interest, such as good safety practices or quality improvements that produce sales that will help them to keep their jobs. Their picture of reality—that which is foremost in their mental models—is different from the view of those who designed the changes. Thus, those who are asked to make job improvements for the sake of increased efficiency may picture a world in which the efficiencies will result in loss of their jobs rather than serve as job-saving measures. Their realities center around job security, while the proponents of change operate from a reality that emphasizes organizational efficiency. Calling for sensitivity to this difference in no way implies that changes should not be made to increase efficiency because people are frightened by a new approach; rather, it is a way of looking at the roots of inertia, which need to be understood if the multidirected energies of the various parties are to be aligned.

In addition, while most advocates of change assume that the rest of the organization experiences a common reality, and while some elements of employees' views of reality may be similar, there are usually significant differences among employees. Thus, those seeking to bring about change should assume that a number of conflicting realities will emerge any time significant change is attempted.

Examples of Multiple Realities in Change Situations

Three illustrations may help to convey the kinds of multiple realities that operate in organizational settings. The first example is a fairly typical situation in which a manager brings together a group of people to launch a change. The individuals may be from the manager's group, or they may represent a mixture of people from various parts of the organization. Figure 4.1 depicts the potential range of multiple realities that exist in the room as the manager unfolds the proposal. To keep things simple, the realities are stated as thoughts and feelings of individuals that are supported by values and worldviews of a more general, complex nature.

Figure 4.1 shows a variety of reactions, including joyful support, self-referent concerns, surprise that the issue is recognized as a serious problem, thoughts of how to improve the proposal, concern that the integrity of the organization will be damaged by the plan, and

Figure 4.1. Multiple Realities in a Typical Discussion of Change.

Source: Adapted from CorelDRAW ClipArt with permission.

so forth. Each of these thoughts is a statement of the reality experienced by that person as he or she contemplates the issue at hand, and each is a reflection of the particular way in which that person has made meaning of his or her general existence within the organization. As Nevis (1987) has shown, these reactions may be seen almost as a map of the terrain of the consciousness (awareness) of this group as it contemplates a problem. They indicate that the people involved have energy either to go to a place different than the envisioned change or to retain the status quo. This is an important point, for it means that all the parties have energy and are not simply passive, unmotivated people.

In this perspective, the first task of dealing with resistance is to accept the reality of multidirected energy fields, and to respect each of these fields as legitimate experience. To do this is to broaden and deepen the perspective both of the initiators of change and of the other organizational members. Then, if heightened awareness is a prelude to informed action, it follows that the way the multiple realities are managed will determine in large part the outcome of the proposed change. We will come back to this point after presenting the other examples.

The second example is a case in which reference group membership played a large role in shaping reality, and in which the presence of several groups resulted in multiple realities. The situation involved a proposal to reorganize some units of the U.S. government.

In the fall of 1993, Vice President Gore's National Productivity Review Task Force on Reinventing Government recommended that the Drug Enforcement Agency (DEA) be merged into the Federal Bureau of Investigation (FBI). This brought forth all kinds of reactions from the parties involved. Based on a study of the published responses, Table 4.1 depicts the multiple realities of three active reference groups confronted with the issue: the FBI, the DEA, and the administrative experts of the Task Force on Reinventing Government.

Table 4.1. Multiple Realities in the Proposed 1993 Merger of the FBI and the DEA.

	FBI	DEA	TFRG
Culture	Analytic values	Intuitive, risk-taking	Objective, unbiased
	Dark suit, white shirt, tie	Informal dress	Casual dress
	Orderly, disciplined	Loose controls	Dedicated to change
	Respectable	"Street types"	"Policy wonks," Ph.D.'s
	Historic role, tradition	Relatively new "club"	Temporary organization
Re: Merger	Our system is better; put DEA under our control.	Flexibility is one of our major strengths.	Merger will save money.
	DEA does not have broad range of required skills.	FBI does not appreciate the uniqueness of our special skills.	Merger provides tighter, more efficient controls.
	DEA are "cowboys"; often break the rules.	FBI is possessive; does not share fingerprints and information.	Better able to integrate crime control with foreign goverments.
	Our worldwide reputation enables us to accomplish more.	We have more experience in working outside the U.S.	Merger brings more to the DEA.
		FBI has too many tasks to be able to devote attention to our mission.	

FBI = Federal Bureau of Investigation
DEA = Drug Enforcement Agency
TFRG = Task Force for Reinventing Government

In this situation, the projected images of each of the three groups were sustained by a lack of any attempt to get the groups to share the different pictures of their current realities and to consider an image of a merged department. By not respecting the legitimacy of each reality and trying to get each group to become interested in a reality other than its own, the idea of merger became politicized, the proposal became "too hot to handle," and the merger never took place. We make no brief for or against the merger; we simply use this example to show the importance of working with multiple realities in change efforts, and to indicate how powerful each reality can be. The probability is high that if a presidential order to merge the departments had been issued, the resulting resistance would have led to foot-dragging and possible sabotage. Use of the power of the president's office might have initiated the merger, but it is doubtful that the merger could have worked without significant effort to reduce the conflict generated by the varying images of the two groups, or without heavy use of all seven of the methods of influence.

The third case, published by Smircich and Morgan (1982), is about an insurance company in which the company's president attempted a significant change. The change was stimulated by complaints from district sales managers that field agents were not getting adequate service from the home office. Service was slow, customers were complaining, and requests to fix things resulted in a huge increase in the volume of paperwork. To cope with this, the president, after consulting with key executives, initiated "Project OJ30" in early May 1979. Table 4.2 presents the memo launching this program. Table 4.3 shows the competing interpretations of reality that resulted after the memo was issued and people began to work on the project. Smircich and Morgan analyzed the situation in terms of the systemic issues involved in creating meaning (their term for creating reality) and showed that it would be a mistake to conclude that any problems were simply a result of poor leadership by the president or of employees who did not care about the health of the company. They indicated that even strong leadership can lead to "trained inaction" if there is not a surfacing and managing of the multiple realities involved.

Implications of the Cases

The above cases show the range of reality constructions that are often in play as a change effort unfolds. They show that from the perspective of organization members there may be very good reasons for not responding to the proposed change. Some of these reasons may

Table 4.2. Memo Launching Project OJ30.

What:	A special program designed to bring all insurance processing activities up to date by June 30, 1979.
Why:	The present work backlog is having an adverse impact on total insurance operations.
How:	1. All departments will make a concerted effort to eliminate all backlogs. The goal is to have work conditions current in all departments by June 30.
	2. All insurance home office employees who have the time will be expected to "volunteer" to assist other departments by performing certain assigned processing tasks until June 30. Procedures relative to this will be developed.
Timing:	Operation June 30 will commence on Monday, May 14, and will terminate on Saturday, June 30.
Priority:	This program has the highest priority. Nothing else in insurance is of more importance.
Reports:	Each staff member will report in writing weekly to Mr. Hall on the status of work conditions in his or her department.

Source: L. Smircich and G. Morgan, *Journal of Applied Behavioral Science, 18* (3), p. 264, copyright © 1982. Reprinted by permission of Sage Publications, Inc.

be expressed directly and others may need to be ferreted out. Some people will not see how the change really helps the organization; others will see what is being asked as beyond their imagination or skill level; still others will believe that the problem has been misdiagnosed. Furthermore, in some cases those initiating change may be correct in their judgment of the problem and in their new vision, but they will be seen as doing a poor job of implementation. The need will be appreciated, but the means will not. These kinds of reactions can be useful if they are integrated into the change effort rather than being driven underground. A classic paper by Don Klein (1976) deals with these behaviors under the heading of "the role of the defender," by which he means that objections may stem as much from caring about the organization as from passivity or noncaring.

Table 4.3. Multiple Realities in Project OJ30.

Framing Experience	Interpretation	Meaning and Action
	The President's Interpretation OJ30 provides an opportunity for the company to work together in the resolution of a problem. It will solve the problem and help develop a cooperative spirit.	For the President OJ30 does much to clear clear the backlog of work and can be judged a success. Meaning framed against an idealized image.
OJ30 frames significant elements of work experience (work backlog, customer and staff complaints), in a form that makes them amenable to action.		
	The Staff Members' Interpretation OJ30 represents another futile act which will do nothing to solve the organization's basic problems. It symbolizes the way we do things here.	For Staff Members Will call for no more than minimal action; do not take too seriously for it can't do much to remedy the basic problem. Meaning framed against past history.

Source: L. Smircich and G. Morgan, Journal of Applied Behavioral Science, 18 (3), p. 268, copyright © 1982. Reprinted by permission of Sage Publications, Inc.

To obtain full appreciation of the power of resistance when it is driven underground, as opposed to when it is treated openly and respectfully, one can go back to earliest recorded time to find tax evasion, religious freedom movements, and uprisings, rebellions, and revolutions of all sizes and shapes. In all of these cases, resistance had no legitimate form of expression and an "underdog" fought against a "top dog." If one identifies with the underdog, resistance can be seen as a laudable action. It is considered to be "desirable," a legitimate position that happens to be held by those with little power, or a reaction to abusive power. One need think only of the resistance efforts of the American colonies prior to the Revolutionary War, or of the underground movement in resistance to the Nazis during World War II, to recognize cases in which many people would applaud the resistance. In these cases, if one takes the perspective of the resisters, one might readily assume that this consciously chosen opposition is a sign of intelligence, maturity, and good mental health, as opposed to being a manifestation of "unruly masses" not following the wishes of those in command.

Another reason for a more respectful reaction to realities other than one's own is that resistance is not an all-or-nothing phenomenon but rather is best seen as ambivalence. People can be *for* something in part, yet perceive a number of negative implications. Even when people appear to be *against* something, some aspect of it may be interesting or acceptable. This ambivalence means that there may be a way to reach people who appear to be well defended against outside influence. This point is often overlooked by advocates of change, who tend to focus on the more stubborn part of the organizational members' negativism, and do not respect it as part of a complex response in which some positive response might flower if approached in a less monolithic manner.

While the number and kinds of these objections may vary from a few to a multitude, they ultimately will need to be addressed in the process of implementing change. Rather than approaching the existence of multiple realities from a negative perspective, it is more constructive to approach it as an opportunity to broaden and deepen one's understanding of the environment in which the transformation must take place. The kinds of questions that need to be asked to surface the multiple realities before they become counterproductive are:

- How is it that others see things differently than I do? Isn't this interesting?

- If we assume that we all have a common goal, why is it that we do not have a common picture of the situation and of what needs to be done?

- How is it that some people do not seem to have accepted a goal, process, or structure that is apparently desirable for them (at least as I see it)?

- Is there anything of value to be contributed from each of the perceptions of reality?

- How can we create a new reality that is more common to all? What should this be?

While these questions are applicable at both the individual and group level, addressing these issues at the group level poses an additional challenge.

Relationship of Multiple Realities to Intergroup Management

One of the most difficult tasks managers encounter is the management of differences among subunits of the organization. Whether these differences stem from honest but different perspectives or from political maneuvering, those who are responsible for integrating the efforts of different groups face this issue daily. In the case of transformational change efforts, the difficulty is magnified considerably as a result of protective and/or defensive reactions of those concerned. This was certainly the case in the contemplated merger of the FBI and the DEA discussed earlier, where the proposed change was aborted because senior government officials did not see a way to manage the intense group differences.

In attempting to manage intergroup relations, managers face two potential traps: the trap of being seduced by one group to accept its position, and the trap of deciding to support one position over the other because it seems to be a better choice. The concept of multiple realities gives managers a way of avoiding these pitfalls because it assumes that both positions are real and legitimate, and that it is not possible to move to a reconciliation or third alternative without initially showing acceptance of and respect for *all* sides. Taking

an essentially neutral position frames the issue as a problem to be
solved jointly by all parties rather than as a need to favor one group
over another. The reader who believes that this is a denial of executive responsibility need only look at the behavior of effective third-
party interveners. President Carter in 1977 could not have
succeeded with Sadat and Begin in moving the Middle East process
along without showing respect for both sides. Similarly, Jan Ege-
land, deputy prime minister of Norway, along with Ron Pundik and
Yair Hirschfield could not have succeeded in negotiating with the
Israelis and Palestinians in 1993 without demonstrating in some way
that they saw each side's viewpoints as expressing a legitimate reality. To be a good arbitrator in any setting would appear to rest in
large measure on this openness of attitude.

This reasoning suggests a tactical position for one who would
manage the dilemmas of intergroup differences and conflicts: act to
get the parties in dialogue and do not align yourself with any one
side, particularly early in the effort. This does not mean that you
abandon your own position, or that you do not express your ideas
and concerns. It does mean, however, that you act to bring about a
resolution that all sides can accept. While there is no guarantee that
this approach will work, the alternative is the use of coercion, a
choice that brings with it the possibility that the differences will
simply move underground and continue to be a problem. In sum,
the concept of multiple realities cautions against falling into the
trap of labeling groups as either good or bad, and helps us to avoid
seeing people whose realities are different from ours as "the enemy."

Relationship of Multiple Realities to Major Phases of Transformation and Methods of Influence

Thinking in terms of multiple realities also enables more effective
application of the seven influence methods to the activities identified in each of the phases of transformation. Here are four illustrations:

1.   *Use of persuasive communication in the Exploratory Phase to create a shared vision.* If divergent realities exist, it stands to reason that the people expressing them need to be talked with differently, using different language and symbols. The aborted merger of the FBI and the DEA is a case in which appeals clearly needed to be tailored to each group. While the leadership may make similar public statements to both sides before bringing the parties together in a more participative mode, it is often necessary for a third party who is trusted by both sides to engage first in a legitimating dialogue with each side alone. This discussion draws forth a picture of each group's reality that can become the starting point for moving toward a shared alternative.

2.   *Use of role modeling in the Generative Phase.* Different subgroups involved in a change may respond to different kinds of role models. The person who is seen as a "hero" by one group may not be appreciated by another group. It may also be necessary to train or coach models on how to relate to different groups. At the macro level, using as a model successful pilot projects from other parts of the organization may be much appreciated by some units or functions but not by others in which a very strong "not invented here" syndrome exists. The latter groups may be better approached with extrinsic rewards or coercion.

3.   *Use of participation in any of the phases.* The call for participation is now reaching a very high level. It makes good sense to harness all the resources available and involve people in things that affect them. There is probably no single better way to get multiple realities on the table and to be respectful of resistance than to get the relevant parties together to share their perspectives. Given the growing awareness of the number of multiple realities to be considered, recent advances in this area include methods for large group interventions in which many stakeholder groups gather together. However, not every problem can be solved through discussion, no matter how complete and authentic that discussion might be. Some people learn more by observing the behavior of others than through

discussion. Exposure to powerful and appealing role models might be much more useful in reaching these people.

4.   *Use of coercion and/or extrinsic rewards in any of the phases.* For some people, no amount of persuasion will suffice to create awareness or generate energy to act without the use of external motivation. For others, such motivation will not be necessary and, as we show later, can actually act as a detriment.

A consideration of these variations supports our conclusion that *no single intervention method is adequate to the task of managing multiple realities.* Nor is it humanly possible for any advocate of change to identify, anticipate, or bring into the open all of the important realities involved in a change effort. The more differentiated the organizational world becomes, the more complex is this task. Therefore, any effective approach to implementing transformational change must allow room for the emergence of these realities and for assimilation of the new reality that is to be developed. The most effective way of doing this is to use more than one point of leverage—in other words, to use the seven methods of influence. Part Two of this book is devoted to an examination of each of these methods.

Since the wisdom of Solomon, or even a group of Solomons, would not be enough to know everything that needs to happen, and since transformation requires the use of multiple methods for reshaping behaviors to support the new organizational reality, the role of the leaders of transformational change is to act as facilitators and orchestrators of the application of all three dimensions of the transformation model. In particular, they must help to reconcile the multiple realities, shaping those realities into a new, shared reality and orchestrating the multiple-influence strategy for resocialization, with special attention to becoming increasingly effective role models of the new behaviors needed to support that reality.

Part II

. . . .

Seven Methods of Influence

An Integrated Strategy for
Transformational Change

5

Persuasive Communication

Enabling People to Envision a Different Future

We begin our review of the seven methods for bringing about change with perhaps the most often deliberately used method: the attempt to be influential through direct communication. From the dawn of human language, human beings have resorted to words and images to deliver information, to instill or change an attitude, or simply to build relationships with one another. Persuasive communication is a method for structuring and delivering information to influence another person to think or act in a way that the "sender" believes to be beneficial, desirable, or preferable.

There are many definitions of persuasive communication. We prefer one that summarizes it as follows: "There is a general consensus that persuasion is an activity or process in which a communicator attempts to introduce a change in the belief, attitude, or behavior of another person or group of persons through the transmission of a message in the context in which the persuadee has some degree of free choice" (Perloff, 1993, p. 5). Significant in this definition is the notion of introducing a message into the awareness of others that they are free to accept or reject, and the notion that if they accept it, they do so with conscious volition.

Persuasive communication may be thought of as the art of presenting a proposal or suggestion so as to maximize the probability that it will be accepted. This act rests on the identification of both the logical benefits and the psychological satisfactions that can result from acceptance. Persuasive communication may be used to change how people think or feel, but it is essentially a method of knowledge transfer in the quest for new behavior. The approach rests on the assumption that knowing and understanding open up new ways of looking at things, new ways of doing one's job, or new ways of working together.

In general, persuasive communication can have three possible objectives: to create for others a vision of desired responses, to shape or reinforce behavior that already exists, and to change the attitudes and/or behavior of others. All three objectives come into play at different points in the transformation process. Given these goals, it is not surprising that persuasive communication is usually the first thing people try when they wish to influence the behavior of others. There is something compelling about the idea that reasonable people need only to have things explained to them to cause them to adjust their way of seeing, feeling, or behaving. Accordingly, when one becomes aware of a problem, one immediately attempts to share one's awareness with others in some fashion to convince them of how best to deal with the matter. Almost all institutional meetings serve this function. In fact, this approach is taken so automatically that people often fail to appreciate what is required for persuasive communication to succeed, or to recognize the limitations of this approach. Consequently, many attempts at persuasive communications—both oral and written—fail to achieve their purpose. The following situation is illustrative:

At Gamma University, the administration had never shared its budget figures with the faculty as a whole. Each department head negotiated a budget with the provost in a "we negotiate whatever we can" mode. Comprehensive figures for the entire institution were not available to any but a select few. Sharing five-year projections of revenues and costs would have been completely out of character. In order to change this, and in the hope of creating support for extra workloads, new projects, and external funding initiatives, the new president decided to share the less-than-rosy financial facts with the entire campus community at a faculty meeting attended by staff and students.

The long-awaited day for the presentation arrived. The newly appointed budget director, an extremely intelligent but shy and unassuming woman, attempted to explain the budget to the faculty by using a chart with hundreds of figures and line items. The material was presented in a tutorial manner. The information presented in the overhead projections was not bulleted and did not isolate important data; it was merely rows and columns of raw numbers.

After years of being in the dark with respect to the budget, the viewers began searching for hidden messages and agendas. A few questions were asked, some very convoluted or confusing, and the speaker found them difficult to answer. The faculty felt that the data overload was meant to obfuscate; the president thought, "Why don't they understand the problems? I've opened the books." What had been touted as a revelation almost spawned a revolution!

The above case illustrates an all-too-common occurrence: well-meaning people assume that for appropriate action to take place, they need merely to explain things to others of goodwill. Think how often people operate on this premise. Billboards cry out to the reader: "Seat belts save lives." "Friends don't let friends drive drunk." "The Surgeon General has determined that cigarette smoking is hazardous to your health." "Just say no to drugs." These messages are founded on the assumption that knowledge changes people, and that if people would just understand the consequences of not wearing seat belts, of drunken driving, of smoking cigarettes, and of taking drugs, they would change their behavior to eliminate all these dangerous pursuits. Similarly, there is an implicit assumption that the explicit warning on a cigarette package will be a reminder every time an individual lights up that there is a body of knowledge on the issue and that *knowing* this will bring about a change in the behavior of reasonable individuals. In theory, once an idea is acquired, it becomes the stimulus for change, and the new cognition or understanding leads to new behavior without the need for additional incentives or supports.

Most people will agree that these messages have had at least some success. Yet people continue to smoke, to use drugs, to drink and drive, and to drive without seat belts. If the exchange of information and ideas is an effective method for influencing behavior, why are seemingly desirable messages not heeded more frequently?

To answer this question, we explore the complexities inherent in the communication process itself, provide some examples of successful persuasion, examine the impact of multiple realities on the use of persuasive communication, and identify the skills and conditions necessary for the effective use of this method in transformational change.

Understanding the Complexities of Communication

To understand how persuasive communication can be effective in transformational change, it is helpful to divide the process into two parts. First, some act of knowing must occur, a comprehension that makes possible the assimilation of a new perspective, skill, or mental model. Second, once this has occurred, it then becomes possible to behave differently. Thus, if one really accepts as fact that wearing seat belts reduces the chance of bodily harm in automobile accidents, it is logical that one will wear a seat belt every time one is in a car. Both parts of this process, the awareness and the implementation, are critical: the first because it gives a picture of the desired behavior and produces readiness for the desired action and the second because it is the opportunity to act on this new recognition.

Unfortunately, the progression from rational argument to behavioral change is not automatic. We have identified five dynamics that get in the way:

1. *The manner in which the leader of change articulates his or her argument may not be powerful enough to provide a picture of the new ways of behaving.* Fundamentally, persuasive communication is based on an inherent human need to acquire information and to organize it in a way that makes it possible to function in a world of many competing inputs. To change behavior, a communication must first be persuasive enough to cause people to look at the underlying assumptions that support their present position and that block their perception of new perspectives and possibilities. When an assumption is accessible to its holder—is available to his or her consciousness—the communicator's task is at least straightforward, although not necessarily easy. However, many of the most basic assumptions exist only at an unconscious level and are therefore not easily available for review and revision. When this is so, the communicator has a far more difficult task. It is much harder, for example, to get a person to stop acting in a racist or sexist fashion if that person is not even aware that his or her behavior is racist or sexist.

Old movies frequently illustrate this point: when they were made, the images and language seemed perfectly normal, but today's viewers cringe at some of the stereotypes and language. The only difference between then and now is that, in general, society's level of awareness has changed. Another example is if an individual is not aware that his or her assumptions about quality standards are very different from management's, management can talk about improvement over and over without eliciting much change. Therefore, a key goal in persuasive communication is to get the attention of those one wishes to influence and help them examine what they would ordinarily not examine.

To do this effectively involves the ability to conceptualize and articulate a message that helps the listener visualize other attractive possibilities. Winston Churchill rallied a nation when he said, "I have nothing to offer you but blood, toil, tears, and sweat," and Martin Luther King Jr. inspired the civil rights movement of the

1960s with his ability to build on his "I have a dream" metaphor. Although most managers are not as eloquent or poetic as Churchill or King, there are numerous examples of effective appeals by corporate leaders. David Kearns of Xerox, for example, captured people's attention when he likened Xerox's transformation to a revolution and articulated the need to "overthrow the old regime" (Kearns and Nadler, 1992).

2.   *Those doing the persuading often fail to recognize the existence of multiple realities.* As noted in Chapter Four, the picture of reality that exists in the minds of listeners may be very different from the picture in the mind of the persuader. For example, while advocates of seat belts frame the issue in terms of safety, many people perceive the laws about seat belts as government intrusion in their lives and a curtailment of their freedom. That these same people will, on the whole, obey the speed limit only serves to underscore the fact that logic alone is insufficient.

Much of the time, managers communicate to others as though there were only one plausible vision. Thus, they see the task of persuasion as that of helping or making the listeners accept this absolute. In an era when critical knowledge was concentrated at the top of the hierarchy and when there were active persuaders and passive subordinates, this approach may have been effective. Today, however, subordinates are not passive, the work force is far more diverse in its perspectives than in the past, and all relevant knowledge is not confined to the senior management team.

3.   *People do not always act in ways that appear to be in their own best interests.* The utilization of knowledge is as much an issue of *emotion* as of *cognition* or understanding. In his creation of "force field" analysis, Lewin (1951) showed how fears and other inhibiting factors work to cancel the apparently logical forces that support change. This effect explains why fitness and weight loss programs have had limited success, although they certainly heighten the participants' awareness of their problem. To become thin deliberately, one needs a vision of what that is like. Persuasive communication

provides such vision, but it cannot by itself overcome the ambivalence (If I'm thin, will I have to deal with unwanted advances?), the fears (What if I'm still not popular?), the lack of discipline (Things are just too stressful right now), or the negative fantasies (I don't deserve to be thin) of the person being persuaded. It also cannot overcome the mixed messages to which the individual is subjected: "Be yourself," "Oh, one little bite won't hurt," and "Gosh, honey, I hate eating alone" are competing messages with significant emotional appeal. In short, getting the message out and creating the vision are useful, but only to a point.

4. *People are bombarded with so many messages at one time and this communication overload may mean that even desirable visions will simply blend into background noise.* There is not enough differentiation between the messages to take them seriously: since everything seems of equal importance, nothing seems of any importance. Too many messages, even important ones, interfere with people's ability to decide what to pay attention to. For example, a parent who constantly admonishes a child may find the child ignoring all messages.

5. *Persuasive communication takes place in a context.* The Gamma University story is an example of this dynamic in action. Presenting budget information to people who have never received it before is not a simple act of sharing numbers. The message behind the numbers is that there is a new way of doing business. To get this message across requires that sufficient groundwork be laid so that those who are listening to the presentation of the numbers have a shared context within which to interpret them. Unfortunately, the administration at Gamma University moved from treating people as though they could not understand budget information at all to presenting them with a sophisticated and detailed report without preparing them with information that would help them interpret the numbers. In a sense, it is the persuader's very expertise that causes this problem. He or she is so familiar with the subject matter that he or she is no longer aware of the myriad assumptions and prior knowledge that undergird the material.

For these five reasons, persuasive communication by itself is seldom enough to bring about significant change. In almost every case with which we are familiar, primary reliance on this influence method has had limited success. In the context of transformational change and the need for resocialization, persuasive communication needs to be combined with role modeling of the new behaviors, listener involvement in the gathering and shaping of the information, and changes to the organizational structures designed to facilitate and support the desired behavioral change. Thus, it is possible to conclude that persuasive communication is a necessary but not a sufficient condition for resocialization and the implementation of transformational change.

Successful Applications of Persuasive Communication

In the organizational world, effective leaders are seen as persuasive communicators when they practice what James McGregor Burns (1978) referred to as "transformational leadership." Such leaders are able to articulate a vision that touches something within their followers, mobilizing them to act. Business magazines are replete with stories about leaders who are very good at gaining attention through sharing compelling visions. Such leaders help followers to derive meaning from their experiences.

Xerox provides an excellent example of how persuasive communication played a significant role in the success of Xerox's transformation beginning in the 1980s (Kearns & Nadler, 1992). A more extensive discussion of the case appears in the final chapter of this book. Here, we refer only to how persuasive communication was used as an influence method.

After CEO David Kearns became convinced of the need for major change, and after he realized that his initial efforts were not working, he started anew with a process for defining a future organizational state for the company. A group of managers called the

"Gang of Eleven" created a slide and audiotape presentation to convince others why Xerox had to care about quality. Those who seemed to support the program were further engaged in seminars and visits to other companies to learn more about quality. Shortly thereafter, a training program was started, beginning at the top of the organization and spreading through the company. Kearns kept up a steady stream of exhortation to his managers, including the use of his revolution metaphor, to get people to understand the importance of the quality effort to the survival of Xerox. This approach launched the effort, but two years later, only limited progress had been made. It took "naming the change" (as Motorola executives dubbed it) and the use of such slogans as "spoiling the customer" and "Xerox: The Document Company" for persuasive communication to reach its full potential for creating an image powerful enough to become the foundation for actual behavioral change.

The Xerox example illustrates the use of persuasive communication in commanding attention and educating people about the developing vision and the seriousness with which the company was approaching the problem. Successful firms often use such methods in launching transformational change. Nevis (1993) observed a similar phenomenon in studying the history of Motorola's quality program over a fourteen-year period.

A somewhat different yet very important use of persuasive communication was exhibited in the "Tylenol problem."

In 1982, someone put cyanide into bottles of Tylenol, killing a number of consumers. This product tampering set off massive hysteria around the world and a huge recall effort. The very stability of the maker, Johnson & Johnson (J&J), was threatened. J&J, a respected producer of health care products, was in danger of lawsuits, loss of consumer confidence, and a severe decline in its reputation in the medical field.

The turnaround of this situation is considered by many to have been due in large part to the way communication with the media and consumers was handled. J&J actually enlisted the media in gathering field data about the problem. In addition, the media and the public were given continuous full disclosure of what had happened and what was being done to solve the problem. Of particular importance was the selection of CEO James Burke and medical director Thomas Gates as J&J's representatives to appear on television. Gates, a warm and gentlemanly person, explained the poisoning, the product recall, and the steps being taken to make the product tamperproof. He sincerely conveyed the message that everything that could be done was being done to make sure that people would be safe. There was no attempt to sugarcoat the situation. In conjunction with fast action (structural rearrangement), this forthrightness enabled J&J to quickly regain consumer loyalty.

In no small way, the manner in which this crisis was handled transformed the way consumer products are packaged.

Analysis of this case (Hartley, 1991) contrasts it with the way A. H. Robins handled the problem of the Dalkon Shield (a contraceptive device); an arrogant denial of responsibility led to a poor image of the company and other problems that eventually led to the bankruptcy of the firm. In 1995, Intel almost fell into the same trap, first by denying flaws in its Pentium computer chip, and then by taking the position that even if there were flaws, the average user would not have a problem. Eventually, the company did reluctantly modify its position, which helped keep its reputation intact. These two contrasting cases illustrate the importance of honesty and openness to the success of persuasive communication, and the importance of keeping people's attention focused on a vision of a different future. These approaches are key to the ability of persuasive communication to begin the process of transformational change.

Articulating a Vision

"Visioning" is of central importance in persuasive communication. A vision is a way of expressing deeply held values. It is essential in creating a picture of a desired future. It is also critical for pulling dispersed and divergent work groups into a coordinated whole. A vision serves as a unifying force. To be successful it must motivate a large number of people to join in the task of bringing it to fruition.

In the computer industry, Digital Equipment's Kenneth Olsen and Apple's Steven Jobs created very different visions, but both were extremely successful in challenging their employees on both an intellectual and an emotional level. These leaders were able to harness dedication far beyond routine attention to one's job by reaching a place within their employees hearts and minds that allowed their very best to emerge. The most effective leaders in all walks of life are able to achieve this. In analyzing Martin Luther King's "I Have a Dream" speech, Lancourt (1994, p. 63) has described King's powerful vision statement as follows:

> In emotionally moving images, he depicts the unacceptable present in terms that resonate deeply for each listener. He knows his audience with his soul as well as his intellect. He calls on what is best in them, and conveys the sense of urgency necessary to overcome the inertia of daily habit. We see ourselves in the vision; it is a rallying point and touchstone. It makes the ideal visible and begs to be communicated, to be told and retold. Above all, it is a call to action that, for many people, redefines the conditions of their existence.

While the compelling nature of King's presentation, delivered in the context of a time of great social change, may seem a far cry from a manager's attempt to rally his or her people, the principles that underlie his call to action are as useful in one setting as in the other. This point is often overlooked in firms where a "vision statement" is prepared and widely disseminated as though it were an engineering blueprint. Unless the vision statement is actualized, unless the vision touches the hearts of the listeners, it will not arouse them to action. Key to this process is the way language is used.

The Importance of Language

While many of the seven influence methods are important in articulating a vision and motivating people to rally around it, persuasive communication may be the most important method in creating the language, images, and symbols that articulate the revolution inherent in multiple discontinuous changes.

When General Motors established Saturn as a new, independent entity, it spoke of "Saturn, a new kind of company," a new way of doing business. When AT&T began its massive cultural change after its breakup, a slogan used by the then CEO was "Ma Bell doesn't live here anymore." When a CEO says, "We are not a project management firm or a matrix organization; we are a knowledge-based network organization," he is laying the groundwork, through language, for a whole new way of conceptualizing what the firm is about. Using language in a compelling way provides new images that can then be used by the organization to describe itself. The more such images are used to describe the organization, the greater will be their assimilation as core values of the firm.

Weick (1980) called attention to the importance of language for effective leadership when he referred to an important task of executives as the management of eloquence. He argued that by using eloquent language, leaders supply subordinates with attractive versions of what the subordinates are doing and put less emphasis on trying to get subordinates to take some specific action. Weick defined "eloquent language" as "the use of fluent, forceful, moving expressions" (p. 18) and called on executives to broaden their vocabulary, especially in the use of metaphors, nuances, or differentiated speech. Today, the ability to speak in this way is seen as an aspect of "transformational leadership" rather than of "transactional leadership." Rather than relying on rewards for services rendered, as in the transactional model, transformational leadership motivates followers to work for goals that transcend self-interest or direct, immediate rewards. Generally accepted masters of this transformational ability have included Winston Churchill, Franklin Roosevelt, Mahatma Gandhi, and Martin Luther King.

We hasten to point out that despite the need for more expressive communication styles, the effective use of language does not require charisma, dynamic personal style, or jumping on tables. Robert Galvin, former chair of Motorola and a quiet man, was nevertheless very effective because he took the time to express things carefully and to coin expressions that had great impact. He perpetuated the importance of "renewal" in organizational life, a concept established by his father, Paul Galvin, the company's founder and guiding light. Motorola has been extremely successful in making truly substantial changes in its business and its products. In referring to its significant initiatives for moving into the twenty-first century, Motorola has been described as "the company that obsoletes itself" (Slutsker, 1993, p. 139).

As noted earlier, senior executives at Motorola have referred to the importance of "naming the change" as a key aspect of successful change efforts. The use of such terms as "Six Sigma" and the "Software Solution" have provided an unequivocal statement of the change goal. All levels of the firm have used these motivational terms to communicate both internally and with customers and vendors.

Avis CEO Bob Townsend used the phrase "We try harder" as a visible summary of the contemplated transformation he subsequently led at Avis. As they tried to be better than "number two," employees at every level responded by working harder and being more flexible than ever before.

In the public arena, Roosevelt named his transformational change "The New Deal" and Lyndon Johnson called his "The Great Society." Whatever one may think about the merits of these programs, the name chosen for each had a huge impact.

In spite of the perceived importance of using rich language and powerful names, many executives have an aversion to using poetic modes of expression. Their preferred terminology is the language of reason, control, and transactional leadership. Unfortunately, such language is not the language of inspirational leadership, and transformation requires inspiration both to guide and, especially, to sustain the difficult journey.

In many cases, the dispassionate, unemotional style is the result of the way most managers have been trained. However, given the magnitude of the changes now under way, perhaps it is time to change the training and enable leaders to become more expressive.

The Impact of Multiple Realities on Persuasive Communication

In Chapter Four we explored the importance of multiple realities to success in creating a new organizational reality. We now examine multiple realities in the context of successful persuasion.

Aristotle described the elements of the interaction between communicator, audience, and subject matter as *ethos, pathos,* and *logos* (the nature of the communicator, the emotions of the audience, and the nature of the message). This is one way of articulating the issue of multiple realities. While it is clear that all parts of the triangle—sender, receiver, and message—*collectively* determine the effectiveness of the communication, for simplicity's sake we examine them individually.

Attributes of the Sender

There are three main reasons why people resist change messages. First, the change advocate fails to communicate the purpose of the change to the audience; second, the listener perceives the present situation differently than the sender; and third, the change initiator is mistrusted or not respected by those being addressed. Use of persuasive communication can help remedy each of these situations, but each situation requires a somewhat different approach.

Communicating the purpose and nature of a contemplated

change requires that above all the communicator must be perceived as authoritative and in command of his or her subject matter. In a number of successful change efforts, the executives recognized the importance of studying the issues in depth as a prerequisite to leading the change. This was the case with Kearns at Xerox and Galvin at Motorola. In addition, selecting a number of obvious experts and having them play a significant role helps in that it communicates the purpose of the change from more than one perspective. Such a team approach is often referred to as having "multiple champions."

In explaining the need for change, the personal characteristics of the communicator are also important. Change leaders who are similar in some way to those they wish to influence are generally more persuasive. People tend to agree more readily with those with whom they can identify, whether in background, career choice, or basic values. Thus, an engineer is perceived to communicate more easily with other engineers than with people of another occupation. On the other hand, it is not necessary for the persuader and the audience to be exactly alike, although when the change advocate is seen by the audience as being very different in important ways, identification becomes more difficult. Advertisers are aware of this dynamic and go to great lengths to use models with whom prospective buyers can identify in some way.

Persuasive communication is also more effective when the persuader is a person admired for success in a field that the audience considers to be of high status. For this reason, the president of the company begins with an advantage.

Sometimes, however, change leaders may need to look further afield for an effective communicator if they need to find ways to confront organizational members with disconfirming feedback that will challenge their underlying assumptions and open the way to a rethinking of their behavior. As noted earlier, when individuals do not see the need for change, merely presenting the message in a rational manner will not suffice; a more engaging approach is required.

In one situation, after months of unsuccessful arguing to convince marketing and division managers that the company's strategy in a significant part of the world was failing, senior management arranged for all concerned to make group visits to customers and political leaders in various locations within that market. These meetings provided the disconfirming feedback in a more powerful way than direct communication from corporate headquarters. The new "messengers" were perceived as credible experts, making it impossible to avoid or rationalize their data in support of the proposed change.

This brings us to the most important conclusion with regard to the attributes of the communicator: *If you are not credible, respected or trusted, your message will not be heeded. If you are credible, trusted or respected, you will be able to do a great deal with relatively modest communication skills.* In short, the ability to connect with the recipient is probably more important for the effectiveness of communication than the polish with which the message is delivered.

This is both good news and bad news. The good news is that one does not have to be a Churchill or a Gandhi to be an effective persuader. The bad news is that many transformational change efforts start from a situation in which unresolved conflicts and past management practices have created mistrust among various segments of the organization. To grasp the power of the resistant forces in an environment of mistrust, one need only consider the monumental task of bringing the Israelis and the Arabs together, of achieving peace in Northern Ireland or Bosnia, or even of the difficulty in settling the 1994 baseball strike. Organizational resolutions may be easier than settling international tensions, but the dynamics and methods are similar.

Therefore, every step of the change process should be designed in such a way that it enhances trust. One cannot merely talk about trust; it requires deeds observed over time. A common mistake made by many managers is thinking that sincere talk or inviting people in for consultation will turn things around. Such actions are a good first step, and trusting actions beget trusting actions, but it is a process. The adage "Actions speak louder than words" is nowhere more true than in leading a transformational change. Management can lecture people about being more responsible for the quality of their work; a more effective approach, however, and one that sends a message of trust, is the elimination of inspectors and overseers.

Attributes of the Receiver

Whenever someone puts out a message to a group of people, he or she is confronting multiple realities different from his or her own. Even though a group of people occupy the same space at the same time, each individual will experience the message in a different way. How do recipients react to a persuasive message? Three attributes of the receiver can affect what they take in:

- *Level and type of experience.* Those who have minimal knowledge in an area need to be approached differently than those who are highly knowledgeable. Recent evidence indicates that people already involved in and thinking about various sides of an issue are more responsive to persuasive communication. This suggests the value of preparation for a persuasive intervention.
- *Needs and concerns of recipients.* Understanding the perspective of the audience is key to eliciting a positive response to the message. Typically, a message is put forth from the perspective of the person advocating the change. Far more effective is issuing the message from the audience's point of view. The best of all worlds is one in which individual needs and organization goals merge, so there is a joining of energy. However, many leaders of change focus solely on the organizational needs and ignore the needs of the individual. Achieving a workable balance is not easy, but it is essential to successful use of persuasion.
- *Differences in susceptibility to influence from others.* There are significant individual differences in how people respond to persuasive messages. This is particularly true with appeals based on arousing fear;

some people respond positively to such appeals, others reject them out of hand.

There is no way that any leader can make consistently good guesses as to what the salient audience characteristics are with regard to a given change. What is important is to recognize the existence of these multiple realities, to create an atmosphere of safety, and to communicate in a way that invites the kind of dialogue that will help the audience make its internal experience public. A major benefit of the newly popular large group meeting designs (such as Future Search conferences, and dialogue groups) is that they begin with an opportunity for all parties to express themselves while others listen without judging. Such an approach allows for each person's reality to be articulated on equal terms.

Attributes of the Message

While advocates of change may have little control over the initial receptiveness of their audience, they do have some control over the content of the message, and the way it is delivered.

Most change grows out of a general dissatisfaction with the current state of being, and because of the pervasive desire to reduce ambiguity, there is usually significant pressure to develop a clear plan for what all the changes need to be. However, the initial goal in transformational change is to raise the awareness of others so they reach the same level of dissatisfaction with the status quo felt by the leadership. The message, then, must paint a powerful picture of what is happening rather than spell out fully developed, clear plans for action. In fact, in the context of transformation and the need for resocialization, having fully developed plans at this point can be counterproductive. As Kearns began his campaign to change Xerox, he used rich, forceful, and clear statements about the status quo to arouse others to join the campaign. In the language of our model, he acted to help redefine the reality of others.

Effective use of words, symbols, and ritual also helps the leader to get the attention of others and to redefine the way followers perceive their world. This management of meaning is key to the effectiveness of the message. In Chapter Four we described the case of the OJ30 program in an insurance company's home office. In that example, the CEO was not very effective in framing the message in a way that resonated with his audience.

Contrast this example with the approach taken by Colby Chandler, chairman of Kodak in 1989. Kodak had suffered the worst performance in its entire history, experiencing an 85 percent drop in net income from previous years, despite growth in sales. To express his dismay, Chandler gathered twenty-five top managers together to discuss the situation. Although he was a soft-spoken person, in the middle of his talk to the managers Chandler raised a machete and began to chop away at the lectern from which he was speaking. There was no doubt in anyone's mind that they were being told to cut costs. Quite literally, Chandler chopped through the existing mental models to loosen the ties that held them in place (Fragos, 1993).

Thus, it is evident that sender, receiver, and message really exist in an interdependent way, and although general precepts and tips can be helpful, it is the constant interplay between these three elements that requires the most thoughtful attention. The sender's listening to the audience's response to the way the sender shaped a message is crucial to the effectiveness of persuasive communication, and messages need to be constantly revised and adapted to particular audiences. Here, one size does not fit all.

Using Persuasive Communication Effectively

Clearly, the shaping of the message is an important factor in persuading others to respond with the requisite bias for action. However, a number of additional skills and conditions are necessary in the effective use of persuasive communication to further transformational change. The following six factors must all be considered if persuasive communication is to be effective:

1. The importance of building trusting relationships

2. Acknowledgment of the emotional dimension of transformation

3. Tailoring of the message to the multiple realities

4. Management of attention

5. Acceptance of the time-consuming nature of the process

6. Integration of messages

We briefly consider each of these factors.

1. *The importance of building trusting relationships.* There is nothing more difficult than building a relationship of mutual trust in organizational settings—especially at a time when downsizing is still so prevalent. However, it *is* possible, even in so inhospitable an environment. One means stems from two of the basic building blocks of trust: openness and honesty. People may not like the message they hear, but if over time they are able to see that their leaders are open and honest, trust will develop. It will no doubt be fragile at first, but consistency over time will strengthen it. Oticon and Semco have made openness and honesty hallmarks of their transformation, and the openness and inclusiveness of their processes have also contributed to creating an atmosphere of trust.

2. *Acknowledgment of the emotional dimension of transformation.* Since the advent of scientific management, several generations of managers have been trained to be logical, rational, and somewhat detached in their dealings with others. This style can be useful in some situations, but it is decidedly not useful when leaders must touch the minds and hearts of their followers. To achieve this, leaders must put forth something more than dry facts. The energy and enthusiasm required for transformational change calls for more powerful expression and an appreciation for the more poetic modes of discourse. The need for this energy and enthusiasm also suggests that organizations must rethink their response to the various pres-

sures in the environment. Typically, people are pushed to solve a problem as quickly as possible, resulting in discussions that often are superficial, that focus almost exclusively on the rational elements involved, and that create a climate in which emotional issues cannot be safely raised. Everyone has experienced meetings in which apparent agreement was reached, only to realize during a hallway discussion that the real issues never surfaced. That the supposed decision is frequently remade should come as no surprise. For persuasive communication to be effective, then, leaders and managers must begin to acknowledge the emotional aspects of change. In transformational change, as we have already pointed out, emotional involvement is critical to successful resocialization. Without it, the requisite commitment and internalization will not occur and the old ways will inexorably creep back in.

3. *Tailoring of the message to the multiple realities.* While most significant organizational change efforts call for more coordination and integration among groups, every message, even those calling for integration, is heard against a background of diverse realities. Thus, if organizations are to go beyond the "not invented here" syndrome, communications forums and opportunities must be created that will enable the multiple realities to be surfaced and addressed.

4. *Management of attention.* In transformational change, people are asked to respond simultaneously to many messages and to make numerous decisions in a small amount of time. The situation is further complicated by the fact that everything cannot come to a halt while people consider the many messages. Keeping people focused not only on the creation of the new organizational reality and the key behaviors necessary to support it but also on the link between the new behaviors and the achievement of the business goals becomes one of the most important roles a leader must play. A varied diet of consistent messages from multiple sources helps support employees as they struggle to make sense of the many changes.

5. *Acceptance of the time-consuming nature of the process.* People must be brought into the change process carefully, and they must

be fully informed of its costs, benefits, and implications. Partial information or glib presentations send signals of disrespect. A dilemma exists, however: the fast pace of today's organizational life makes it hard to find the time to convey the messages in a thorough, engaging way. Use of one of the whole-systems or large-scale change methods explored more fully in Chapter Six can be of significant help in this regard.

6. *Integration of messages.* Everyone has been bombarded with messages that promise something that never happens. This is certainly true in the political arena, where many voters have been turned off by the ever-present rhetoric. In the business world, many organizations hop from one program to another, making followers feel that they are being fed the "flavor of the month." The cynicism generated by these experiences makes it more difficult to deliver new messages with any degree of credibility. Add to this the complexity and comprehensiveness of transformational change and it is immediately apparent that there is a need to articulate the connections that exist between the various activities and messages that make up the process of transformation. If in attempting to draw these connections no connection seems possible, people should seriously question why a program or activity is being done. Raising questions is part of good communication, and eliminating programs that do not explicitly contribute to transformation will help increase the credibility of leaders' commitment to the new reality and enable organizational members to better focus their attention on the few things that really matter.

Summary

We have looked at persuasive communication as a necessary but not sufficient method for implementing change. There is a need for managers to be more persuasive and to use themselves as instruments of change. Today's uncertainty and rapid changes are leading to a new paradigm of leadership in which the development of vision and the management of attention are vital. Creating or redefining reality is an ongoing task of management, one that in the new organizational paradigm substitutes for command and control.

Persuasive communication is only one way of being influential, and as we have pointed out, it is a method with a number of inherent limitations. Therefore, in any resocialization strategy, it is vital to plan for the use of other influence methods as well.

6

Participation

Creating a Shared Reality Through
Joint Endeavor

Pick up any journal or book that deals with management or organizational issues and you are likely to find something about
employee participation, involvement, or empowerment. No matter
what the industry, from high tech to designer-label women's wear,
companies are embracing the idea that employee participation
is good for what ails them. This is the idea expressed in any total
quality program; it forms the basis for self-managed and high-
performing teams; and it has become one of the tools in the toolkit
of any modern manager. Indeed, it is not an exaggeration to say,
"Everybody's doin' it." But what, exactly, is it that they are doing?
How does it work? And why do so many managers and employees
still find it so frustrating?

In this chapter we examine several cases in which employee participation proved to be problematic, and we identify some of the
key causes of these difficulties. We briefly explore several of the con-
ceptual dimensions of participation; we discuss the environmental
and organizational issues that are making its use highly desirable;
and we develop guidelines for the successful application of a participatory method in the context of organizational transformation.
Finally, we identify some of the skills and conditions necessary to
its success.

Examples of Unsuccessful Participatory Management

In *Stewardship*, Peter Block (1993) provides an example of how a participatory method can be derailed:

> The European Sales Office of a large U.S. computer company decided to make those who would be using some new office space responsible for the design of that space. Multiple teams from all levels and subunits met with interior designers and suppliers to explore ways of balancing their various needs. The final plan was a large living room with comfortable chairs for reading, tables for small meetings, and computers on carts that could be plugged in wherever a person wanted to work. No distinction was made between managerial space and that available for everyone else. The arrangement supported a sense of community across the different functions, cost about 20 percent less than previous comparable space, and the office became an example of the "office of the future." Delighted, the European Regional Office adopted the design as the model for future office layouts. With enthusiasm, they translated the design into standard requirements and timetables, and then required offices to implement it. To their surprise and consternation, many offices failed to comply, and others dragged their feet. The Regional Office's response was to develop a more elaborate rationale for the program, stressing its cost effectiveness, and the fact that by not having assigned space, the sales force would be forced to spend more time in the field. Their argument had little impact on the implementation success rate, but they managed to sell the program to Corporate Headquarters in the U.S. Still, offices failed to implement the guidelines, and

the program was soon abandoned due to lack of field support or compliance [pp. 186–189].

What went wrong? Why was the regional office unable to spread the award-winning design to other local offices? One answer is that they unwittingly made a common mistake: by taking the "product" of the "process" and trying to implement it across the organization, the regional office short-circuited the very process by which commitment to the new design had been developed. Trained to focus on results rather than processes, the regional office did not realize that the model office's enthusiastic support for their design had more to do with the process by which the design had been developed than with the actual features of the design itself. As Beer, Eisenstat, and Spector (1990) comment, letting people "reinvent the wheel" within some broad parameters contributes significantly to the successful implementation of any change. In other words, involvement in defining and shaping the change minimizes resistance and allows for the generation of good ideas as well as the support and commitment necessary for implementation.

Let us consider a second example of a participatory approach that did not generate the expected benefits.

Having been told by the senior vice president to whom he reported that the information systems (IS) division of a global high-technology company had accepted the goal of implementing Total Quality Management (TQM) in the division, the manager of sales IS called his management team together to determine how they would implement the TQM program in their department. As a first step, they scheduled a "tools" training workshop for their subordinates, and two of the more interested managers decided to take a TQM course themselves. At a departmentwide kickoff meeting, the sales IS manager made an impassioned speech about the importance of quality and promised his full support. A steering committee was set up to suggest areas that the continuous improvement teams (CITs) should investigate, and to make decisions concerning those recommendations. Teams were established, topics agreed to, and data collected. As the work proceeded, the management team also began to discuss the incompatibility of trying both to "delight" their customers (the sales force and the corporate IS and sales offices) and to produce technically excellent systems. The systems design life cycle, they concluded, had its own "requirements," which neither set of customers understood; and in any case, the wishes and needs of their two customer populations were often diametrically opposed to each other. To add to the difficulty, "corporate" kept changing its mind as to how it wanted to measure the sales force, and sales IS found itself redoing a system it had released for implementation only the previous month. At the CIT level, data from one of the teams indicated that any number of improvements would make it easier for salespeople to access information they needed in order to be effective, but the IS senior vice president felt that given the current corporate priority on tracking sales dollars, now was not the time to address the needs of the sales force. The team was told to put its report on hold. As competitive pressures grew, the sales IS management team had less time to devote to the CITs, meetings were postponed or canceled, and after a year the effort fizzled to little more than a bitter memory of hopes raised, with no results to show for the effort expended.

This example illustrates several other common mistakes. First, those involved in the process were given no opportunity to develop a shared frame of reference. The business reasons for adopting TQM were never explained, and TQM was never tied to an explicit set of business goals. As a result, when participant priorities shifted, it was easy to push TQM aside. Lack of a common frame of reference also meant there was no shared context in which to resolve the conflicts that existed among the participants' differing sets of priorities.

Second, the conflicting priorities represented not only differences in organizational goals and metrics but also significant differences in views of the world—of how things worked and of what was important. To the IS "experts," socialized through years of technical training, the word "quality" meant something quite different than it did to the sales or corporate "experts." In this example, participation was viewed narrowly—as a problem-solving technique—and the need to create a cross-functional forum in which a common vocabulary could be developed was never considered.

The view of TQM as a tool applied by management to "the troops" also meant that the managers never saw themselves as active participants in the TQM process. As a result, no management infrastructure was developed to support the effort, and the management teams continued to operate much as they always had.

Finally, the CIT members experienced no sense of personal empowerment as a result of their participation. The mixed messages to which they were subjected—first, the impassioned kickoff, implying a high level of management commitment to employee involvement, followed by a shelving of the CIT recommendations when their data proved to be inconvenient—left the CIT members feeling less empowered than ever. Their cynicism and resistance to the implementation of future changes increased as management's credibility decreased. In this respect, a frustrating experience with participation can be worse than no participation at all.

Clearly, the effective use of participatory systems as a method for organizational transformation is not without its pitfalls. These examples illustrate some of the problems encountered in its use: there is too little of it, sprinkled like dew drops across a web of mixed messages. It is misunderstood, used too late in the change process, or too intermittently. It is introduced with fanfare, only to be abandoned by the organizational roadside at the first sign of difficulty. Is it possible to ever get it right?

One of the difficulties in "getting it right" stems from the widely different meanings ascribed to the words "employee participation," and it is somewhat ironic that developing a common understanding of what is meant by participative strategies is never a part of the process. To avoid compounding this error, let us examine some of the many facets of participation in the context of organizational transformation.

What Is Participation?

In their assessment of participatory approaches in three countries, Foy and Gadon (1976) point out that "the word participation itself means something different in each country. Americans tend to give it a fairly narrow definition—a management style with overtones of McGregor's 'Theory Y.' To the Swedes, participation involves a passionately held belief in a cooperative society with social equality between workers and managers" (p. 72). In Israel, the model of participation prevalent in the kibbutz factories is based on an ideological commitment to group ownership and democracy. In what was formerly Yugoslavia, participation took the form of Workers Councils, and in many European countries, the laws require that workers have an opportunity to influence decisions in their enterprises. There are American models, such as the "cooperative committee" system of the Tennessee Valley Authority, and the "gainsharing" feature of the Scanlon Plan, and some writers even consider collective bargaining to be a form of worker participation despite its adversarial flavor.

Work simplification, Socio-Technical Work Redesign, and high performing work teams are more recent forms of employee participation; and of course, no catalogue of participatory models would be complete without mention of the total quality movement. First through Quality Circles, and more recently through TQM, the quality movement has made some form of employee participation a feature of virtually every major corporation in the United States, Europe, and Japan.

In the United States it is also common to hear participation spoken of in terms of decision making in which those who have relevant knowledge are invited to take part. In the popular management literature one also finds authors and advocates speaking of participation as a thinking and learning process, and as a way to create boundariless organizations. Other writers define participation as a system of management that allows members to influence organizational decisions. The form of participation and the degree of influence may vary widely. It may be formal or informal, direct or indirect; it may be limited to decisions on local work methods, or it may influence organizationwide policy.

Other writers remind readers that the use of participation has frequently been no more than a thinly veiled attempt by management to co-opt or neutralize a militant opposition, or to cope with a deteriorating set of labor relations, thereby avoiding the threat of unionization. One does not need to search far to find examples in which involvement of employees in minor or very operational points of implementation serves to divert attention and energy from the fundamental issue of the employees' dependent relationship to management. In fact, many working-class radicals and union activists can point to evidence that participation has been a means of obscuring the fundamental ways in which workers' interests differ from those of management.

Clearly, participation is as complex, multidimensional, and value laden a concept as one is likely to find. The debate as to its nature, purpose, and benefit is steeped in fundamental value differences, in vastly differing views of the world, and in the very paradigms and mental models that shape people's thinking. At the heart of the debate, however, lies the issue of power, and of whether or not or to what degree the participatory process will involve a significant shift in the locus of power and control. Does any given participatory process or system enable employees to define, influence, shape, or change the nature of a given decision or solution? Does it in fact empower them to increase their ability to define, influence, shape, or change future decisions or solutions? And does the scope and nature of the decisions in which they participate remain fixed, or is it open to expansion? It is in this context that the concept of pseudoparticipation or the application of labels such as "authentic" and "inauthentic" become relevant.

Of all the difficulties to be encountered in transformational change, without a doubt power sharing is the most difficult, because for many executives, middle managers, and supervisors, the very definition of their roles has been to plan for and control others. Further, it is almost a truism to say that no one willingly gives up power. Is it any wonder that ambivalence shows itself in instances when, without intending to manipulate people, managers zigzag between offering opportunities for participation and withdrawing or modifying the offer in some way?

Why Participatory Systems and Strategies Are Needed

Externally, the environment in which corporations now exist is driving people to rethink every aspect of their organizations in order to remain competitive. Internally, the ability to rethink and transform an organization to meet new environmental demands is more and more dependent on the ability to obtain a deep, personal commitment to corporate goals from each employee. In this quest, there are four driving forces that need to be managed:

- *Perpetual change:* Change has become the order of the day, not an occasional happening.

- *Speed of change:* Response times have narrowed considerably to keep up with changing requirements.

- *Complexity of change:* Required knowledge bases have grown exponentially; no single person or group can provide the expertise needed.

- *Scope of change:* "Fixing" something means improving or changing entire systems and cultures.

Given these four drivers of change, survival and success increasingly require fast, flexible, on-the-spot decision making based on immediate customer need and ephemeral windows of opportunity. There is no longer time for the hierarchical forms of planning and control; there is no time for decisions to be made remotely, or to go up and down a cumbersome chain of command in order to obtain permission, make an exception, or take an action. With knowledge spread widely throughout a firm as opposed to being concentrated at the top, there is a need to involve many people in order to make a good decision or design and implement an effective project. Furthermore, the difficulty of the changes being called for today means that the full commitment of many people or groups is required for success. A participative method, then, is based on two premises: (1) the involvement of everyone concerned with an issue leads to higher-quality decisions; and (2) the involvement of everyone concerned results in higher commitment to programs and decisions.

It is the need to meet these two conditions simultaneously that gives participation its appeal. Although working in a participative mode is often time-consuming and often looks like a sloppy, inefficient process, research and practical experience demonstrate that it is one of the few ways to achieve both the knowledge and the commitment required for a high level of organizational effectiveness. But participation is not merely a matter of "being in on things." It can also be highly empowering in that it allows those who possess the required knowledge to *act* without having to go through levels of approval. Moreover, by bringing leadership and followership levels together, participation makes it possible for organizational members to share information about corporate goals and strategies, customer needs, and environmental pressures. Participation serves to create a partnership in which there is significant alignment between organizational vision and individual needs, so that the realization of one requires and ensures the realization of the other.

Finally, participation is one of the best ways to obtain a picture of the multiple realities that exist around each and every problem. No manager can be insightful enough to know what these are; participation is a method for allowing people to share their world-views and their models so that everyone's perspective is broadened and deepened. Perhaps more than any of the other methods, participation provides an opportunity to manage multiple realities, or what is more often thought of as "resistance."

Multiple Realities: Working Through Resistance to Change

One problem typically faced in dealing with individual and organizational resistance is treating them as if they were monolithic and unidimensional. In fact, resistance is a highly complex, multi-dimensional phenomenon. In general, people resist change for three reasons: they view the change from a perspective different from that of the change agent; they are expressing the normal, healthy human fear of the unknown; or they disagree substantively with the specifics of the proposed change. As we noted earlier, to label any of these reactions as resistance is itself a problem, for it fails to respect the reality and the validity of these responses. A more useful approach is to become deeply interested in what people are thinking and feeling when they do not go along easily with what appears to be a highly desirable change. To engage people in a joint inquiry at such times is to enact one of the most powerful forms of participation.

In addition, all three types of resistance tend to be treated as if they had a single cause. Everyone who expresses some form of resistance is lumped into a single category—that of deviant. When this happens, the typical response is to mount a counterattack upon the opposition. Unfortunately, this usually results in more entrenched resistance. The following example illustrates this phenomenon.

After almost six months of exploring alternatives and hammering out a set of corporate goals and value statements, the board and senior executive team (SET) of a nationwide consumer products company concluded that to remain competitive they would have to reengineer many of their core business processes. In a two-day kickoff meeting, complete with multimedia presentations and detailed charts, the SET introduced the reengineering process to the company's top one hundred managers. The managers were told that the process would be participatory, with the design teams drawn from all parts of the company. In a rousing appeal at the end of the meeting, the CEO spoke of the need for everyone to support the effort if the company was to succeed. He concluded with the exhortation, "If you're not with us, get out of the way. The train has left the station."

The following week, the SET presented summaries of the reengineering process to the entire work force in a series of local meetings. The employee reception was lukewarm; questions were perfunctory and expressed skepticism as to the need for such dramatic change and for the proposed solution. In a postmortem of these meetings, the SET expressed anger and frustration. The company had incurred considerable expense in order to communicate directly with all the employees. The unenthusiastic reception was quickly labelled resistance and when, in the ensuing weeks, stories of middle management "concerns" came to the SET's attention, they deemed the questioners "subversive." If such resistance continued, it would become necessary to fire a few of the "troublemakers" in order to "send a message to the organization that lack of support for the reengineering process would not be tolerated."

This scenario is all too typical of the way many change efforts are launched. Sadly, what the SET had forgotten was that their own acceptance of the need for reengineering was the result of their having spent six months exploring in depth both the corporation's problems and a variety of potential solutions. During those months, they had multiple opportunities to question, challenge, argue, and disagree with one another. They had shared their differing interpretations of the business data, they had put their different views of the organization and its future on the table, and many a Rubicon had been crossed before the beginnings of a consensus emerged as to an appropriate solution. In short, the SET's own participatory process proved highly effective in overcoming their own resistance to the changes that needed to occur.

Unfortunately, in announcing "if you're not with us, get out of the way," the CEO in effect declared illegitimate the very kinds of questions and challenges that employees needed to ask, for from the employees' local geographic and organizationally functional perspectives, they simply did not see the severity of the problem. Their perspective did, however, encompass many painful memories of how previous changes had been managed. Solutions had been defined by the corporate staff and then forced upon the organization. Twice, implementations had been halted, once in an ineffective attempt to remedy a program's deficiencies and once when it was decided to scrap a program altogether. To the line employees, despite the face-to-face communications and the promise that line people would be involved, this project seemed no different from past projects. Moreover, since the SET had offered no overarching, positive, and compelling vision of the future state of the company, the employees were left with no new vantage point from which to view the proposed change. They had only their own individual perspectives: "How will it affect me?" or "We're doing OK here in St. Louis. Why should we be punished because they've screwed up in Dallas?" What the SET labeled resistance was in reality simply a different view of the problem. Had multiple opportunities for real dialogue been encouraged, with no questions off-limits, the SET could have created a common understanding of the seriousness of the company's position, which then would have enabled greater support for the solution.

Another company addressed this problem in the following way:

Having recognized that the organization's middle managers had a parochial view of the company, a nationwide financial institution decided they had to find multiple ways to bring the managers into the transformation process early in the game. Their first step was to set up a series of small-group, half-day meetings in which the management steering committee (MSC) presented a picture of the problems the company was facing. These presentations included detailed financial information and a thorough picture of the competitive and regulatory environment with which they were currently faced, and the sessions provided the opportunity for the managers to wrestle with the information, discuss it among themselves, and then direct questions to any of the MSC members.

Rather than replying defensively to the many challenging questions, the MSC first acknowledged the validity of the concerns being expressed. Questions were explored, with the MSC sharing their perspective but recognizing that actionable understanding could only develop over time and that building trust required an effort to understand one another's points of view. They also agreed to continue the exchange in a second series of meetings.

The participants in each of the small group sessions represented a cross section of the organization's geography, functions, and management levels. During these meetings, it became clear that while these middle managers knew their own geography or function in great detail, they had very little appreciation for the larger context, or of the challenges facing the organization as a whole. As a result of input from these sessions, the MSC supported the creation of a communications team composed of a broad cross section of middle managers. The team's charter was to continue the two-way dialogue, push it down to the local employee level, and identify materials and resources needed to ensure that a shared understanding of the problems could develop.

By involving all the middle managers in an ongoing participative communications process, the MSC created a forum in which the managers' multiple realities could be forged into a common frame of reference. As a result of these meetings, the middle managers actually came to view their worlds differently, and their new, shared perspective formed the foundation for their support of a reengineering process. Their continued active involvement also provided them with a helpful anchor in what was otherwise a sea of uncertainty. As part of a broad-based communications team, they came to feel less isolated. Although their fear of the unknown future could not be eliminated, they felt that at least they would not be the last to know, and that from this new vantage point, they would have multiple opportunities to influence how the future unfolded.

This interactive process also enabled the MSC to identify specifically where substantive disagreements did exist. In many cases, they were able to provide additional materials and insights that resolved the disagreement, and in those cases in which they were not able to persuade a manager to change his or her point of view, the respectful nature of the out-in-the-open dialogue minimized the negative effects of the disagreements. In other cases, the employees' substantive objections actually helped to identify aspects of the problem or solution that the MSC had not explored sufficiently, and in those instances, the MSC more than once modified its position. The MSC's ability to remain open to dissent was key to developing a synergy and synthesis of the employees' multiple realities, and to creating a climate of collaboration and partnership.

In the course of such participatory activities, then, people discover that they are not alone in their sense of loss, or in feeling fearful and anxious. Isolation tends to increase anxiety, whereas sharing it with others seems to reduce its intensity. Often, simply knowing that what one is experiencing is normal reduces its power. All too often, however, managers short-circuit this crucial process, viewing it as a refusal to move into the future.

Participatory systems can also help overcome the sense of loss by giving people compensatory roles to play. For example, in many change efforts, middle management digs in its heels and resists. This is due to their accurate perception that the changes will have a dramatic and negative affect on them. TQM, after all, shifted significant parts of the supervisory role to line employees. Reengineering is frequently about eliminating layers of middle management, and the success of self-managed teams is making it clear that if somehow managers' jobs do survive, the role they will be asked to play will be very different from the one they filled in the past. However, instead of leaving them to gripe and throw monkey wrenches from the sidelines, involvement can shift the personal meaning of this phase from negative to positive. Somehow, ambiguity always seems easier to deal with if one is doing something about it rather than just waiting helplessly for something to happen. Another example will help make this clear.

In recognition of the potential for middle management resistance, one company decided to involve its middle managers as change implementation leaders. While this did not guarantee them jobs in the reengineered organization, it did give them a very particular and important role to play in the transition. During the training and coaching process for this new role, an implementation leaders network (ILN) was developed and chartered to identify changes in current policy necessary to support the organizational transformation, to design any new procedures that would be needed and new reporting relationships that would facilitate the change, and to create any task forces necessary to address transition issues. They were also charged with identifying new skills needed to manage the transition (for example, facilitation, problem solving, conflict resolution, and team building). The ILN (primarily through a series of small group telephone conferences, with periodic face-to-face meetings) was also given the responsibility for sharing local implementation successes throughout the company, for facilitating joint problem solving as issues arose, and for defining ways to measure and monitor the progress of the implementation. With little prompting, the managers created their own steering committee to ensure that the small group networks were functioning, and to ensure that all the networks were linked together. The steering committee put "meat on the bones" of the charter, and in rapid succession initiated a series of contacts with the reengineering teams, developed and had approved a set of implementation criteria, and proposed a model (ultimately agreed to by senior management) for including several ILN managers in the prototyping of the reengineered processes. These managers were then able to return to their work locations and spearhead the rollout of the new process.

By actively involving the managers, and by providing resources and support, this organization turned the traditional middle management resistance into active support in a short period of time. In large measure, this network was able to reduce the managers' resistance to the upcoming changes because it compensated for their sense of impending loss. It also decreased their sense of isolation, temporarily reduced the ambiguity of their position, and provided a means by which they could influence what was happening. It was also a way they could gain new skills and contribute creatively to the shape of the new organization. Participation in the network in essence provided the managers with the opportunity to develop a sense of positive meaning during what would otherwise have been a highly negative experience.

As these examples show, using a variety of forms of participation can significantly diminish the existence of resistance to change by providing opportunities to examine the change from multiple perspectives. This process enables the proponents of change to make some assessment of the nature of the resistance and to undertake a set of activities to address the specific underlying causes. Through participatory systems the organization can also begin to forge a shared perspective, mark the endings, compensate for the sense of loss with new roles, decrease the participants' sense of isolation, and enable the development of new, more positive meanings.

Bringing Organizational Knowledge into the Decision-Making Process

In a business environment that is both as infinitely complex and rapidly changing as the current one is, richness of information and perspective is a lifeline to the future. What is ultimately needed is not a few experts, but as diverse a collection of viewpoints and interpretations as it is possible to gather. Information can then become a rich source of knowledge and wisdom as people interact and relate to it, and "the more participants we engage . . . the more we can access its potential and the wiser we can become" (Wheatley, 1992, p. 65). One of the basic assumptions about participation is that better decisions will be reached if those who have knowledge about the issue being considered take part in the decision-making process.

Unfortunately, the very design of organizational hierarchies has been to act as filters that narrow the range of perspectives that surface. Although it is claimed that good information is central to the ability to operate, those who gather it have been virtually enshrined in elite strategic planning groups, far from the "hurly-burly" of frontline activity. Inevitably, as information wends its way up the hierarchy, messages are either garbled or not received at all. To consign the gathering and interpretation of information to an elite group (be it the strategic planners or the executive team) is to rob information of its richness and potential.

The problem of losing the rich variety of potential meanings or realities can be addressed through the use of participatory systems and strategies. Several new methods have recently emerged to facilitate the process of engaging large groups of people in gathering and interpreting information in organizational environments. These methods have several additional benefits in the context of organizational transformation: because they engage a broad cross section of people in the gathering and analyzing of information, they are able to significantly increase the level of participant commitment to carrying out the activities and actions necessary to the transformation, and are therefore able to increase the speed with which the changes can be made. Though this approach was used as early as the 1960s (for example, by Beckhard in 1967), it has not been popular until recent times.

While these various methodologies (future search conferences, large-system or whole-system change models) may differ in format and detail, they are all based on a similar set of principles:

- They begin with a multiple-day (three to five) meeting.

- Diverse groups of stakeholders, both internal and external, from all levels, functions, and geographies are connected to each other in an immediate, real-time way. The meetings bring whole systems into the room, and the number of participants can range from fifty to five hundred or more.

- The meetings begin by having everyone share their "information" on the past and current internal and external organizational environment. Frequently, there is initially a sense of information overload, and people feel overwhelmed after the first day. However, by the second day patterns begin to emerge.

- The development of a common database or picture of the past and of the current internal and external organizational environment enables everyone to see how all the pieces fit together as parts of one system, and to see how their piece fits into and affects the larger system.

- The meeting enables everyone to develop a fuller appreciation of the problems to be solved, and to vividly understand the forces and constraints with which they will have to contend in making any change.

- This common picture constitutes a new, shared reality, a necessary base from which all participants can move forward together.

- Through a mix of cross-functional small groups, interactive work groups, and large group processes, participants develop a shared view of the organization's desired future.

- The mix of group processes is repeated as participants identify the action steps necessary to bring about the desired future.

In the space of a few days, these methods break through organizational boundaries, come up with coherent, coordinated sets of actions based on shared assessments of the current organizational environment and of the desired future. Real-time relationships are forged as working subgroups are formed and reformed, and commitment to implementation is high because the participants created the picture and action steps themselves. These methods have now been popularized by the writings and experiences of Weisbord (1987, 1992), Jacobs (1990, 1994), and Troxel (1993). Their growing use indicates a move from the Traditional Phase to the Exploratory Phase, as described in Chapter Three. A brief example will help to convey the power and potential of these methodologies.

Lockheed Missiles and Space Company needed to reinvent itself in the face of dramatic shifts in the defense industry. The research and development (R&D) division recognized it would no longer be able to depend on U.S. Department of Defense for a steady source of funding. To address this need, the division head brought together all fifty-two managers of the different research labs. Over the course of several days, in a series of small groups, they listed concrete images of what they wanted to see in place in five years and they identified the major impediments to achieving the desired future. The process used focused on organizational barriers to effective performance. The groups identified major blockages, and proposed new ways to address these barriers. Thirteen immediate action proposals resulted in implementation steps to be achieved within ninety days. At the close of the session, participants were amazed at how much had been accomplished and the extent of agreement reached. Task forces came up with key indicators of business health, a process for "fast buy," a cryogenics marketing workshop to push themselves toward the "new marketing mentality," and a proposal management center that doubled the number of proposals issued. Division managers met informally each week, customer cadres were created, an R&D services Yellow Pages was developed, a "From the Labs" newsletter was issued, and each of the divisions held their own "action planning" events. Within three months, everyone in the organization was actively engaged in the transformation—all as a result of one large-scale meeting [Tuecke, 1993, pp. 71–92].

Using this and other methods that involve large numbers of people (between three hundred and five hundred is not unusual), organizations draw in from the periphery an increasing amount of unique or disconfirming information—the kind of information that is almost completely lost when only a few strategic planning experts examine data to identify current trends. These new, highly structured participatory processes are able to take those bits and pieces of information and amplify them in ways that offer glimpses into potential futures, futures that employees can help to create rather than futures to which they can merely respond after they have happened.

Not only do these highly participative processes serve to provide organizations with better data on which to base decisions, but they also create a powerful sense of ownership for the actions that need to be taken. If change leaders want employee ownership, accountability, and commitment, this is one of the most powerful ways to achieve it. Getting the whole system into the room creates a sense of community, and having a common frame of reference and a common language and set of tools enables people to get to the core issues far more quickly. These meetings provide a highly structured way for this to occur, and the message that most people leave with is an optimistic belief that they can create a better future.

What these processes recognize both implicitly and explicitly is that the critical variable is not the transmission of bits of information but the interactive processes in which pieces of information are combined and recombined and invested with common meaning to create new knowledge and new possibilities. Simply transmitting information, in electronic memos or otherwise, does not enable these powerful results. What participatory processes, systems, and events enable is an increase in an organization's ability to facilitate the flow of productive and creative energy through expanded and expanding webs of relationships and connections.

Empowering Employees

Participation in these "whole systems" processes also contributes to increasing organization members' sense of self-efficacy and competence. By visibly incorporating their specific inputs into the creation of the various "pictures" (past, present, and future) of the organization, participation validates the value of employees' perspectives; and by engaging them in the creation of the future direction and action planning, participation graphically demonstrates the importance of employees' input in and commitment to the future success of the company. Further, participation is empowering in a collective sense: no longer is the individual a lone cog in the wheel of an impersonal machine; rather, he or she has been transformed into an active contributor to a human network and process that personally engages him or her in the creation and implementation of the company's future.

Like participation itself, empowerment is one of those words that has come to mean everything and nothing. This lack of clarity stems in part from the ambivalence many people feel about the word that lies at its heart: *power*. One executive bluntly admitted, "I don't want them to be empowered because then they could decide something different from what *I* want them to do. But I can't really say that to them." Some executives, when they cannot get others to do their bidding, bemoan their own lack of empowerment. The definition of power as power *over* others is part and parcel of our prevailing organizational paradigms, shaped by the mechanical, Taylorist models of fragmented structures in which power is vested at the top. In the Taylorist model, leaders and managers do the thinking and workers execute the tasks that have been designed, and they are controlled by those above them. It is fundamentally a model of employee dependence and management control. Therefore, although leaders frequently talk about wanting an empowered work force, many organizational structures and processes still produce employee dependence and powerlessness. In every part of the organization—the top-down, fragmented organizational structures; the decision-making processes and communications mechanisms; the competitive, individualistic reward systems; the high-control, failure-focused models of supervision; and the approach to job design—forces are at work that create dependence, a sense of powerlessness, and low levels of commitment. In the name of stability and control, the industrial-age organizational systems have been exquisitely and often explicitly designed to disempower people—including managers. More often than not, being "empowered" feels like an admonition to take on more responsibility and more work, with no additional resources and no change in organizational context.

Many companies, however, have moved aggressively to push authority and decision making down to lower and lower levels. Self-managed, high-performing teams have become realities in many organizations. A number of companies are using whole systems change methodologies to include broader and broader segments of their employees in environmental scanning, strategic planning processes, and the management of change implementation. Asea Brown Bovari (ABB), Oticon, Semco, and W. L. Gore are but four examples of companies in which the entire organizational structure and infrastructure has been altered to enable broader, more fluid participation and the placing of both accountability and resources into the hands of entrepreneurial frontline units.

The purpose of empowerment is to give employees the autonomy and authority to make decisions that will solve customers' problems as quickly and as effectively as is humanly and technologically possible. To do this requires changes in the organizational environment, and the use of participatory systems and processes to develop empowered employees.

According to Conger and Kanungo (1988), the literature on empowerment falls into two categories: empowerment as a relational construct and empowerment as a motivational construct. As a relational construct, empowerment is a function of the dependence or independence of a person or group as they try to cope with organizational problems—in other words, how many levels do I have to check with before I can act as I see fit? Empowerment is also about the type and number of resources (financial, symbolic, expertise, information, and punishment) an individual or group has at its disposal. Do I have the ability to easily bring the needed resources to bear to do what needs to be done? Accordingly, empowerment would be defined as those organizational changes that delegate or decentralize both the decision-making power and the control of or access to the resources necessary to carry out those decisions to the frontline levels of the organization.

In the more networked, flexible organizations like ABB, Oticon, and Gore, the thinking/doing split has been erased, and employees are able to configure and reconfigure themselves into whatever temporary structures are needed to take advantage of the fast changing windows of opportunity. In companies such as these, delegated and decentralized decision making have not only been woven into the structures, processes, and cultures, but the resources and support needed to make the accountability viable have also been located at the lowest possible level.

As a motivational construct, empowerment refers to an individual's belief in his or her own ability to be effective and self-determining. Here, empowerment is about the individual's sense of his or her ability to deal with organizational demands. Do I feel competent and confident that I can produce a desired result or achieve a certain performance level? In this context, an empowered person or group is one that knows that it has the skills and abilities required and that it has sufficient belief in its ability to enable members to take on situations that might otherwise be intimidating and to persevere in the face of adverse experiences and obstacles (Conger & Kanungo, 1988).

By providing opportunities for personal autonomy and self-determination, decision making and collaboration, networks of emotional support, and a more varied set of roles, participatory systems and processes provide building blocks for the creation of empowering environments and empowered employees. Thus, the very act of participating directly in reshaping or transforming one's environment in meaningful ways engenders a psychological transformation of sorts. People move from a condition of low self-esteem (the result of feeling unable to influence the things happening in one's life) to a sense of increased effectiveness (the result of being able to shape one's environment). Participation, then, is helpful in the achievement of both the relational and motivational dimensions of empowerment (Conger and Kanungo, 1988).

Organizational models at ABB push responsibility, accountability, and resources right down to the bottom, investing line managers with tremendous decision-making power. Companies such as W. L. Gore, with its "lattice organization," expect people at all levels to take leadership in a variety of situations. New "associates" at Gore rotate through different areas of the business before settling into a specific concentration, and every associate is encouraged to experiment and pursue a potentially profitable idea to its conclusion.

Gore has no R&D unit, yet its number of patent applications and innovative products is triple that of Du Pont. The company strives to "provide multiple opportunities for everyone to participate in the organization and multiple ways for them to be rewarded for their participation. . . . Gore has gone beyond the ideal of a democratic, capitalistic organization to an egalitarian, participative, entrepreneurial society" (Shipper and Manz, 1992, p. 60).

It is no more than a statement of the obvious to say that changes of this magnitude do not happen overnight. To transform disempowering organizational structures and processes and to develop in individuals a renewed sense of their own competence and potential requires a powerful and compelling vision of what is possible, a fixedness of purpose, a willingness to engage in repeated struggle, and a determined commitment to stay the course.

The key word here is *commitment*. Compliance, perhaps adequate in other contexts, is not enough. To transform an organization, change leaders need to tap into what has been called people's "discretionary" energy. This is not something one gets by paying people. It is what people give because they want to—because they have come to feel and know in their hearts that the goals of the transformation and their own deeply held personal goals are inextricably intertwined. They have come to see that they cannot reach their own goals unless the organization reaches its goals, and the organization will reach its goals if they can reach theirs. This alignment is the essence of commitment, and is an indication that resocialization and internalization are taking place.

The Development of Commitment

As with the concepts of participation and empowerment, employee commitment is generally spoken of as some sort of general good, but time is seldom taken to define what is meant by it, why it is needed, and what needs to be done to get it. In this section, we will define the important dimensions of commitment, why it is so important for organizational transformation, and how participatory systems and strategies can be instrumental in creating it.

According to Kanter (1972), commitment arises at the intersection between the organizational requirements and the personal orientation of its members. Commitment exists, Kanter says, when people are willing

> to do what will help maintain the group because it provides what they need. . . . Commitment links self-interest to social requirements . . . [and] a person is committed . . . to the extent that he sees it as expressing or fulfilling some fundamental part of himself; he is committed to the degree that he perceives no conflict between its requirements and his own needs; . . . When a person is committed, what he wants to do . . . is the same as what he has to do . . . and thus he gives to the group what it needs to maintain itself at the same time that he gets what he needs to nourish his own sense of self" [pp. 66–67].

What is striking about this description is the mutuality of the need satisfaction. Both the individual and the organization must get their needs met in order for commitment to be the result. Thus, according to Kanter (1972, p. 68), commitment results from (1) a series of decisions and choices concerning the costs and benefits of involvement, (2) the development of strong interpersonal and emotional bonds between participants, and (3) a moral assessment that the norms and values of the organization are ones that the individual wants to uphold. These influences form the three important dimensions of commitment. In one way or another, if employee commitment rather than compliance is to be obtained, organizations will need to create environments that enable the individual employees to meet these three criteria. Not surprisingly, participatory systems and strategies are one of the most powerful ways to do this.

Since a crucial part of creating sustainable commitment depends on the existence of a deep alignment between the core needs and vision of the organization and those of the employees, vision work must engage the individual at a moral and emotional level. Typically, this means that the organization and its employees must wrestle with and make explicit the core values concerning how it treats customers, employees, the environment, and the communities in which it operates, and how it views its overall mission and purpose. If these values are congruent with the employee's core values and sense of overall mission and purpose—and they should be if the employees have had a genuine opportunity to help create them—then alignment and commitment will be forthcoming. Unfortunately, most so-called visioning work takes place at either too general or too operational a level to have any effect on the development of commitment.

Through commitment, the individual also has the opportunity to develop a rich web of emotional and interpersonal ties to others in the organization, and to increasingly experience the new reality as an integrated entity. By increasing the importance of these ties, and the satisfaction derived from them through the provision of mutual support as everyone struggles to learn the new ways, participation also serves as a way to reduce the connection individuals have to the old ways. Peer support and peer pressure to continue learning and to avoid backsliding can be very powerful in detaching people from the old behaviors and in increasing their commitment to act in new ways. Through increased participation, as individuals gamble that their involvement will pay off, their motivation to continue the journey also increases. Therefore, the more quickly and more deeply individuals become invested in the journey to organizational transformation, the more likely it is that they will be motivated to learn the new ways, and the easier it will be to minimize the appeal and power of the old ways. It is also through commitment that new loyalties can be developed, and the more intense the involvement and the more one's personal satisfactions are derived from that involvement, the more willing people will be to work out the conflicts and tensions involved in the process of transformation.

Using Participation Effectively

Several key conditions seem to influence the effectiveness of a participatory approach to organizational work. They are organizational characteristics, skills training, and group dynamics.

Organizational Characteristics

According to Levine (1990), some form of gainsharing, job security, guaranteed individual rights, and measures that promote group cohesiveness correlate positively with the success of participatory approaches in the workplace. "In the long run, sustained and effective participation requires reward for the extra effort participation involves" (p. 87). This gainsharing frequently takes the form of base compensation and a variable reward based on some target measure of profitability or group productivity, and there is some evidence that participation in both decision making and gainsharing works more effectively than does either one individually (p. 90). Semco and Oticon's effective use of profit sharing and participation support this point (see Chapter Ten).

Long-term employment relationships also increase the success of participatory strategies because they promote longer time horizons, and measures that build group cohesiveness also have an impact on the success of participatory strategies. For example, group-based gainsharing promotes cooperation rather than competition, and it helps maintain high performance because peer pressure is effective in sanctioning workers who do not contribute their share to productivity. Semco and Johnsonville Foods are examples of this effect (Semler, 1993, 1994; Talbott, 1994). Another facilitating activity is the kind of team-based training used by Xerox in the early days of their transformation.

Levine also notes that the guarantee of individual rights is also important in creating the climate of trust required for effective teamwork and organizational cohesiveness. Hewlett-Packard (HP), for example, has incorporated this sense of fairness into its culture through policies that ensure due process and just cause for actions taken, rather than seeking the freedom of an employment-at-will environment. From HP's perspective, the gains from participation and productivity outweigh any loss of managerial sovereignty.

An environment of mutual trust means that disagreements and conflict are seen as natural and resolvable. In such an environment, people feel free to speak their views and share their feelings without fear of reprisal. This freedom in turn increases group cohesion, creating a mutually reinforcing cycle. One caveat: cohesion is not the same as conformity, and for an organization to obtain the real benefit from the use of participatory processes, there must be minimal pressure to conform. As the proponents of the science of chaos and natural systems suggest, energy for growth comes from the disconfirming pieces of information at the boundaries of organizational systems. Therefore, of the conditions that support the effective use of participation, tolerance of—indeed, encouragement of—diversity must rank high on the list.

Skills Training

Another internal condition considered to be crucial to the success of participatory systems is adequate skills-based training. First and foremost, we would list conflict management skills as essential. By definition, bringing together people with different points of view will involve conflict. If these groups are not provided with the negotiating and consensus-building skills necessary to constructively address those conflicts, the outcome will be frustration, disgust, and an understandable unwillingness to participate in the future. Development of these skills can contribute to a group's ability to confront multiple vested interests and to build consensus among people with differing perspectives (in other words, multiple realities). *More than any other skill, the ability to manage conflict can make or break a participatory process.*

Critical thinking skills, listening skills, meeting facilitation skills, group process skills, managing-diversity skills, teaming-building skills, and negotiation skills are also important to the effective functioning of participatory systems. Without sufficient skill in these areas, participation frequently can and does flounder and die in a sea of frustration as participants spar, pass judgment, blame, miss deadlines, remake decisions that were made in a previous meeting, see little or no result from their efforts, and generally feel that their involvement makes no difference.

Group Dynamics

Groups are more than the sum of their individual parts. When people interact in groups, the process of interaction itself inevitably influences the outcome. Therefore, it is not enough simply to give people the opportunity to participate and then to hope for the best. We have noted the importance of training, but that too is not sufficient. In addition, several phenomena must be kept in mind which, if not consciously addressed, can detract from the richness of the group's output. The most troublesome of these is the phenomenon of groupthink.

In most organizations, in fact, in most social systems, there is a great deal of pressure to conform to the prevailing norms. Deviance is tolerated only within narrow limits. Getting along is valued, and "don't rock the boat" and "don't make waves" are dicta learned at an early age, while many conflicts are addressed by sweeping them under the rug. Norms of politeness, deference, and friendship can all work to keep issues off the table, and to inhibit feedback from being offered in a constructive or timely fashion.

These dynamics play out in several ways. Often, people are reluctant to challenge one another to stretch their thinking, and when someone suggests what at first blush may seem like an impractical or unusual idea, the tendency is to denigrate it. If someone proposes a new perspective, the first response is not typically, "Oh, what an interesting idea. I wonder how we could make that work," but rather, "Oh, that'll never work because . . ." As a result, group discussions tend to remain within familiar and safe bounds, and the group's thinking process can become stale and incestuous. This is particularly true when the membership of a group remains stable over a considerable period.

Further, in the desire to skirt issues of difference, avoid conflict, and achieve agreement, people frequently find they have settled for the lowest common denominator, by which the decision has been reduced to something about which no one really cares. The decision offends no one, but neither does it please anyone. In the desire to be polite, people frequently do not voice their objections, even if they do not want to do something. They keep silent on the mistaken assumption that someone they do not want to offend (a friend or superior) wants a particular outcome, or they may remain silent because they do not want to be seen as not being a team player. Harvey (1988) referred to this phenomenon as the Abilene Paradox. In deciding whether to make a trip to Abilene, none of the individuals in the group really wanted to go, but each thought they were the only one who did not want to go, so no one voiced their objection. In the absence of any objection, the group decided to make the trip. Thus, everyone went to Abilene, even though no one wanted to go.

These issues are important because they highlight the need to actively and consciously work against the pressure toward group-think and lowest-common-denominator outcomes. There are several ways this can be done:

- Create group norms that sanction the explicit exploration of differences and support the examination of underlying assumptions.

- Purposefully compose teams so they are cross-functional. This need for cross-functional, cross-boundary input is becoming more critical to effective decision making and to overcoming the organizational fragmentation that serves to maintain the old organizational reality.

- Explicitly value functional, customer-based, cultural, racial, gender, or stylistic diversity. This can help ensure that engineering decisions include the marketing perspective, that engineering and manufacturing departments collaborate on design for manufacturability, and that management styles do not make it difficult for people of other races, genders, or cultural backgrounds to participate comfortably.

- Ensure that employees participate on multiple teams, and that membership on any given team does not become cast in concrete.

- Develop group norms that view conflict as not only acceptable but also desirable.

These procedures will only succeed, however, if they are paired with conflict resolution skills, meeting facilitation skills, dialogue skills, and negotiation skills that enable teams to work through their differences in constructive ways.

Summary

Participation is a concept with multiple meanings, few of them simple. Fundamentally, employee participation involves a shift in the locus of power, and much of the difficulty experienced in the use of this method stems from ambivalence toward this issue.

Most often, participatory systems have focused on decisions that affect the day-to-day work environments of employees, because traditional wisdom has it that employees are more comfortable and more interested in being involved in issues that most directly affect that environment. Certainly, management is more comfortable with this level of participation.

Somewhat less common, but gaining in popularity, are the large-system change models and future search conferences, in which a broad cross section of the employee population participates in the development and/or assessment of higher-level organizational visions, strategies, goals and action plans. However, there are still categories of issues and decisions that have not been open to participatory systems. These include compensation, downsizing, strategic investments, mergers, and divestitures. Exclusion of these issues from the arenas of participation can be a limiting factor in transformational change efforts. If people are exhorted to think more like empowered owners of the business, it is difficult to justify excluding their ownership decisions. There is nothing inherent in any of these issues that makes them either appropriate or inappropriate candidates for participatory input. It is more a matter of general ambivalence toward giving up old notions of power and control. Semco, for example, has opened virtually all issues to employee participation, as has Oticon, and there is evidence that a number of other companies such as Johnsonville Foods are beginning to open compensation design and decision making to employee input.

No matter where an organization comes out on the participatory continuum, the complexity, scope, speed, and continuousness of the changes occurring in the organizational environment indicate the need for an empowered work force. Empowerment is impossible to achieve without genuine participation. Participation, then, becomes both means and end. As a goal, it becomes a characteristic of the transformed organization. As the means for achieving that goal by providing a process for taking into account the multiple realities of organizational members, it is central to an organization's ability to work through the normal resistance to change. It also enables the broadest base of organizational knowledge to be brought into the decision-making process, and it is central to the development of the commitment necessary to sustain the long hard work of the transformation itself.

7

· ·

Expectancy

Using the Power of Self-Fulfilling Prophecy

Persuasive communication and participation, explored in the two previous chapters, are the change methods most often thought of by managers as ways to motivate people or to bring about transformational change. They may be thought of as "explicit methods" in that they rely on relatively obvious, formal interventions. We now turn our attention to what may be thought of as "implicit methods": expectancy, discussed in this chapter, and role modeling, discussed in Chapter Eight. These two approaches are more subtle than persuasive communication and participation; they seek to create an environment in which people are encouraged to change by eliciting from them or displaying to them new behaviors and attitudes. Effective use of expectancy and role modeling is so powerful that when understood and used appropriately, they can create deep and lasting results. They are particularly useful in bringing about and supporting new behavioral norms; expectancy, for example, sets up *anticipated* productivity standards, while role modeling provides a *visible* example of desired behavior for achieving those standards.

Expectancy is often referred to as the inducement of self-fulfilling prophecies, in which expected behavior becomes a reality. The first elaboration of the concept was made by Robert Merton (1957) in describing how people, fearing that banks would fail in the Great Depression, withdrew their money from the banks, thereby ensuring that they would fail.

Expectancy phenomena occur when a prediction made by one person about the behavior of another is realized as a result of the actions of the person making the prediction. The predictor makes some assumptions about the target of the prediction and then acts in such a way as to make the predictions come true. Eden (1990) refers to this method as "the manager as prophet." In acting as prophets, managers influence people to consider a better or different world. This role is particularly important in the early stages of transformational change, when effective use of expectancy can make a big difference in the success of the effort. Combined with persuasive communication and participation, expectancy provides a potent element in creating and embedding a new vision.

Use of expectancy is essential to the process of resocialization, particularly in focusing and motivating people to persevere in difficult endeavors. Expectancy provides both a vision of a desired end-state or goal and the supportive power of belief that the goal can be attained. It is through the expectations and related actions of initiators of change that the words and pictures contained in the persuasive communications develop into full-bodied visions capable of being turned into reality. In the following pages, we provide examples of the use and misuse of expectancy, discuss the importance of the method in transformational change, and explore its dynamics in detail.

Use and Misuse of Expectancy Methods

A few examples of how expectancy has been used and misused can begin to show how expectancy works in practice. The cases we present make the point that if a leader wants his or her followers to achieve high levels of performance, the chances of their doing so will increase if the leader believes that people are capable of attaining those levels *and then acts on that belief*. Similarly, if a leader believes that people are "no damn good," and then acts on that belief, the people will achieve poor levels of performance; they will live "down

to" the expectations. Douglas McGregor's famous "Theory X–
Theory Y" model is based on these two distinctions.

The power of expectancy can be found everywhere—in business
organizations, the military, education, sports, and family settings.
We will look at examples in each context.

In a recent attempt at transformational change in a business
organization, top management started with an assumption that
introduction of the new program would be received with great resistance by members of the organization—a negative expectation
about cooperation. Acting in accordance with this negative expectation, top management designed the program around ways of
inhibiting or controlling this resistance. Although the program was
launched with an upbeat, positive-sounding plan, the launch was
accompanied by very tough exhortations such as, "If you're not with
us, you're against us." In addition, no one—neither executives nor
those at lower levels—was allowed to express any negative responses
or offer alternative suggestions.

As signs of resistance increased, those leading the change effort
increased their admonitions and began to label some organizational
members as "troublemakers." A negative cycle developed, with resistance increasing as top management attempted to tighten its control of the situation. The more top management perceived the
feedback as being negative, the more it attempted to overpower it,
which only served to generate more resistance from unhappy people. The initial prophecy of high resistance (a judgment call)
became a reality, confirming the basic premise of expectancy. Subsequently, it took more than a year of hard work, the use of external consultants, and the development of more optimistic
expectations about people to see a positive prophecy confirmed.

Perhaps the first organizational study of the power of positive
and negative expectancies can be found in Livingston's paper "Pygmalion in Management" (1969/1988). Building on the George
Bernard Shaw play *Pygmalion* (later adapted as *My Fair Lady*), in
which Professor Henry Higgins's expectations of his student Eliza

Doolittle form the basis for her change from a Cockney flower girl to a lady, Livingston's paper captured the promise of expectancy. He applied the concept to a study of life insurance salesmen whose performance was characterized as "good," "average," and "poor." Assigned quotas based on their categories, the "good" did better than their quotas and the "poor" did worse. The surprise was that the "average" did better than average. Interviews by Livingston with members of this group indicated that their manager had insisted to them that they had more potential than even the "good" group. He stimulated them to higher productivity by giving them an "above average" expectancy rather than an "average" one.

In a related case, in one of America's largest banks, lending officers who had a higher than average number of poor loans were given further restrictions as to what they could approve. This lowered their loan volume, and consequently, to make their quotas, they began taking further risks and ended up making more "bad" loans. Seen as bad performers and then constrained by the system, they unwittingly acted to live "down to" their reputations.

Numerous studies conducted by Eden (1990) in Israeli combat command training bases showed similar results. In a typical case study, groups of command trainees were randomly identified to their instructors as having either "high," "regular," or "unknown" command potential. At the end of fifteen weeks of intense training, those who had been identified as "high" had achieved performance scores substantially better than the scores of their classmates. Those labeled as "regular" performed well, but at an average of fifteen points less than those considered to have high potential on a one-hundred-point grade scale. Those identified as "unknown" performed midway between the other two groups. Eden noted that based on their initial ranking, the different trainees were treated differently by the same instructor, who had a mix of all three categories in his class. In some powerful yet subtle way, it appears that the instructors dealt with the "highs" differently than with the others, in essence *expecting* them into "highness" and expecting the "regulars" to do only reasonably well.

In the field of education, the concepts of expectancy and the self-fulfilling prophecy had a significant impact on minority education in the 1960s. Scholars argued that black children should be treated as though they were capable of learning. Jules Richmond, former director of Judge Baker Children's Center in Boston and surgeon general in the Carter administration, helped create the Head Start program, which is based in part on the concept that if children are reached early enough in life, they can avoid the vicious cycle of negative self-fulfilling prophecies.

A May 1983 *New York Times* article described a case in which a fifth grade science teacher in an Indianapolis inner-city school organized a chess club for students who knew nothing about chess, generally considered an elitist activity. Although many of the students' friends and family thought the students were wasting their time playing chess, the teacher kept entering them in tournament after tournament, building on their innate competitive and street-smart instincts to stay with it until they learned how to win. Three years later, in competition with teams from some of the most prestigious school systems in the United States, this club won the 1983 National Elementary School Chess Championship. A similar true-life phenomenon was the subject of the movie *Stand and Deliver*, in which James Edward Olmos portrayed a Los Angeles teacher who inspired his ghetto students to win a calculus competition.

In a well-known tale that has come to be known as "Sweeney's miracle," a Tulane University professor created his own Pygmalion effect. In the early days of computers, Professor Sweeney set up a computer center in the basement of a campus building. Often working into the night, he became friendly with the night janitor, who began to inquire about what he was doing. Sensing the janitor's interest, Sweeney asked him if he would like to learn how to operate a computer. The janitor demurred, saying that since he lacked education, he could not possibly achieve such a skill. Sweeney's persuasiveness prevailed, and the janitor not only learned to operate a computer but rose to the position of manager of the university's biomedical computing center. While this may seem like a one-in-a-million success story, we have now collected dozens of similar anecdotes, such as secretaries who have become managers after exposure to those who acted toward them in the belief that they could perform at higher levels.

Tales abound about successful sports teams that manifest strong expectancy effects. A coach refuses to believe that an aging team cannot compete and creates a vision of competitive strength derived from internal fortitude and experience. Witness George Allen and his Washington Redskins "Over-the-Hill Gang," a Super Bowl winner in the 1970s: a focus on pride and prayer induced a positive expectancy. Consider the power of New York Yankee "Pinstripes" and Boston Celtic "Green": for several decades, putting on the uniform of one of these teams meant taking on the mantle of a winner; players joining these teams were convinced they were special, and they expected to win. One new player for the Celtics during the Larry Bird era said, "These guys expect to win every time they play!" Strong positive expectations took the Dallas Cowboys from being a losing team to being a Super Bowl winner. In interviews, Coach Johnson articulated the role that expectations had played in the four-year turnaround (Johnson, 1993).

Finally, a pioneering study of twenty-five women who became CEOs and owners of businesses in the United States (Hennig and Jardim, 1977) indicated that almost all of them had fathers who expected they could succeed at anything they wanted to, including male-dominated professions such as management:

> As I think back, Father was something special. As far as I can recall I was Daddy's special girl. There were always special times set aside for him and me to be alone. He taught me to skate when I was four and he used to show

me off to all his friends who had sons older than me. "See," he would say, "You may think that she is just a girl, but watch her outskate those boys of yours."

My dad was a railroad executive. . . . Often he got called out on weekends and he would take me along. I am probably the only woman alive who walked railroad tracks under construction at the age of five! Sometimes we would walk several miles stopping here and there to talk with work crews. Sometimes we would ride on the work trains. They were always warm and smoky, filled with sweating and dirty men. I loved those times and all the men knew me and talked to me. My dad was very proud of me and often joked with the men about me becoming the first woman train engineer. They would all laugh and then he would get very serious and say that he didn't know what I would do but since I took after him I'd do something famous and unusual.

These examples require little elaboration; the power of expectancy speaks loud and clear.

Having examined a number of examples, we now explore the various ways expectancy can be used by transformational leaders.

Expectancy and Transformational Leadership

It may seem that we are simply preaching optimism about human nature; however, negative expectations also are extremely powerful. A parent may tell a child, "Don't be so clumsy," and after a prolonged period of such statements, it is almost impossible for the child not to behave clumsily, thereby fulfilling the prophecy. There is an old adage, "Expect nothing and thou shalt not be disappointed." People who have such a negative attitude will see their worst prophecies come true.

The real issue for management is whether altered expectations can be used to help change behavior in a desired direction. Can this phenomenon be harnessed to increase the possibility of eliciting a broad range of new behaviors, such as an increased sense of responsibility, proactive sharing of information, and skills in dialogue and conflict management?

Admittedly, the hardest things to modify in any large-scale change effort are the norms that define how work is done and what is considered to be an acceptable level of performance. Anyone who has ever tried to change a cherished method or significantly alter output has experienced this difficulty, even when the people involved could see the merits of the change. Once set, expectations are notoriously difficult to modify. Somewhere in the organization's past, a vision of what was expected, accepted, and plausible took hold and became internalized as a set of expectations about how to do things. Success in carrying out this process becomes a barrier to the adoption of new ways.

A classic example is found in the railroad industry's definition of its business. As long as the industry was defined in terms of railroad transportation only, there was no way to see potential in newly emerging trucking and airline opportunities. Railroad managers dealt with each other and with employees so as to reinforce narrow images and expectations around "railroading," rather than defining opportunities in terms of the transportation business in general. As has been well documented, the industry began to decline and missed a window of opportunity from which it was otherwise in an ideal position to benefit.

To counteract the forces of such inertia requires leadership in the creation and actualization of a new set of expectancies. The resetting of expectations, then, becomes one of the key activities in transformational leadership.

One of the most important expectations a leader must set has to do with the generation of optimism, hope, and aspiration, especially in the context of transformation, a change process that unfolds over many years. Optimism, hope, and aspiration are best conceived in statements and actions that say, "We can solve our problems," "Change is a normal, healthy, human response," "Change can be exciting," and "We have the ability to create a more desirable world." Implicit in these statements is an enhanced faith that engaging in a difficult effort will have a fruitful outcome. This faith involves faith in oneself, in one's leaders, and in the process of transformation itself—no small order in today's cynical world, but it is essential to develop this set of beliefs as a foundation for transformational change.

Without such beliefs, the ambiguity inherent in transformational change, and the inability at the outset to articulate specific behaviors and performance standards, can overwhelm even the most willing participants. Therefore, in a variety of ways leaders must continually convey their expectation that the desired future state is achievable and that the struggle will be worth the effort. One way of doing this is provided in the following example (which we will discuss more fully in Chapter Twelve).

At Balfour, CAD-CAM was introduced in a setting that had previously had tools and dies made by artisans with years of experience. The new technology demanded a significant shift in paradigms on the part of the tool and die makers. The engineer in charge of the project made constant use of expectancy by repeatedly telling people that he had a great deal of confidence in their experience and in their ability to master the new technology. In addition, he set forth challenging productivity goals, which were met in half the targeted time. He then challenged people to a higher level, which was also achieved within the allotted time frame. In other words, he concentrated on convincing others that they could live up to a high level of aspiration.

A second way of creating optimism, hope, and aspiration is in the development of a new vision that is actualized by the leaders themselves. This method goes far beyond merely developing a new vision statement. A vision is an explicit statement of expectations, but to actualize it requires that leaders themselves change the way they interact with others. It means they understand that there is a different way of *being*, and that their own behavior and attitudes will reflect this understanding. Many change attempts have failed because organizational leadership tried to bring about change before or without changing their expectations of themselves.

The transformation that occurred at Du Pont's Belle, West Virginia, plant is an excellent example of this approach (Knowles and Brown, 1992). Until Richard Knowles, the plant manager, was able to acknowledge his own need to become more comfortable dealing with feelings, to stop thinking in terms of either/or, and to always be right, strong, and John Wayne–like, his management team was unable to move beyond the "flavor of the month" approach to change. In an act of true courage and leadership, Knowles learned how to let go of his need to control, and to invest his energy and time in a mutual exploration with his team of what they wanted to become, and what they needed to do to get there. After considerable personal struggle and soul searching, Knowles became what Peter Block (1993) calls a steward or servant to his organization. In effect, Knowles's new perspective said to everyone in the plant, "My expectation is that you are capable of transforming this organization, and I will support you in every way I can." And over the course of several years, he did just that.

In a context such as that just described, the aim of visioning is to reach people on a deeper emotional level—to touch the passionate side of their nature—than do the rational approaches of persuasive communication, extrinsic rewards, and structural rearrangement. Visions, which embody a set of expectations, are important because they crystalize desired values and standards of performance in a way that is intended to stretch members so that each person "is raised to a higher level of motivation and morality" (Burns, 1978, p. 38).

Expectancy is at the heart of transformational leadership in that it positions the desired outcomes or standards in an emotional and ideological context that is elevating, mobilizing, and inspiring. It is based on a psychological as well as an organizational level of relationship in which the leader's and the followers' purposes become fused.

Bass's research (1985) indicated that transformational leaders show the following characteristics:

- They emphasize high intellectual standards.

- They get people to work longer and harder and to do more than they expected to do.

- They treat people as equals, even those who are less accomplished than they are.

- They are good listeners, but firm in expressing their own opinions.

In essence, transformational leaders convey a set of beliefs or expectations about what people are capable of, and *by acting on those beliefs,* they generally elicit the behaviors they hoped to see. Often, the leader will articulate what is already in the hearts and minds of his or her followers (for example, Martin Luther King Jr.). The leader's task, then, is to act in such a way that the vision unleashes the potential that already exists but that needs nourishment and shaping in order to be brought to fruition.

To do this, transformational leaders use themselves in ways that bring their expectations to life. In face-to-face and small-group interactions, when "managing by walking around" or when holding meetings, leaders convey to others what the leader believes they can achieve together. Leaders do this not only through direct statements or in what they choose to talk about, but in their stance, in the images they use, and in the closeness they display. Whatever the form of expression, leaders convey expectations that inspire others and portray a "possible dream." And then they continue to act in ways that will make that dream come true. They encourage people, they support them with resources, they listen to them, they challenge them to stretch, and they trust them, even when something goes wrong—as it is bound to do in any complex, experimental, creative pursuit.

Indeed, there is something quite remarkable about the interlocking flow of energy that occurs between the person setting the expectation and the person(s) responding to the expectation. In a way, they become one.

Given the power that expectancy has in shaping future behavior, and given the subtlety of the dynamics involved, it is worth examining these dynamics in somewhat greater detail.

The Dynamics of Expectancy

To get some idea of the power of expectancy, consider the following scenario: As the executive in charge of an operation, you are told by an associate that you are very fortunate that Manager "A" has been transferred to your group as she is an excellent performer with whom people enjoy working. As you define the job you have in mind for her, you recall the comments, and scope out a kind and level of responsibility that is in accordance with this expectation.

Now, consider an alterative scenario: As the executive in charge of an operation you are told by an associate that he feels sorry for you that Manager "A" has been transferred to your group as she is a poor performer with whom few people want to work. As you define her job, you recall the comments and scope out a kind and level of responsibility in accordance with this negative expectation.

Everyday experience and a considerable body of research show that the dynamics of the two scenarios are dramatically different. In the first, a positive expectation is generated, and the executive, without even being aware of it, will act to make the "prediction" become the outcome and the person will work up to the expected level. In the second scenario, the opposite is true. Set up to expect less rather than more, the executive unwittingly defines a situation to bring about a lower level of performance. In dealing with people for whom positive expectancy is held, executives not only define their job tasks and challenges at higher levels; they also meet with them more often, look at them more directly, stand or sit closer to them, provide them with more positive feedback, and use different language with them than with those for whom they have negative or poor expectations. Gestures and facial expressions are also different. Thus, in both of the above cases a self-fulfilling prophecy was set in motion that took place largely outside the awareness of the parties concerned, including the associate who spread the "good" or "poor" message to the executive.

How Self-Fulfilling Prophecies Develop

Although some expectancy assumptions are supported by fact, research shows that people most often make such judgments on the basis of limited data. To the extent that managers carry biases about people, they bring that baggage into the workplace. Even when substantial data may be available, the conditions producing those past behaviors may no longer be present. The past may not be a "prelude to the future," but rather just "the past." This is especially true in the case of organizational transformation in which an explicit goal is to change the conditions that produced certain kinds of behavior. Figure 7.1 summarizes the consequence of expectancy for positive and negative behaviors.

If managers believe that workers will produce error-laden output, they will create a group of inspectors to find and correct the errors. Consequently, workers will feel that quality is someone else's job and abdicate that responsibility, believing "that's the job of the inspectors." Workers may think, "*We're* responsible for output; *they're* responsible for quality." The workers' behavior continues to allow errors (for inspectors to find and correct), and management concludes that its initial assumptions were correct: workers cannot be trusted with the responsibility of quality. The workers, in essence, say to management, "We are what you think we are."

Figure 7.1. The Dynamics of Expectancy.

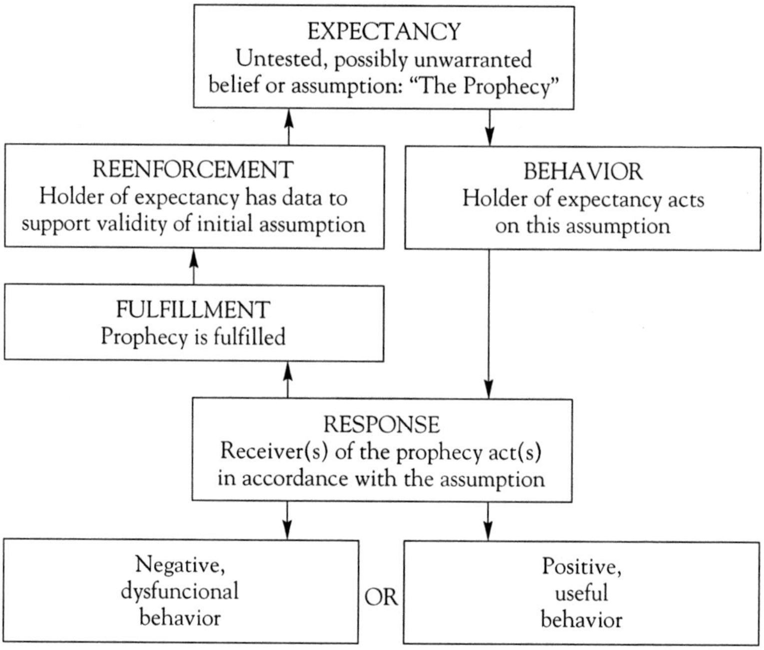

Conversely, consider the optimistic expectancy that creates an attitude of "zero defects." Many programs of total quality, continuous improvement, and zero defects have demonstrated that changing the expectancy to predict that workers can be trusted to do high-quality work has resulted in the elimination of inspection by management and a substantial decrease in errors. Figure 7.2 summarizes the sequence for negative self-fulfilling prophecies, and Figure 7.3 summarizes the sequence of positive self-fulfilling prophecies.

Expectancy can become a powerful motivating force. If certain people are consistently invited to important meetings and others are consistently left out, it does not take long for a prophecy about "contributors" and "noncontributors" to become established. Those invited *do* contribute, and are then invited again as members of the contributor group; by contrast, the uninvited members are seen

Figure 7.2. Low-Trust Self-Fulfilling Prophecy.

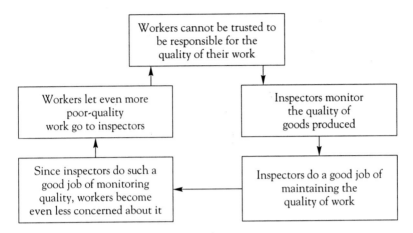

Figure 7.3. High-Trust Self-Fulfilling Prophecy.

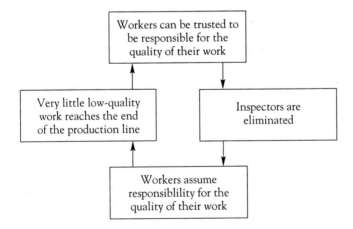

even more strongly as noncontributors. How can they contribute if they are never invited to do so?

Thus, expectations fulfill themselves because the cycle becomes self-perpetuating. In the context of transformational change, however, it is important that leaders and managers—indeed, all organizational members—learn to use this most subtle of dynamics to propel the transformation forward.

Applying Expectancy to Transformational Change

An example of effective use of expectancy in a transformational effort can be seen in the case of Oticon (which will be covered in detail in Chapter Twelve). This Danish manufacturer of hearing aids decided to transform itself into a knowledge-based company that provided a much broader range of products and services for application to all kinds of audio problems, such as acoustics for concert auditoriums. Lars Kolind, the CEO, led the development of a new vision that he called "revolutionary," and he began to act to help people see that they had the ability to succeed in the effort.

Kolind began to treat people as though they were capable of doing more than the narrow definitions of their jobs. Departments and job titles were eliminated, and replaced by self-defining project teams. Kolind supported this move with an expectation that all employees would work on at least two projects of their own choosing. One project would be in the area of their major experience and knowledge, and the other would be in any other area in which they were interested or thought they could add value. With the CEO setting an example by selecting a project outside his own area of expertise (use of role modeling), a great deal of energy was unleashed that supported the goal of looser boundaries around the notion of who does what.

Another interesting example is found in the case of "Team Zebra," Kodak's revitalization of its black-and-white film operation beginning in 1989 (Fragos, 1993). To speed up the response to a very critical situation, the manufacturing executive in charge of the endeavor announced to the twenty-five managers involved that they had to implement a major redesign of the manufacturing flow within two weeks, rather than a kickoff planned for four months later. In a very optimistic reply to the managers' shock, he reminded them that they had been planning the change for two years and that they really knew what to do to implement it. He did not sugarcoat the difficulties they would experience, but he acted as though there was no doubt in his mind that they could succeed. Of particular interest is that Fragos, the manager who would direct the implementation, reports that upon hearing this, "I felt my excitement rise and pulse began to race. . . . I honestly believe that it might have taken another year to get the film flows rolling if we did not have marching orders to begin that very morning" (pp. 43–43).

While this incident demonstrates a not-so-subtle use of expectancy, and involves an implicit use of coercion as well, it shows the power that leaders have when they are clear in putting forth desired performance standards. Similarly, given the perceptions of Kodak's managers that problems were studied "until rendered harmless," the executive in charge of the project made it clear that it would not be business as usual as they undertook the company's first major overhaul in a hundred years. To further show faith that people could achieve the desired results with an accelerated timetable, this leader met with two thousand Kodak employees to tell them that he expected they could do the job in six months. The book describing this case (Fragos, 1993) tells how participation, persuasive communication, and role modeling were all used to complement and strengthen the effort to create a positive self-fulfilling prophecy.

This last case gets us close to an understanding of how expectancy—which we have generally talked about as close-distance influence—can also be used in motivating large numbers of people. It illustrates that CEOs and other leaders of large groups of people need to be sure they are bringing about positive self-fulfilling prophecies through both their words and their behaviors.

Putting forth a vision and a target is not enough; it is necessary to *act in every way possible* to make that belief come true.

Using Expectancy Effectively

If expectancy effects are so powerful and can be demonstrated to occur in all walks of life, why are managers as a group only dimly aware of their power, and why do they continue to set up expectations that produce the very negative behavior they wish to eliminate? We have identified four reasons for this unfortunate state of affairs:

- Lack of awareness as to the subtle ways their own behavior brings about the realization of their assumptions

- Lack of understanding as to how environmental factors impact performance

- Failure to reexamine old stereotypes and judgments

- Discomfort with emotion

Self-Awareness

To harness the concept of expectancy in the service of the behaviors they wish to promote, managers must begin to look at their own self-fulfilling prophecies. The first thing required is the *development of heightened insight* into one's own expectations and their impact on others. Increased awareness will enable managers to consider alternative ways of dealing with the "recipients" of their expectations. Is the prediction held for the other the only prediction warranted? Is it an inevitable conclusion, or is it amenable to change? Without the possibility of a reconsideration, the present behaviors will continue unchanged.

Second, managers must be willing to *look at how their behavior plays a role in the way others behave*. They must ask the following questions of themselves: To what extent is the other's behavior a reaction to mine? Am I using the right approach with this individual? Would changes in my behavior have a strong impact on the other's behavior? Without asking such questions, it will be almost impossible for managers to use expectancy in a powerful way, or to interrupt an unwanted self-fulfilling prophecy.

Understanding Environmental Factors and Reexamining Stereotypes and Judgments

Along with self-insight, managers need to *cultivate a more balanced view of human nature*. Is it possible that environmental factors, including one's own behavior, have brought about undesirable behavior and have constituted a barrier to the ability of others to actualize their own greater potentials? For example, managers must be able to give up past judgments and be willing to reexamine stereotypical images they have formed, because impressions of past performances, if broadcast in an individual's new setting, may make it impossible for someone to shed a label and have a fresh start. Obviously, data must not be suppressed, but certainly it should not be used in such a way that an individual is set up to fail in a new situation before he or she has a chance to show what he or she can do. Managers who receive negative reports must be very judicious about how they evaluate and share such reports.

Emotional Involvement

To utilize expectancy is to be emotionally involved. Whether at the level of overall organizational vision or in the day-to-day motivation of people, the effects of expectancy cannot be generated by remote control from a command post. They require visible and highly contactful behavior that has an element of passion, even if embodied in a disciplined executive manner. As with the use of persuasive communication, to which expectancy is closely related, emotional as well as cognitive factors need to be combined in order to be most effective. To the extent that managers who are unemotional in their behavior and who substitute logic for passion continue to be developed and rewarded, the use of expectancy will be impaired.

This last point is critical, for it gets to the heart of the resocialization process. For this process to be successful, emotionally powerful experiences are required. Just as parents and teachers do not shape the behavior of their children and students by logic alone, the good manager must create relationships and pose dilemmas that arouse their employees, sometimes in unsettling ways. It is in the confrontation of these emotion-laden situations that deep learning takes place. The executives used earlier as illustrations, however, are not interacting with subordinates simply as benevolent parental figures; they are acting to "stir the emotional pot" and to establish an atmosphere of expectancy that will support the attainment of difficult objectives. Without integrity in this process, they will be seen only as manipulative cheerleaders.

It can be seen from the preceding material that one of the major skills required is the use of routine, often small, day-to-day behaviors, as a way of influencing others. This means devoting greater attention to the quality and quantity of time spent in face-to-face interaction with those one wishes to influence. Unlike the use of extrinsic rewards, structural rearrangement, coercion, and some forms of persuasive communication and participation, expectancy depends on close interpersonal relations. Nevis, DiBella, and Gould (1995) have referred to the use of expectancy as "involved leadership," citing the management styles of Wal-Mart's David Glass and Motorola's Robert Galvin. This more personal and tailored approach will also enable transformational leaders to adapt their expectations to the ever-present multiple realities that exist in the organization.

Multiple Realities

The existence of multiple realities complicates the use of expectancy in that differences in at least two factors must be considered. First, there is the issue of self-perceived competence to achieve the new vision. Some people will feel more insecure or impotent than others to do what is being asked of them; some will feel very confident, but may not agree with the changes being contemplated. Similarly, more may be asked of some groups than of others. These differences require the articulation of different sets of expectations and the use of a different set of leadership behaviors.

Second, there are issues concerning the degree of cynicism or mistrust in different groups. If trust is high, establishing positive self-fulfilling prophecies is easy. However, where mistrust is high, efforts by leaders to set positive expectations may well be seen as manipulative attempts to get people to work harder. Thus, the credibility of the leader will be very important in determining how to best use expectancy. In some cases, use of positive expectations may need to be coupled with the use of extrinsic rewards.

Effective use, then, depends on a leader or manager's willingness to sincerely question his or her own role in producing a set of behaviors in others, and on a willingness to let go of past history, to engage at an emotional level, to tailor expectations and behaviors to the multiple realities within his or her domain, and above all, to *act* in a way that helps others play to their strengths.

Summary

In this chapter we have added expectancy to the important individual change methods that contribute to transformational change. Just as self-fulfilling prophecies have been established in the current organizational reality, new ones must be developed to support a new vision. This is a major task of transformational leadership, one that requires making new predictions about people and then *acting* to make these a reality. Almost every successful transformational change that has been documented shows the creation of powerful new expectations by change leaders. These expectations serve to make people more comfortable with and more excited about the change process itself. Managers establish expectancies whether they are aware of them or not. We argue that raising awareness about these dynamics of expectancy will enable its more purposeful and productive use in furthering the process of organizational transformation.

8

Role Modeling

Showing How It's Done

Role modeling, or the setting of an example through one's actions, is a powerful method for shaping behavior. For better or worse, it is the major way of learning for children, whether it be playing "house," pretending to drive a car, making pretend phone calls, or drinking alcohol or smoking marijuana. These behaviors are shaped by observation of social cues that people are often unaware of observing. This phenomenon is sometimes referred to as *vicarious* or *social learning*: children learn by watching behaviors performed by someone else and then performing them later through practice. Concern about the impact on people, particularly children, of violent and sexually explicit behavior shown on television is testament to the perceived power of role modeling.

On a positive note, consider the millions of audiotapes and videotapes sold each year to teach people new sets of skills, such as how to be better athletes or how to pronounce foreign words. Similar phenomena can be seen in the workplace. Apprentices in construction trades and manufacturing jobs generally watch those who have mastered an operation before trying it themselves. The quality of machine parts, for example, would be an uncertain thing if the parts were made by people who had never seen others making them. An employee promoted to the role of manager might have little idea of how to proceed in the new role without having previously seen managers in action. In addition, not only do learners observe the content and behaviors involved in the operations they are seeking to learn, but they also often adopt the *style* of those they have observed—or take on another style that is suggested. In short, people learn a great deal about how to play a particular role by watching others play that role as either positive or negative models.

This point is of great importance in implementing transformational change. If significant change involves new roles and behaviors, it follows that such change will be more successfully carried out if living examples of the new ways are visible to those being asked to cooperate in the change. Yet, most change programs are carried out with minimal attention to this point. Through persuasive communication a vision is drawn of the desired new behaviors, but that vision may only exhort people to behave in ways that they have never seen performed. Structural rearrangement may provide an environment more conducive to the development of new roles and responsibilities, but it does not in and of itself make available the behavioral models and skills necessary to carry out these roles and responsibilities effectively. While extrinsic rewards may make it more attractive for people to perform in desired new ways, the question still remains of *how* to perform the behaviors to be contingently rewarded. Role modeling adds a critical dimension that is lacking in these other influence methods.

Role Modeling in Transformational Change

The challenge of using role modeling in transformational change lies in finding role models who can actually model the new behaviors, yet who are appropriate enough to the old culture to be acceptable. Meeting this challenge requires a very delicate balance, for it is hard to get people to give up their identification with current role models and emulate a new model that seems disconfirming of the old. In short, new role models need to be both acceptable to the old culture and different enough to generate interest in the new vision.

A good example of such a model may be found in Lee Iacocca,

who took over the Chrysler Corporation at an extremely difficult time in its life. *Fortune* magazine published an article about Iacocca's presence at a large meeting to introduce a new car: "Chrysler invited the plant's 2,300 hourly workers, many called back recently from layoffs and retrained to operate new equipment, to watch with the usual political and industry bigwigs and journalists. When Iacocca stepped out of the glistening Dodge Lancer he had driven into the spotlight, those workers let out a roar worthy of the crowds in Latin American soccer stadiums. . . . There wasn't an atom of ambiguity about who they were working for—the man they believed saved their jobs, their mortgages, their children's tuition" (Flax, 1985, pp. 35–36).

This example illustrates the power of identification at work on a large scale. Iacocca was acceptable to the Chrysler culture because he was "an automobile man." Yet, he role modeled a colorful marketing approach and a high degree of confidence, both of which had been lacking in the demoralized setting he had entered. In the use of this example we do not mean to imply that transformational change cannot be accomplished without bringing in people from outside the organization. There are numerous cases in which transformation was accomplished with existing personnel.

In one study at a manufacturing facility (Westley, 1990), existing managers were able to role model the new behaviors after being exposed—through the use of new, collateral structures and sessions with consultants—to a new structure and a new way of managing. Some of the managers went through a profound personal change, perhaps because they already possessed some of the attributes and skills desired, although they had not displayed them under the old system. Other managers made a deliberate attempt to change their style, even though they did not fully grasp what was being asked of them. Westley considers the latter group to be made up of people with strong loyalty to the organization; they might not have been the best role models of new skills, but they were examples of people willing to give the new approach a good try.

Perhaps even more compelling evidence that transformational change can be led effectively by insiders who first transformed themselves is to be found in the case of Semco under the leadership of CEO Ricardo Semler (Semler, 1993). In trying to discover why Semco had more "stone cutters" than "cathedral builders," Semler followed a chain of analysis that led right back to himself. He, like his other senior executives, came in early and left late. Meeting until midnight was not unusual. This schedule was symptomatic of the whole culture at Semco: rigid controls and long, stress-inducing hours.

After he passed out one day during a visit to a plant, Semler realized that "before I could reorganize Semco, I had to reorganize myself" (p. 61.). He changed his hours, leaving every day by 7:00 P.M., no matter what. He stopped working on weekends; delegated, delegated, and delegated some more; stopped wearing a watch; and began to value his intuition over expert advice. These changes were made visible to others in a number of ways. The complex, numbers-driven budgeting and control system, which consumed countless hours of everyone's time with little visible improvement in output, was eliminated. When Semco was awarded a Brazilian labor relations award, an employee committee member, rather than Semler, accepted it from the Brazilian president. In his determination to streamline his work, Semler also began to work at home. This behavior conveyed a message of trust: I don't have to be there to make sure you're doing a good job. By doing his own filing, he also found that he saved a lot of paperwork, to no ill effect. At one point, by ceremoniously throwing into the trash an enormous file documenting a problematic order, he stimulated a radical rethinking of what was really necessary to make a decision, and the underlying uselessness of leaving a paper trail in an environment operating on principles of trust. One-page memos and terse, to-the-point reports became the norm; after all, who wants to watch a hundred hours worth of work being thrown into the trash?

Whether new role models come from within or outside a firm,

it is necessary for those models to act as the embodiment of new values and new ways of behaving. Despite evidence showing how important this behavior is, ineffective use of role modeling is rampant in organizational change efforts. Boxes on the organizational chart are rearranged, but the same people are simply shifted into the new boxes, with little consideration as to whether they really know what the new roles require or how to act in those roles. Even with massive training, which works on the cognitive level, the more deeply held, emotionally supported role behaviors of the old system remain strong barriers to the assimilation of new behaviors. To facilitate a better understanding of this point, we next present some examples of changes that failed, in large measure because effective role modeling was missing.

Misuse of Role Modeling

Two cases of failed change efforts show what happens when new role models are not available to support the effort.

In the early 1970s, the new CEO of a highly respected paint and chemical company began a program to diversify into the then-burgeoning home improvement market. The aim was to develop a chain of retail stores in which paint and related products, such as wall and window coverings, carpeting, and so forth, could be sold to the do-it-yourself market. The firm had a long history of loyalty to its people, who responded in kind with great loyalty to the company. Thus, it was decided to take a large number of current sales and management people and train them for the roles required in the new organization.

The people chosen had worked with paint contractors and bulk buyers of coatings throughout their careers, and all of their experience was at the wholesale level, not with retail customers. Other than bringing in an advertising manager familiar with retail marketing, the new organization was staffed entirely by retrained members of the old company. After several years of trying to remold the chosen staff, it became clear that the retraining had failed to teach them how to behave in a customer environment different from the one in which they had "grown up." Some sales and marketing people were hired, but by that time the program had lost momentum and the window of opportunity had closed.

In the early 1980s, the CEO of a manufacturing firm spearheaded an attempt to create an environmental services company, a longtime passion of his. Parts of the existing business were sold to enable a focus on the new company. To launch the new business, the CEO chose a few people from the old manufacturing area. For several years, this group struggled to get the business off the ground, with very limited success. Hiring a highly experienced environmental services expert as the manager made a noticeable difference, but he was unable by himself to overcome the manufacturing mind-set that existed in the old-timers. Subsequently, two acquisitions of small environmental companies were made. This provided a number of new role models with additional knowledge and experience, but these changes took place over six years, during which the business was seldom profitable. As a result, the board of directors ultimately decided to exit the environmental business.

Both of these examples show how a lack of critical role models can hamper change. In both cases, considerable resources and time were devoted to reorienting people, but the emphasis was largely on skills training and on learning through trial and error. There were almost no visible examples of the desired customer service behaviors that people could actually observe.

The highly touted practice of bringing in a new senior manager also has its limitations, however. While it does provide a new role model, it puts the weight of change on one person's shoulders and it offers only one role model rather than several that might be useful. As one frustrated CEO remarked, "I'm tired of being the only champion of change." Needless to say, his endeavor was not successful, and the CEO eventually left the company when it became apparent that the transformation was failing.

An equally dysfunctional approach is when leaders tell people to change their behavior but continue themselves to role model the old behaviors. Even when leaders try to lead by example, they are often ineffective because the way they behave sends counterproductive messages into the organizational system. It is one thing to talk collaboration; it is another thing to live it. This point is illustrated in two revitalization efforts discussed by Beer, Eisenstat, and Spector (1990):

> Singer (the CEO) asked all his vice presidents to go back to their groups and find out what the reaction would be from their people if we took away a week of their vacation. So at the next meeting, my boss (the divisional vice president) reported that it would be a disaster. That's what the feedback was. Well, Singer immediately took my boss on: "You lousy sons of bitches from Construction! No wonder you're all screwed up." And all the other vice presidents at that meeting went silent [p. 196].

> In Specialized Products. . . the unit's general manager stifled innovation and revitalization despite his public support for change. . . . "He was a hard-hitting goddamnit personality," said one manager. "Every time I saw him," remembered another, "he would greet me by saying, 'Well, Bob, what have you screwed up today?'" [p. 198]

These cases show that role modeling can be a powerful negative force, and unfortunately, time after time the recipients of the role model's message adopt the message even when they find it distasteful or inappropriate—for example, studies have shown that people who abuse others, such as child abusers, often were abused by their parents. Subordinates of Harold Geneen at ITT did not like his aggressive, often belittling manner, but it nevertheless became the managerial style during his reign as CEO. On the positive side, however, because he was such a powerful role model, managers also attended to his financial acumen and learned to emulate it. We are what we observe, whether we are aware of it or not—and whether we like it or not!

The Dynamics of Role Modeling

Role modeling operates on two levels. The first has to do with the *learning of specific behaviors*, such as driving a car or learning to swim. Children and young adults generally observe these skills for a long time before they practice them. Similarly, employees who regularly attend meetings observe the leadership of those meetings well before being asked to conduct one themselves. Thus, some learning occurs that is independent of overt practice or direct rewards. The implication is that skill development begins before it emerges in actual behavior. Such learning is also independent of trial-and-error learning or the sink-or-swim approach, in which people are thrust into a role and expected to perform.

Examples of role modeling are abundant. It is a crucial part of all apprenticeship learning systems, in which a "master" and a learner are put into the same work space for periods of time. Almost all teachers take advantage of this principle. For instance, it is hard to conceive of someone learning to play a musical instrument without having seen the particular techniques demonstrated. In addition, many studies have shown the power of role modeling in teaching social behaviors such as stopping one's car to help a motorist in trouble or putting money in Salvation Army collection boxes. In these studies, a role model has been used to demonstrate a particular behavior while the learner is watching. The learner is then observed to see if he or she manifests the new behavior.

Some management development programs take advantage of role modeling. Porras and others (1982) describe a program in which this approach was used. Ten useful supervisory behaviors were selected for a training program. In addition to discussions of the behaviors and their use, videotapes demonstrating each principle were shown. Follow-up months later showed that the trainees had retained the learned behavior skills and that productivity and group labor relations had improved.

The second level on which role modeling works has to do with the *process of identification* with someone whose values or way of being in the world are attractive. The attraction can be of different kinds. Sometimes it is to the role model's demonstration of a craft or skill that becomes a possible career choice. Other times, the attraction is to specific attributes of the role model, such as the way he or she accomplishes work, or the way he or she handles conflict. In addition, the attraction may be to a general lifestyle that presents a vision of a desirable way of life or a commitment to a mission. Finally, the attraction can be defensive, allowing the learner to avoid threatening situations by emulating the behavior of the role model. The process of identification is complicated, but it is part of every human being's developmental history. Some would say that a person's maturity can be measured in part by the nature of the role models with whom she has identified.

An example of a model who evoked strong identification in others is Gandhi, who attracted people to himself and his cause through the mission he embodied in his everyday way of being. In the world of sports, Magic Johnson and Michael Jordan attract identification by countless young African Americans.

An illustration of the power of role modeling in creating identification can be found in the way Ralph Nader, the consumer affairs and public interest critic, stimulated bright young lawyers to work very long hours at very low wages. Nader was able to accomplish this by role modeling the behaviors he wanted to see in others. Nader set the standard for seven-day weeks and working into the night by working those hours himself. As is evident in the following comments made by one of the young lawyers working for him, one of Nader's strengths was his ability to convey through his behavior an energizing curiosity about the way the world worked. Furthermore, he did not simply talk about getting things done; he did them, in a visible and compelling way.

> Ralph's been the best teacher in the world because he doesn't teach you. What he does is to project a wonder and a curiosity about the world and the way in which society is organized, and so lead you to make the best use of your energy, education and talent. . . . Ralph made it clear to me that what he had in mind was a seven-day-a-week job. I remember his sitting back and saying, "Maybe sometime, every few weeks, you could take off on a Sunday." What Ralph does for you when you start working with him is to show you what it feels like to get things *done*. He lets you know that what you're going to do is going to set the world on fire . . . and in fact, I've never worked so hard in my life as I have for Ralph Nader [Whiteside, 1973, pp. 54–55].

An important aspect of the above example is that it shows how identification is supported by motivational forces created *within* the individual rather than by extrinsic rewards. This "ownership" factor makes the learning that follows far less dependent upon outside conditions than when behavior is dependent upon contingent reinforcement. The goal of organizational socialization is in large part to influence people to internalize values and norms without having constantly to rely on tangible rewards. This is an important consideration in today's transformation efforts, in which business conditions are putting restrictions on the enhancement of extrinsic rewards.

Learning through role modeling need not be restricted to observation without action. There is also *participant role modeling* in which the role model and the learner carry out an activity together.

A competent swimming coach teaching people to dive frequently will take the hand of a fearful student and jump into the pool while holding hands. On other occasions, the coach swims alongside the student. Another example is when a teacher and student jointly fly an aircraft. This approach provides protective support for trying the new behavior while allowing some degree of self-directed performance. The implications of this form of learning for transformational change are great. Unfortunately, all too often senior leadership asks people to do things that make them anxious, without providing direct support for the attempt.

Participant role modeling is a way for the advocates of change and their subordinates to venture into the unknown together. An important example of this is provided in the behavior of Robert Galvin, then CEO of Motorola, when he initiated Total Quality Management back in 1979. Galvin personally attended the first quality training as a student along with other employees, and he participated along with students in later activities after he began to gain competence himself. He was role modeling the role of a student to set an example, and to communicate that an ambiguous new situation can be approached with some confidence. A similar illustration is found at Home Depot, now considered to be one of the best-managed companies in the United States. In this very large firm, the CEO and the president personally lead training sessions. Says CEO Bernard Marcus, "Nobody else does training this way. It's time-consuming, it's hard work." He goes on to comment, "How else do you instill the right culture in a company?" (Jacob, 1995, p. 60).

In looking at the dynamics of role modeling, it is important to understand the difference between identification and imitation. *Imitation* is the duplication of the actions of others. Implicit in imitation is an attempt to copy the behavior by incorporating it into one's own way of being. Children are prone to do this, as are people who are very dependent and prone to introjection, the blind swallowing of the behavior of another. *Identification* is a more active process, often supported by the development of new mental models. It often involves purposive choice and a "chewing over" before assimilating the behavior. It is a creative adaptation of the role model's way of being, rather than a carbon copy. Helen Vassallo calls this "adopt, adapt, adept."

The Impact of Multiple Realities on Role Modeling

To avoid simple imitation, it is useful to expose the learner to several role models with varying backgrounds, experiences, and personal styles. While observers may attend more to some role models than to others, they rarely adopt all the qualities of their preferred models. Studies have shown the value of multiple role models in demonstrating the range of possibilities without demanding that everyone follow the same path. Multiple role models allow an observer the opportunity to choose parts of the behavioral patterns of different role models. If learners see only one way of being, it is much more difficult for them to develop their own creative synthesis of the various possibilities. A case in the training of psychotherapists and organizational consultants at the Gestalt Institute of Cleveland illustrates this point and shows how imitation can be avoided.

In the early years of the institute, trainees were strongly influenced by the charisma displayed in videotapes of Fritz Perls, one of the founders of Gestalt therapy. In their practice sessions with clients, these trainees attempted to act just like Perls, and of course failed. There was just no way their imitations did not seem awkward or jarring. As a result of this experience, the institute faculty decided that one or two of the most experienced teachers would do demonstrations for the students. This was a little better, but then the students began to imitate those teachers. Finally a solution was found: the students would be exposed to demonstrations by at least six teachers. This made their learning task harder, but it forced them to take in several role models and to integrate what they observed into their own style. For thirty years now, this approach has worked well.

This example makes an important point about diversity in an organization. Most often, the issue of diversity is raised in connection with the changing nature of the work force or because of heightening awareness of the need to manage work groups composed of diverse minorities, such as African Americans, women, Hispanics, or foreign workers in European countries. The concern here is to see what is required to help these people adapt to the prevailing culture. This is a problem-oriented perspective, and it fails to appreciate the opportunity that diversity provides at all levels of the organization. A heterogeneous work force at all levels automatically provides a range of role models in terms of cultural differences and life experiences. While the management task may be harder with heterogeneous groups, the advantages are not to be overlooked. Sophisticated multinational companies, such as Unilever, Shell, and Asea Brown Boveri have for years moved managers into countries other than their own. The value of this strategy goes beyond the developmental experience provided to these managers. It makes available to local people a role model different than would be possible in a homogenous culture.

Role Modeling and Mentoring

A final point about the dynamics of modeling leads to the distinction between role modeling and *mentoring*. Role modeling is a part of mentoring in that persons who have mentors are almost always allowed to observe their day-to-day behaviors. Mentors also provide opportunities for their protegees to observe other role models. One example of this is the case of twenty-five senior Motorola executives who selected three hundred champions of a new change initiative. These executive mentors were, in effect, inviting their "champions" into a rich observational environment. This action involved taking on a more active political role on behalf of their protegees in that a mentor acts as a guide or sponsor who takes deliberate actions on behalf of a chosen other. The actions can be limited to giving advice or coaching, or they can include full participation in the mentor's decision-making process. The role can be performed by peers as well as those in higher positions. Mentoring is a useful way of preparing high-potential people for greater responsibility and status, but although it involves the role modeling of behaviors, it involves a great deal more as well.

With this in mind, we now look at some successful applications of role modeling in the organizational world.

Successful Applications of Modeling

A very rich example of organizational change strategy using many influence methods is Blue Cross–Blue Shield of Ohio (BCBSO). In 1987, BCBSO ranked seventy-second out of seventy-three national Blue Cross plans in industry measures of performance. By 1993, it had moved into first place under the leadership of Jack Burry.

> Jack Burry doesn't fit the picture of your average CEO. Described by his employees as half grizzly bear, half teddy bear—the grizzly part is demanding and hard to satisfy, the teddy is approachable and understanding—he wears flannel shirts on bad-weather days and gets his own coffee as a matter of course. Though his strategies are often controversial in the insurance community, Burry's intelligence and unwavering commitment to his company gain his employees' respect. "When he says he'll do something, he does it," says one of them. "He hasn't wavered in his commitment to us and to the company." This commitment has taken many forms, from tangible investment in training for all employees to less tangible but strongly symbolic gestures such as selecting high-energy, nonmanagerial talent to help lead the changes. "The CEO's attitude," says the employee, "has served as an energizing surprise. No one counted on Burry's zest and vision to take BCBSO where it has gone" [Smith, 1994, p. 24].

This case reveals the importance of having a leader who is both respected and distinctive. It is reported that while implementing the quality program, upper-level executives were coached about their behaviors and the messages they were sending. Note also that one can emphasize both toughness and support, and that in the case of Jack Burry, both of these were observable to others.

One of the best examples of how successful role modeling has been applied over a long period is Motorola, considered to be one of America's most admired and best-run companies. This case, touched on earlier, illustrates effective use of multiple role models rather than sole reliance on the CEO.

When the quality initiative began, Bob Galvin, then CEO, used himself as a model by being a student in the workshops and seminars developed to learn about quality. Moreover, he changed the way he conducted his operations review meetings by starting each meeting by asking each business and function executive to report on what he or she had done to improve systems for quality since the last meeting. In the first such meeting one of the participants gave a very brief report and then started to discuss operational numbers. According to this person: "When I finished, Galvin asked me: 'Bill, is that all?' I replied, 'But Bob, there is a lot to cover in this meeting, and I want to present my results.' He replied, 'I've got plenty of time. Let's discuss quality in more detail.'" To underscore his interest and seriousness about quality, in subsequent meetings, Galvin continued to have the reports on quality systems go first and then often left the room, allowing his second in command to lead the discussion of the numbers.

As several years went by, the executives in charge of the quality initiative realized that there were now a lot of knowledgeable people who could act as champions that would enable quality management to take hold throughout the company. They identified and enlisted a group of people who cared about the project or already possessed some knowledge in this area to serve as "champions" in different parts of the company. Motorola executives consider this to be a highly important contribution to the success of the quality program, which resulted in the company's winning the first Baldrige Award in

1988. In a more recent initiative, started in 1992, the concept of multiple champions or role models is one of the important strategies
being used. First, a group of twenty-five senior managers was formed
to be responsible for leading the effort. Then three hundred people
who already possessed some of the attitudes and skills required to
advance the new initiatives were recruited from all parts of Motorola
to serve as advocates throughout the company. It is interesting to
note that although the twenty-five senior managers identified a seven-
year time line for this project, their first step was to educate themselves. Second, the training and development of the three hundred
champions came well before any rollout of the program to the company at large [Nevis, DiBella, and Gould, 1993].

The Motorola case is an example of how the power of role modeling multiplies when the presence of numerous desirable role
models is added to that of the CEO. The presence of multiple role
models also sends a message to the rest of the organization that a
particular change effort is to be taken seriously. Two further implications derive from this case. First, successful change requires a
period during which the ground is laid for a more massive intervention. Second, transformational change cannot be accomplished
overnight; it may require several years of focusing on readiness-
producing activities before a broader momentum can be developed.

Using Role Modeling Effectively

Role modeling occurs as a function of the role model just being who
he or she is. It is not about occasionally acting in a certain way, and
it does not require the exaggeration of any particular behavior. Role
modeling is most likely to be effective if it is seen as natural behavior. Therefore, the most effective role models will be those who
have a good sense of identity and high self-confidence.

Although the *concept* of role modeling is a simple one, role modeling itself is a complex, powerful phenomenon that is often misunderstood or unappreciated. To some extent, this is due to the fact

that most of the time people are not consciously aware of what they are role modeling. Anyone who is in a position of leadership—a parent, a teacher, or a manager—acts as a role model whether or not they are conscious of doing so. They are constantly observed by those around them, who see and judge their behavior. The picture is further complicated by the fact that what an individual thinks is "critical influencing behavior" may not be seen that way by an observer. I may think that the main thing I am communicating in my way of being is a friendly, generous style of managing, but others may find my intelligence or my disciplined work style more compelling and worthy of emulation.

While managerial presence in any situation evokes things in others simply as a function of the manager's being there, heightened awareness of *what* is being role modeled is important for distinguishing between that which supports change and that which supports resistance. Thus, behavior of senior managers in the earlier example who acted in punishing ways may have been seen by the executives as displaying the requisite no-nonsense decisiveness, but that behavior cost the senior managers their credibility.

Selection of appropriate role models at the beginning of a change effort is therefore extremely important. In situations of significant change, the best role models may be those seen as "different" in some way. In their study of culture and performance, Kotter and Heskett (1992) found that the firms involved in renewal that did not bring in a new CEO from outside selected from within an executive who diverged from the prevailing norms.

However, regardless of where the new role models are from, to be effective at role modeling, the role models need to act toward others like teachers or coaches, and they need to pay attention to what they evoke in others.

As noted before, use of a variety of role models and hence a variety of styles is not only possible but desirable. One model may believe that the best way to teach others is by a straightforward sharing of his or her experiences. Another may project a more mysterious manner and create attention through an air of wonderment and awe, such as a Zen master does. Another may take great pains to show others exactly how he or she performs some task. Yet another may display a dazzling intelligence and an acute perceptiveness of the world. And still another may model a paternal patience, including an acceptance of others' resistance.

Although not a limitation inherent in role modeling, one of the ways its potential is diminished is by management's failure to appreciate that different subunits and referent groups often require different role models. It is hard for salespeople to identify readily with accountants or engineers. Similarly, racial and gender differences can lower the effectiveness of a role model. A frequent complaint of women managers in recent years is that they do not have enough female executive models from whom to learn and with whom they can identify. This does not mean that only same-race or same-sex role models can be effective, but it does mean that role models need to be seen as attractive to the groups they are to influence. It is naive to think that these differences do not matter, yet little attention is paid to them in many change efforts.

For an organization to gain the greatest possible benefits from role modeling, attention needs to be paid to those who supervise new employees. In many instances, this does not happen. Yet studies of the early experiences of management trainees and entry-level professionals indicate that the quality of orientation constitutes a critical difference between those who had good learning experiences and those who did not.

Another tactic that is useful in role modeling to achieve behavioral change is job rotation. This strategy not only provides a new set of tasks and roles for the person who is rotated, but it also offers a new set of role models to a given organizational unit and the opportunity to see the same behaviors performed in a different style. Apprenticeship periods can also be a valuable way to take advantage of the power of role modeling to reshape behavior.

Perhaps the most important organizational support for learning through role modeling is the frequency and duration of people's opportunities to observe role models at close range. Making it possible for people to attend important meetings, even as observers, is very helpful in this regard. Watching one's manager present a report on which one worked allows one to observe both one's own manager and others. Increasing the number of people at meetings and the number of meetings that individuals may attend may seem unwieldy, but the inconvenience may be offset by the learning opportunity.

Summary

Role modeling is a highly effective influence method. People are models of what they truly believe, not of what they preach. The leaders of change would do well to realize that role modeling is not, by itself, enough to sustain and improve the performance of what is learned. Unless there is later reinforcement through practice opportunities and incentives, that which is learned will likely remain a limited skill. While this may be easy enough to do when learning a specific behavior, it is not easily done with the more complex and difficult roles of a manager, in which more general identification and attitude change is involved. Any implementation plan involving new role models must provide opportunities for those they influence to try out new ways of behaving, and it must ensure that there is encouragement and praise for those who do. For some people, monetary incentives may indeed be necessary.

In addition, role modeling is much more intangible than other approaches. It is often not clear to managers how role models influence others, and there is a tendency to see role modeling as a method that deals with "soft stuff." As we said earlier, learning that occurs through observation is not immediately apparent in performance. Accustomed to achieving a quick return on investment, senior management may have difficulty with the more long-term nature of the results that role modeling involves.

Role modeling takes time. As in the case of Motorola, a truly internalized change requires several years to develop role models other than that of the CEO. However, role modeling is a powerful shaper of behavior—one way or the other. Therefore, in the context of organizational transformation and resocialization, the development and deployment of role models capable of effectively modeling the new behaviors will help speed the transformation.

9

. . . .

Structural Rearrangement

Shaping the Work Environment

No matter what the need—to reduce expenses, to eliminate bureaucracy, to improve customer satisfaction and productivity, or to utilize new technologies more effectively—the instinctive response of managers seems to be to rearrange the organizational structure. Historically, structural change—defined primarily as a rearrangement of the boxes and lines on the formal organizational chart—has been the intervention of choice in addressing many organizational issues.

There are several explanations for this preference. One of the most important is the human need to minimize ambiguity. In the uncertainty that organizational change represents, structures are one of the most tangible aspects of the change, certainly far more so than the many human and interpersonal aspects that have to be managed. The very word "structure" conjures images of things solid and stable—bricks and mortar! Indeed, it is not difficult to see how this mental picture of physical structures has influenced the view of organizational structures as a series of well-defined boxes or "rooms" connected by a series of lines or "hallways" along which communication between the rooms can travel.

This need for something solid to hold onto has led to many debates concerning the "best" structure, that is, how various "rooms" of the organization should be aggregated or disaggregated to achieve a given goal. In a global, high technology environment, for example, market focus and information sharing have been addressed through decentralization, while cost control and resource sharing have generally suggested the need for centralization. Typically, these management conversations explore the relative merits of functional units versus business units, or the advantages of an industry focus versus a geography focus. If a company is organizationally sophisticated, it may also wrestle with how to manage the inherent tension between these polarities, rather than choosing one over the other. This need to balance conflicting priorities often leads to the implementation of a matrix structure, and dotted line/solid line relationships—and headaches—have become a permanent part of most organizational vocabularies. Nevertheless, for many people the ambiguity of this management structure violates their deeply felt need for something clear and simple to grab hold of. For most employees, the relationship with their boss is one of the more tangible aspects of their relationship to the organization, and at the first hint of restructuring, the question "Who will I be reporting to?" or "To whom will my group be reporting?" is uppermost on everyone's mind. This is part of the normal desire (and hope) to exert some control in a complex and ambiguous situation.

In fact, structural rearrangement has been one of the primary ways to control what is going on in an organization. Since the advent of the industrial era and Frederick Taylor's efforts to control work by reducing a given job to the smallest unit of tasks, organizational structure has concerned itself with issues of control: of the work through division and coordination of labor, and of decision making through the arrangement of organizational authority and power.

In the context of organizational transformation, however, this conception of structure is too limited, and unless structure's less tangible dimensions are more completely appreciated, it will be impossible to take full advantage of its contribution to transformation. A growing number of organizations have been experimenting with structural rearrangements that embody the principles of the "new science" paradigm, introduced in Chapter One. These companies vary in size, industry, and nationality, but they all seem to have at least two things in common. First, they have recognized that continuing to tinker with their current hierarchical, "mechanical" organizational structures will never enable them to produce the kinds of individual and organizational behaviors necessary for success in the currently turbulent business environment. Second, they have all demonstrated a pioneering spirit, that is, the willingness to explore new territories and chart new courses.

Two companies that have succeeded in this area are Oticon, a Danish hearing aid manufacturer, and Asea Brown Boveri, a worldwide electrotechnical company. A number of other companies have ventured into this territory as well. W. L. Gore, an American company, has a long history of success, which it attributes in large part to its "lattice" organizational structure. By developing a radically new, boundariless "satellite" structure, Semco has managed to remain extremely successful, despite Brazil's highly volatile economic climate. Johnsonville Foods, a Wisconsin-based sausage maker has developed a results-based "membership" structure and has recognized that in order to take full advantage of its core competencies, it would have to abandon its hierarchical organizational structure. In Japan, the Kyocera Corporation is transforming itself into what it calls an "amoeba" structure, able to fine-tune itself to the changing conditions of its environment. Even the U.S. Army, long considered a bastion of authoritarian, hierarchical command and control structures, has instituted a series of structural innovations aimed at transforming itself into a more flexible, rapidly deployable, innovative, reflective force capable of quickly learning from its experience.

An exploration of how these companies have reinvented their organizational structures as a way to transform organizational behaviors will be helpful in understanding the multiple dimensions of the link between structural rearrangement and behavioral change. This chapter explores these multiple dimensions, first by examining cases that highlight some of the difficulties that have been encountered when structural rearrangement is too narrowly defined. This examination will form the basis for an expanded definition of organizational structure. Based on this definition, we will examine how structural rearrangement works to shape organizational behavior, and we will also suggest the need for a new paradigm to guide thinking about structural rearrangement as a method of organizational transformation. We will then provide examples of how structural rearrangement has been successfully used to transform several organizations. Finally, we will discuss the skills and conditions necessary for the successful use of structural rearrangement in transformation.

Problems Encountered in the Use of Structural Rearrangement

While rearranging organizational boxes and lines forms one dimension of the use of structural rearrangement in organizational change, increased sophistication concerning the dynamics of organizational change has helped detect the crucial importance of several other dimensions.

Faced with a significant loss of market share, a global computer company decided to restructure. Product development was taking too long, and too many "windows of opportunity" had been missed. Customers complained that it was too hard to do business with the company, and salespeople frequently spent more than 50 percent of their time negotiating the internal system to get the customer support they needed. To address these concerns, the executive team announced that the company would move from being a functionally and geographically based organization to operating with a business unit structure. Each business unit would have profit and loss responsibilities, and each could buy the services it needed, either internally or externally. This new structure was expected to instill an entrepreneurial mind-set throughout the company. Yet, eighteen months later it was still missing "windows of opportunity," customers were still complaining, and employees were still spending inordinate amounts of time getting the resources they needed. The solution? Another restructuring—this time to a global industry focus. Global industry teams were formed, and time was devoted to the creation of industry methods, goals, and financial targets. Unfortunately, this restructuring proved to be no more effective than the one that preceded it. One frustrated participant commented that the repeated organizational restructuring was like watching the crew of the Titanic rearrange the deck chairs.

One reason that the structural changes described in this case had little effect on the success of this organization's change endeavors was that while virtually all the organization's energy went first into creating a large number of customer business units and then into repeating the process with a set of industry business units, the functional and geographic structures remained in place—the old structures were merely overlaid with the new. The existing organizational and management infrastructures remained intact (including strategic goals and metrics), and only minimal attention was given to the alignment of functional, geographic, customer, and industry structures. While considerable effort went into a high-level delineation of the roles and responsibilities of the new structures, only a minimal concurrent effort was made to redefine the roles and responsibilities of the functional and geographic structures, and even less effort was devoted to creating an integrated set of roles and responsibilities. As a result, there were few changes in the behaviors of those in the functional and geographic "silos," and the substructures often worked at cross-purposes, creating tensions and frustrations that were never resolved. In addition, little attention was paid to the presence or absence of new role models or to the development of new skills and competencies.

A second reason the structural changes had little effect on the day-to-day organizational behaviors of a large part of the organization stemmed from the fact that the changes were based neither on a redesign of the work processes themselves nor on a systematic redesign of the organizational infrastructure once the new structure was in place. These two omissions meant that the messages being sent to employees about priorities—and therefore about how they should behave—were on the one hand still firmly rooted in the past, and on the other hand, frequently in conflict with each other.

The issue of the impact of work processes as a component of organizational structure on employee behaviors is an important one, and the power of these structures to influence behavior is often greatly underestimated, as the following case illustrates:

> During a visit to one of Terex's manufacturing plants, the new CEO concluded that the plant needed an infusion of up-to-date equipment. He ordered the plant manager to install two computer-numerical-control cutting tables right away. Two months later when he again visited the plant, he was surprised to learn that the equipment had not even been ordered. Expressing his concern, he was told that they were still "studying" the matter. He reissued his mandate; yet a month later, he found that although the paperwork had been processed, they had not yet selected a vendor. During a subsequent visit, he learned that although the equipment had been installed, several employees were still working on a cost justification because all purchases had to be cost justified; even though it would be after the fact, it would at least confirm that the right decision had been made [Sheridan, 1989].

This example clearly shows the power of existing organizational work processes in defining employee behaviors. Despite repeated direct orders, it was the work processes that determined the employees' actions. Not only are direct orders insufficient, but often partial changes in work process are similarly ineffective. Many sincere efforts at self-managed teams fail because taking responsibility is not simply a matter of being told to take it. Success requires having the knowledge, skills, and authority to explore alternatives, make decisions, access resources, and learn through experience. It also requires changes in, for example, the training, information systems, and reward infrastructures that support the behaviors.

Experience has taught many change leaders that when they think of structural rearrangement as a method for organizational transformation, they must think not only in terms of the "hard" aspects of an organization's structure and infrastructure but also in terms of many of the "soft" aspects. However, as the two examples that follow demonstrate, taking the soft aspects into account is also, in and of itself, no guarantee of success.

In an effort to increase customer satisfaction, growth, and profitability, a large financial institution decided to restructure many of its departments. Reporting relationships were changed, departments were merged or co-located, teams were implemented throughout the organization, and telephone operators were trained in telephone techniques and listening skills. However, despite these structural changes, there was little change in employee or management behavior, or in the level of customer satisfaction, growth, or profitability. In an effort to understand why, the company began to examine its underlying values. They discovered that what the organization really valued was keeping things orderly and unambiguous, maintaining harmony at all costs, responding promptly and accurately to all requests, and making the numbers, no matter what.

In this case, the behavior-changing effect of the formal structural rearrangement was minimal because the organization's underlying values and culture remained intact. Three factors potentially account for the inability of the new structure to overcome the power of the old values. First, the restructuring arose not out of a redesign of the actual day-to-day work but from a high-level reshuffling of the boxes and lines. Second, teamwork cannot work if conflicts are swept under the rug. Third, no amount of training and skill development will help create more customer-focused behaviors if the behavior that gets rewarded is "making the numbers no matter what."

While redesigning an organization's culture is crucial for organizational transformation, the next example illustrates how failure to focus on restructuring the day-to-day work creates problems.

Multiple organizational layers made it difficult for U.S. Financial to compete successfully in the newly deregulated banking industry. Responsiveness and accountability were lacking, and there could be no doubt that the management style was cautious and conservative. Even knowledgeable loan officers were unable to exercise their own judgment. Determined to make the company competitive, the new CEO and senior management team began to articulate the need for a new organizational culture. Together, they developed a new corporate vision and a statement of values, both of which were communicated throughout the organization. The values were incorporated into the company's performance evaluation program and into many of the company's training programs. A matrix structure was developed to flatten the organization and to manage the product/market segments, and a pay-for-performance program was put in place to create a more performance-oriented culture. However, to everyone's surprise, these changes did not help to make the company more competitive [Beer, Eisenstat, and Spector, 1990, pp. 25–29].

In this example, the CEO and the executive team took vision and values into account, rearranged the organizational structure, and made sure that important aspects of the organization's infrastructure were changed to support the organization's new values and focus. According to Beer, Eisenstat, and Spector (1990), these changes failed to affect behavior because they put the proverbial cart before the horse. In other words, these structural and infra-structure changes were not based on a restructuring of the actual work. Beer, Eisenstat, and Spector call this "task alignment, a . . . redefinition of work roles, responsibilities and relationships. . . . [It is a] process of realigning how people and departments should work together" (pp. 45–46), and it "capitalizes on the power of social context to change individual behavior" (p. 60).

What appears to be needed is a deeper and more holistic definition and understanding of the concept of structural rearrangement. To be sure, any definition would include the redesign of the organizational boxes and lines. However, before rearranging these more visible manifestations of organizational structure, there must first be a focus on the redefinition of the roles, responsibilities, and relationships embedded in the day-to-day work processes. In addition, there must also be concern about the redesign and alignment of what is generally referred to as the organization's supporting infra-structure (for example, the budgeting or resource allocation processes, the performance appraisal processes, the information systems, the reward and compensation systems, and the full array of management processes that focus on decision making, communication and training, and the management of multiple organizational tensions). The infrastructure must be brought into alignment with the new work processes, roles, responsibilities, and relationships. Finally, for structural rearrangement to be successful as a method for organizational transformation, it must also recognize and encompass the softer aspects of the organization's cultural infrastructure—to wit, the effect on behavior of organizational and individual values and visions.

All these dimensions create what may be called the environmental context in which organizational behaviors take place. Consideration of this context brings to the fore the fundamental issue in the use of structural rearrangement to achieve organizational transformation: the use of these structural dimensions to shape individual and organizational behavior.

Dynamics of Structural Rearrangement

Everyone has had direct, lifelong experience with the effects of structure in producing and shaping desired and appropriate behaviors, be it the structure of the family, of the community, or of the larger social institutions with which everyone inevitably comes in contact. All these structures of relationships give messages in a complex variety of specific and subtle ways as to how people should behave in relation to the world around them. They tell people who is in authority (for example, fathers, bosses, CEOs, presidents), and they provide the signposts or pathways that guide people's behaviors as they travel through life. As people negotiate these multiple structures, they receive from them constant cues and directions about what to do and how to do it.

Schools, for example, transmit and teach far more than the standard menu of sanctioned bodies of knowledge packaged as course offerings or subjects. Based on the current structure of most educational experiences, students play (and are rewarded for playing) an essentially dependent role. From the first, the classroom structure makes it clear that the teacher is in charge. Students respond to assignments they are given or to teacher-led discussions. The behaviors of reading, writing papers, studying, taking tests, and competing for grades all take place within parameters determined by others. Students learn early that math and English and science are separate subjects. Grades reflect individual effort only, and with class standing frequently based on a bell curve, there is little incentive for collaboration. Over the years, students proceed through a set curriculum divided into predetermined grades that must be taken in sequence.

All this structure elicits certain behaviors from people. For the most part, they learn to accept the overall structure put in place by others, even if they do not like it. They learn to follow school rules and norms of behavior, to play the role of student—that is, to sit through classes, raise their hands when they have something to say, study subjects whether they are interested in them or not, write papers, take tests, and for the most part, accept what the teacher says as fact. Independent study, and independent thinking, if they occur at all, are a small part of the overall experience.

If, however, school were structured differently, as a flexible smorgasbord of self-directed study, for example, people would learn to behave quite differently. In a self-directed study structure, students might see their "teachers" only sporadically. In such a structure they would have to take full responsibility for developing their own proposals and projects, figuring out what to incorporate, what to read, to whom they should talk, and with whom they needed to collaborate. Their explorations would most certainly cut across "subjects," as is the case, for example, in the current use of the theories and insights from quantum physics, chaos theory, and biological ecosystems to better understand organizational dynamics and behavior.

Digging a little deeper reveals that these different structures are actually composed of differing patterns of roles and responsibilities. Roles are an entirely social phenomenon. People play them in relation to one another, and they are recognizable as roles because they are composed of patterned sets of behaviors that conform to the expectations of those with whom one interacts. According to Weick (1979), structure is the "interlocking behaviors," consisting of "reciprocal actions that are repeated over time" (p. 90).

In this view, structure is relational and is the recognizable outcome of a set of patterned behaviors or roles that two or more people have set in motion. This understanding helps explain why simply rearranging the organizational boxes and lines does not always produce the desired result. Concepts such as centralization or decentralization represent, at best, a generalization about the specific sets of relationships involved. To be successful, structural rearrangement needs to go beyond the concept and focus specifically on rearranging the roles, responsibilities, tasks, and relationships. Structural changes will then be firmly rooted in the day-to-day work life of the employees and will, over time, "teach"

a different set of behaviors. It is this ability of organizational structure to elicit, teach, guide, shape, and reinforce a pattern of reciprocal, expected behaviors on a daily basis that makes structural
rearrangement *as we are defining it here* so powerful a means of
changing behaviors. This is what Beer, Eisenstat, and Spector
(1990) discovered in their study of organizational renewal, and what
Bartlett and Ghoshal (1993) found in their work with Asea Brown
Boveri (ABB).

At ABB, organizational transformation was initiated not by
defining how the various departments or divisions would relate to
one another but by understanding and redefining the cluster of roles
that collectively define the social structure of the company and
in which the core management processes were embedded (Bartlett
and Ghoshal, 1993, p. 44). This view is based on the belief that
everyone is capable of both initiative and shirking, collaboration
and personal opportunism, learning and inertia. Which of these
behaviors is actually manifested depends on the individual's predis-
position *and* on the context in which the person finds himself or
herself (p. 45). The process of resocialization, then, can be greatly
facilitated by the conscious application of structural rearrangement.
As one manager in Beer, Eisenstat, and Spector's (1990) study of
organizational renewal said emphatically, "No matter what the hell
you do, if you don't permanently change the organization's structure [and] infrastructure to force behavior change, it isn't going to
happen. The organization, that structure, is stronger than anything
else you can do and it's going to pull it right down to the old environment unless you permanently change it" (p. 95).

Methods for Changing Work Processes, Roles, and Responsibilities

The importance of changing the organizational environment,
the work processes themselves, and the roles and responsibilities of
organizational members in order to effect organizational change is

currently reflected in three popular methods: the Socio-Technical Systems model, the Total Quality Management model, and the Business Process Reengineering model. An exploration of these three methods offers important lessons for the use of structural rearrangement in organizational transformation, and helps to expand understanding of why and how structural rearrangement works.

Socio-Technical Systems

The Socio-Technical Systems (STS) approach embodies one of the more important keys to the sustainability of change and transformation: the integration of the social needs of the individual with the technical needs of the work process. The advocates of STS designs discovered more than fifty years ago that this integration is the basis for generating and sustaining what has come to be known as high-performance teams. This "new industrial revolution" was originally seen as a way to overcome the Taylorist fragmentation of work and to integrate the human resource perspective that sought to apply to the work setting the emerging understanding of human behavior and the related concepts of human dynamics. Unlike the industrial engineering approach to work design, which focused exclusively on the design of the technical aspects of the work, the STS model recognized that every organization is made up of both technical and social systems. When either system is not taken into account in the design of both the work itself and the organizational systems that support the work, organizational productivity suffers. The aim of STS is the full utilization and integration of both the human and technical resources available.

To achieve this integration, STS begins with the premise that technical systems are only one part of the work process. Traditionally, the focus on technical systems led to the application of rationality and efficiency as the primary criteria for designing work in a way that would increase productivity, with task simplification, standardization, and specialization as the means for achieving those objectives. Unfortunately, or perhaps fortunately, this approach did not produce the desired levels of productivity. What was needed, practitioners discovered, was an equal focus on the so-called higher-order needs of the employees. These needs, explored by numerous behavioral scientists, have been articulated over the years in a variety of ways. They include:

- An environment of continuous learning, and support in development of the competencies needed to perform effectively

- An understanding of how an individual's work fits into the organization's mission and goals

- A collaborative management style to support the self-directed STS teams

- Skill in resolving team and cross-functional conflicts

- Two-way, open, nondirective forms of communication

- The information and authority to make decisions that enable appropriate response in a variety of situations

- Opportunities for career growth

- Regular feedback on performance, and recognition for good performance

- The opportunity to produce quality products that result in a sense of pride and commitment to one's work

A social systems analysis focuses on issues such as who needs to talk to whom, the interdependencies between various parts of the work, who has the most information about various aspects of the system, and how to arrange the work layout and processes to maximize the flow of information and create a sense of ownership for the work. Such an analysis also focuses on the informal relationships and networks that exist in an organization, as well as on the impact of the physical environment on behavior. Many of these issues are subtle and nuanced, and implicit in STS is a recognition of the importance of participation, expectancy, and role modeling in creating environments that are able to engender trust and openness. Unfortunately, most managers are uncomfortable dealing in such intangibles; yet time and time again it becomes clear that when these human issues are ignored, the work redesigns do not produce the kinds of behaviors the initiators of change say they want to see.

To take human needs into account in designing a work system represents, then, a considerable shift in thinking about how to go about designing the work of a group or of a company. Taken as a whole, the STS assumptions lead to a focus on integrated work processes, the creation of both highly cohesive work teams and an organizational infrastructure (in other words, management processes and practices) to support the work teams as the basic unit of the organizational work structure.

Fundamental to the STS approach is the belief that it is the work team itself that has the knowledge necessary for redesign of the work. Self-management, in which many of the tasks traditionally performed by a supervisor are now performed by the team, is a logical extension of this principle. As a result, the roles and responsibilities and the web of relationships change dramatically for both the work team and the former supervisor. This shift has not always been easy, especially for the supervisor or frontline manager who sees himself or herself as losing status and power. This difficulty simply reinforces, however, our fundamental premise: if change leaders want people to behave differently, they must redefine roles and responsibilities. Unfortunately, the adoption of high-performing, autonomous, self-managed or self-directed work teams has most often focused on redefining the roles and responsibilities of the team itself, with little attention to or empathy for the now apparently marginal supervisor or manager. The results, predictably, have been managerial behaviors ranging from apathy through resistance to, in extreme cases, sabotage of the organizational changes. However, if the basic STS tenets are used to redefine the roles, responsibilities, and relationships of the frontline supervisors and managers, the behavioral outcomes can be quite different.

Despite its revolutionary insights and important contributions to an understanding of the impact of structure on behavior as an approach to redesigning work, the STS model has a number of important limitations. While STS includes in its redesign methods the analysis of variance and the scanning of customer and stakeholder environments, these processes are not powerful enough to solve design problems that exist beyond the realm of the teams' influence. They are not powerful enough by themselves to change the expectancies or the skills of those involved or to inculcate an attitude of continuous improvement. In practice, STS has been only partially successful when it is not combined with other approaches.

Total Quality Management

Adding a missing piece to the tools for structural rearrangement, Total Quality Management (TQM) focuses on the continuous improvement of work processes. This is accomplished through the use of sophisticated tools for the analysis and control of process variance and through a deep understanding of customer needs. By sharpening the emphasis on process improvement as the single most important key to improved product quality, and on customer focus as the key to customer satisfaction, TQM has been responsible for sweeping structural rearrangements. W. Edwards Deming's belief in the importance of process in determining employee behavior is so strong that he asserts that if employees are not doing a good job it is "not because they lack the motivation but because they are dealing with poor systems and processes" (Deming, quoted in Persico and McLean, 1994, p. 15). To improve work systems and processes it is necessary to begin with customer needs rather than the needs of the products. This is a profound shift that inverts the traditional organizational pyramid. The customer rather than the CEO is king, the frontline workers (be they in sales, manufacturing, or service) listen to the customer directly, and the entire management structure and system is cast in the role of support to the line.

In many respects, the structural rearrangement inherent in TQM has become a method for organizational transformation. In those companies that have succeeded with this approach (for example, Xerox and Motorola), TQM has become a way of life for everyone in the company, and the resulting changes in structure have helped shape and support significant changes in behavior.

This systematically structural approach to change is evident in the history of the transformation of Xerox into a total quality company (Kearns and Nadler, 1992). Early in the process, David Kearns recognized that to achieve this, the work processes had to change, the reward and compensation system had to reward TQM behaviors, and promotions needed to be based on role modeling of "quality" behaviors. Communications and information systems were changed so that on a daily basis assembly line workers received detailed information on defects, and the training system was changed so that training in the use of TQM tools and processes started at the top and was cascaded down by the managers themselves. In addition, the organizational vision and goals were revised, with customer satisfaction replacing the troika of customer satisfaction, market share, and return-on-investment as the supreme corporate goal. The structure of the operational review meetings was altered to reflect the key importance of the company's progress on quality, and benchmarking was used by virtually every department in the company.

A study of Motorola's fourteen-year experience with TQM showed an identical approach with similar results (Nevis, DiBella, and Gould, 1995). As with STS, however, TQM has some important limitations. When the gap to be closed with a competitor is large, or when the appropriateness of the work process itself is in question, continuous improvement is simply not enough. In general, although TQM has focused firmly on process improvement, it often does not integrate processes in a systemic way.

Business Process Reengineering

Business Process Reengineering (BPR) emerged in response to the corporate need for something more than continuous improvement, and in recognition of the fact that most major organizational processes cut across traditional organizational boundaries. In BPR, organizational processes are viewed as the primary organizing principle for the corporation. The so-called supply chain process—from order entry to product delivery and the provision of follow-on services—serves as a unifying model for the rearrangement of organizational roles, responsibilities, and relationships that cut across existing and entrenched functional boundaries. Functionally "stovepiped" organizational forms are recognized as dysfunctional when the goal is to develop a seamless process that can more rapidly and flexibly meet customer needs. The need to overcome the functional fragmentation that exists in most organizations and the need to integrate work across organizational boundaries seems obvious. Jack Welch of General Electric uses the term *boundariless organization* to describe this way of thinking.

In the context of the work process itself, BPR aims at making deeper changes than TQM does. As a work design methodology, BPR asks a more basic set of questions: Do we need this process at all? Is there some entirely new way of thinking about how to get the tasks done? This approach has been variously called "breakthrough thinking," "out-of-the-box thinking," "frame breaking," or "thinking outside the nine dots"—but the theme is the same: to take a fresh, unfettered view of what tasks need to be done and how those tasks could be organized. Not only does BPR ignore existing internal functional boundaries but it can also ignore organizational boundaries. In an increasing number of instances, whole functions or subfunctions may be eliminated or combined as better, more efficient processes are designed, and organizational boundaries are becoming increasingly blurred as outsourcing and having customers and suppliers perform many sets of tasks become popular alternatives.

Given the inefficiencies that have crept into organizational work processes, and given the enormous challenges posed by the current turbulent environment, there is little question as to the need to reengineer many business processes, both to eliminate inefficiencies and to change organizational and individual behaviors. To date, however, BPR has fallen short in its ability to actually implement many of the radically redesigned structural arrangements of work processes, roles, responsibilities, and relationships. Several factors appear to have contributed to this problem.

First, in and of itself BPR has proved to be something of a paradox. On the one hand, the shift involved in thinking in terms of business processes rather than in terms of business functions is significant. It involves a rethinking of the basic mental image of how an organization should be organized, and it quite literally turns the structures inherent in the current divisions of labor, processes for coordination, and decision making on their ears.

However, to think beyond what currently exists or is known, to throw out thousands of preconceived notions, to suspend assumptions and break through to new levels of creativity, unhampered by current reality, is very difficult to do, and although BPR calls for breakthrough thinking in terms of business processes, it has itself remained rooted in the Newtonian, hierarchical paradigm of the organization as giant machine. Evidence of this may be found in its almost exclusive focus on the technical aspects of the business processes it is seeking to redesign; in the elite, hand-selected composition of its process redesign teams; in its treatment of design and implementation as discrete, fragmented, sequential processes to be carried out by different groups of people in a linear fashion; and in its failure to simultaneously recreate the organizational infrastructures and cultures needed to support the newly designed processes (Lancourt, 1994).

Further, in failing to incorporate the social and organizational dimensions into the design of work processes, and by viewing the business or technical process itself as of far more importance to the business than the people, BPR is essentially a machine-age methodology. In this paradigm, people are viewed as interchangeable, disposable commodities, and the close association of BPR with "downsizing" is no accident.

Be that as it may, if organizations are serious about needing employee behaviors that are more flexible, customer focused, responsive, collaborative, knowledge based, committed to organizational goals and methods, accountable, creative, proactive, boundariless, and able to deal with complexity and speed, then STS, TQM, and BPR are by themselves insufficient to the task. In fact, the prevailing organization-as-machine paradigm is, in significant measure, responsible for the current rather static and fragmented conception of organizational structure. What is needed is a new lens through which to view the construct of organizational structure.

A New Paradigm for Structural Rearrangement

To support organizational transformation and elicit the behaviors we have identified, structural rearrangement needs to be thought of as both means and end. In examining STS, TQM, and BPR, we have explored structural rearrangement as means. Unlike the Newtonian model, the organic, self-organizing systems paradigm offers a model of structures that are fluid, open, relational and weblike. In this model, relationships between and among the parts become more important than the parts themselves. Rather than controlling and eliminating variation, the self-organizing paradigm suggests that amplifying the disconfirming bits of information may promote growth. Rather than hardwiring organizational structures, temporary, flexible structures must be created that emerge as needed to facilitate the flow of relationships. In such a model, the organization of tasks and hierarchies gives way to the organization of relationships, and roles are viewed not as fixed jobs but as changing patterns of relationships. Information generated and shared with everyone seeds creativity and innovation, and diversity sparks and releases the vast reservoirs of human potential. Unity is no longer a synonym for sameness, and order and control are not the opposite of change and autonomy. Disequilibrium becomes the beginning of new growth, and the dynamic tensions between individual and team, top-down and bottom-up, or internal and external are managed as the paradoxes they are rather than as either/or dichotomies (Wheatley, 1992; Lancourt, 1994).

Several examples of organizations that have consciously attempted to implement structures suggested by this new paradigm will help illustrate how structural rearrangement is both means and end in support of genuine organizational transformation. While there is clearly no one best or right arrangement of the various structural elements inherent in this new paradigm, there appear to be a number of common themes in how each of these companies has implemented this approach.

Roles and Responsibilities

In the new paradigm, senior management has moved from a role of command and control to one of architect, designer, steward, and guide, responsible for the development and maintenance of structures, processes, and behaviors that would create an organizational environment and culture supportive of an empowered work force. This shift has been well-articulated by Ralph Stayer of Johnsonville Foods: hierarchies create dependent employees and dependent behaviors. The real boss is the company's customers. Thus, Stayer's role shifted from controlling and delegating work to creating a culture of trust and ownership. Empowerment at Johnsonville Foods came to mean "not the right to do as we please, but to be pleased to do what is right for our customers" (Savage, 1994, p. 13).

At ABB, CEO Percy Barnevik and his senior team focus on ensuring constant organizational renewal through the "shaping and embedding of corporate purpose," role modeling collaborative behaviors, setting objectives, creating stretch performance standards, and providing everyone in the organization with something more than just the bottom-line numbers in which to take pride—in other words, his job is to create the overall social context that will shape and reinforce the desired behaviors (Bartlett and Ghoshal, 1993, p. 38).

At Semco, the role of CEO rotates among six "counselors." In this model, "when financial performance is one person's problem, then everyone else can relax. In our system, no one can relax. You get to pass on the baton, but it comes back again. . . ." According to Semler, "the old pyramidal hierarchy is simply unable to make [the] leaps of insight, technology, and innovation [that we need]" (Semler, 1994, pp. 64–74).

Even the U.S. Army has "loosened" its hierarchy in what it calls its After Action Reviews (AARs). AARs occur after every battle or training event, and specific behaviors of everyone, from senior command to private, are open to question and critique from everyone else, no matter what their rank (Wheatley, 1994, p. 52).

One of the most significant changes to occur when a company's structure is based on the new paradigm is a change in the roles and responsibilities of its middle management. At Oticon, middle managers have become project leaders, and they are part of the day-to-day work team. At ABB, middle managers are accountable for "reviewing, developing and supporting" frontline entrepreneurial initiatives, "linking skills, knowledge and resources" across organizational boundaries and "creating and maintaining a climate of organizational trust." Frontline managers are charged with creating and pursuing opportunities, managing operational interdependencies, developing personal networks, and managing the tension between short-term and long-term performance goals (Bartlett and Ghoshal, 1993, p. 38).

Semco has pushed the departure from tradition even further. There are only three levels in the company and "responsibility for any task belongs to the person who claims it. . . . Whoever holds the spear is completely in charge of bringing down the mammoth" (Semler, 1994 p. 72). Major project coordinators, frequently chosen from outside the company, are charged with putting together a project plan, chairing meetings at which everyone involved shapes the decisions about the plan's final form, lobbying for the people they want, and then ensuring the coordination of the work. Moreover, they are not the single authority on the project; those working on the project are answerable to everyone.

Oticon has abolished the traditional notion of the job and organizational structure, finding it more productive to think in terms of project teams based on core competencies, knowledge, and individual interest. Every employee is expected to work on several projects, at least one based on their core competency and one based on other competencies or interests. At ABB, frontline employees are directly accountable for face-to-face customer relations and customer satisfaction, as well as for viewing their work from an entrepreneurial perspective. To support this, ABB has restructured itself into a federation of thirteen hundred companies with five thousand profit centers; each center is small enough to make sure that everyone can touch the customer (Kets de Vries, 1994).

Organizational Relationships

Collaborative relationships appear to be key in virtually every company, with teams of one sort or another forming the basic unit for organizing the work. At Oticon, project teams form and reform as the work changes. This promotes the free flow of knowledge and a sharing of lessons learned throughout the organization. Similarly, at ABB, personal and organizational networks become channels for sharing knowledge and fuel organizational learning. At Semco, key relationships extend beyond traditional organizational boundaries to encompass the company's extensive fluid satellite structure of contractors, suppliers, and even competitors. Semler points out that "This is a borderless system of short-term, noncontractual task assignments often using Semco's own fixed assets, some of it in Semco plants and some dispersed at a dozen sites that don't belong to the company" (Semler, 1994, p. 64). Semco, like Oticon, sees this fluid, eclectic mix as a kind of creative stew that both drives and supports people to "look at everything we do and ask why we can't do it better or cheaper or faster or in some entirely novel way" (p. 70).

The Japanese Kyocera Corporation's "amoeba" system of relationships promotes similar behaviors. Amoebas are organisms finely attuned to their environment, taking on changing roles and relationships as the situation changes. The "leaders" become dispersed cells, and new leaders emerge at the "seeking head" of the new organism. The seeking head is simply those amoebas that move the fastest. Once the new food source is found, the head becomes the base on which the follower amoebas build. Eventually, this "structure" collapses, dispersing the individual amoebas, and the process begins again. At Kyocera, each "amoeba" unit is small (three to fifty people) and fairly self-sufficient, and each competes, subcontracts, and cooperates as the work demands. "Depending on the demand . . . amoebas can . . . move from one section of the factory to another, or integrate with other amoeba departments . . . [and] heads of amoebas lend and borrow members and so eliminate losses caused by surplus labor" (Zeleny, Cornet, and Stoner, 1990, p. 166).

As each of these examples illustrates, the underlying theme appears to be the notion of flexibility, flexibility, and more flexibility.

Organizational Infrastructures

Oticon and Semco have created information systems that support sharing virtually all information with everyone. At Semco, the company books are available to the union, and all meetings are open and optional, an approach that helps undercut and eliminate the filtering and "horse trading" of information that goes on in most traditional companies. Oticon's unique open physical space also supports and encourages maximum interaction and sharing of information.

In summary, the contexts created by this web of structural changes foster learning, collaboration, creativity, and the taking of initiative in every area of a company, and the various structures have all been designed to require and facilitate the following behaviors:

- An almost obsessive focus on customer needs

- The free flow of knowledge throughout the organization

- Integration across all organizational boundaries

- An entrepreneurial spirit throughout the organization

- Fluid, dynamic, and innovative work teams

In each of the preceding examples, all of these structures are interactive and mutually reenforcing of organizational context, management action, and individual behavior.

Using Structural Rearrangement Effectively

By now, there should be little doubt that structural rearrangement can be an effective means for transforming organizational and individual behaviors. As should be equally clear, however, there is no one organizational design that will fit all organizations, and there is no one way to go about rearranging organizational structures in order to ensure success. But experience has provided four general rules of thumb that appear to enhance the chances of successful application of this method: (1) there are no quick fixes; (2) top management support is necessary; (3) begin with the work; and (4) a holistic approach is the key to success.

No Quick Fixes

Structural rearrangement is not a quick fix. It is the ability to guide and reinforce new behaviors on a daily basis *over an extended period* that makes structural rearrangement so powerful a tool for broad-based transformation. While some results may be evident in the short run (for example, increased communication when two groups are co-located, or an increased sensitivity to customer needs when customer visits become a regular part of the job), the more profound behavioral changes do not occur as quickly (for example, becoming a coach rather than a controller, becoming a steward rather than a traditional CEO, or becoming a knowledge-networked organization rather than a functionally stovepiped company).

In addition, while the structural rearrangement itself may constitute a revolutionary change (in other words, a fundamental recasting of the organization's roles, relationships, infrastructures, and culture), the rearrangement process, like the metamorphosis of a tadpole into a frog, frequently unfolds in an evolutionary fashion. Xerox's structural rearrangements continued to occur over a period of years, and are still occurring as a normal part of organizational growth and repositioning. Semco's satellite structure also illustrates this point, evolving over the years from an experiment with the Nucleus of Technological Innovation group and other attempts to ride the roller coaster of the Brazilian economy. In a series of interviews with senior executives of ten companies in the process of transformation, all agreed that despite their initial expectation that the structural changes would be complete in a year or two, roles, relationships, and infrastructures continued to evolve. Now well into the process, all have stated that the kind of structural rearrangement necessary for transformation is at least a five- to ten-year process, and many of them have admitted that it is likely to be a process that will never end (Lancourt, McGowan, Stroh, and Holland, 1993). This response supports one of the goals of transformation, the creation of an organization that is *inherently* flexible and *continuously* adaptive.

Top Management Support

Structural rearrangement generally requires the support of top management. In fact, we know of no case in which significant structural rearrangement was successfully implemented without the support of top management. In Oticon, ABB, Xerox, Johnsonville Foods, the U.S. Army, and Semco, it was the CEOs themselves who were responsible for initiating the use of structural rearrangement as a method for organizational transformation. Each had become deeply convinced that their companies could no longer compete successfully by continuing business as usual.

Each of these leaders also possessed an experimental mind-set. Oticon's Lars Kolind announced the transformation with the statement that he was "100 percent sure that we will *try* this" (emphasis added; LaBarre, 1994, p. 24). The history of Semco's transformation is the story of a CEO willing to try even solutions that at first appeared outrageous. Xerox's Kearns approached his company's transformation with an exemplary willingness to learn and evolve. When something was not producing the hoped for results, he did not abandon the effort; rather, he moved to reshape it. His reframing of corporate goals from the original three (customer satisfaction, market share, and ROI) to one (customer satisfaction) is an example, as is his use of the training infrastructure to shore up the quality focus when leadership realized that they had "forgotten" to train people in how to inspect (Kearns and Nadler, 1992).

Begin with the Work

Successful structural rearrangement needs to begin with a focus on the work itself, and on the redefinition of roles, responsibilities, and relationships necessary to perform that work effectively, rather than on first changing the formal structures. Further, experience also indicates that knowledge of both the technical and social/ psychological perspectives and methodologies of work design should be considered critical skill sets for the effective implementation of structural change.

There is always a lot to learn about the real requirements of new roles in terms of skills and behaviors needed, systems and processes required to support the new work, and the personal characteristics that will most contribute to successful performance in the new organization. First, systems and structures that are designed too quickly can result in shaping the wrong behaviors. This finding is congruent with the understanding of the emergent nature of the more organic, self-organizing, self-renewing structures described by Wheatley (1992) and others. Leaders need to be careful that they do not try to "nail things down" too soon.

Second, putting people into the new roles creates a "pull" for skills training and team building, as well as for changes in the supporting infrastructure, such as performance appraisal, compensation, and information and measurement systems. This pull serves to make training, for example, far more effective. Typically, training is "pushed" on employees before they really understand why it is needed, the context for its application, or what particular aspects will be of greatest use to them. When people are put into their new roles first and held accountable for their new responsibilities, they are able to bring to the training a keen sense of why the skills and behaviors being taught are important, an understanding of the context in which the new skills and behaviors will be applied, and a focus on the particular aspects of the training that will be of the greatest use or relevance to them (Beer, Eisenstat, and Spector, 1990).

Mandating restructuring too early also models a behavior rooted in the old organizational paradigm—that the top leadership or an elite design team has "the" answer, or even that there is "an" answer. A more tentative revision of structures, however, not only helps nudge behaviors in the right direction without sacrificing the much-needed flexibility, but it also begins to create the expectation that the idea of a "final" organizational structure may also be an artifact from the past.

A Holistic Approach

Given the complexity of the resocialization process and the power of the structural messages sent in this process, a more holistic, iterative approach to organizational restructuring needs to be taken. Such an approach would help deepen understanding of the unarticulated structural assumptions embedded in an organization's mental models and culture, and of the need to develop the kinds of systems thinking skills that will enable identification of the hidden structures and patterns of behavior that so frequently hold organizations prisoner to old, dysfunctional ways of operating. A holistic view also helps people shift from seeing organizational behaviors as unconnected events to understanding them as manifestations of deeply embedded systemic structures.

Our advocacy of a holistic approach should not be interpreted as a suggestion that everything must be dealt with all at once. What it does mean is that we acknowledge the importance of focusing on the interconnections, deeper levels, and systemic nature of the undertaking.

Summary

In this chapter, we have examined several cases of the ineffective use of structural rearrangement. These cases help pinpoint the importance of anchoring structural change in the day-to-day roles and responsibilities of the work itself. We also expanded the definition of structure to include the underlying, less-tangible aspect of values and culture, and the human needs embodied in the sociotechnical approach to work redesign. In examining the limits of STS, TQM, and BPR as methods of structural rearrangement, we highlighted the importance of the need for a new paradigm that will enable organizations to create more organic, fluid, weblike structures held together by the free flow of information, virtual teams, the autonomy to respond to local markets, the movement of decision making to operational units, and flexible, informal, transparent, permeable boundaries.

By exploring a number of companies that have successfully used structural rearrangement as a key means of embedding these traits in their organizations, we have demonstrated a vital point: there is no one best way to design such a structure. There are themes, however: the role of management shifts from control to enablement, and the role of employee becomes more fluid, competency based, and entrepreneurial. Structure in the old sense of fixed boxes and lines has actually disappeared in some of our examples, but in all cases, boundaries have become fluid and permeable, with an emphasis on relationships and forms that continually adapt to larger organizational needs. Similarly, infrastructures such as information, reward, and performance management systems—another key aspect of our definition of structure—change to support the new, more fluid forms.

Paradoxically, key success factors appear to be the active involvement of senior executives in orchestrating a participative approach. To be successful requires these executives to proceed in a more holistic, nonlinear fashion and to work with both the hard and soft aspects of structural rearrangement so as to build in the guidance and support for the desired behaviors.

· ·

10

Extrinsic Rewards
Reinforcing Transformative Behaviors

This chapter discusses a second method derived from the environmental change perspective of organizational transformation. Like structural rearrangement, the use of extrinsic rewards has been a customary practice for managers since the early days of the industrial revolution. The concept is quite simple: structure the work contract so that desired behaviors are reinforced by a desirable reward. The reward is given only if the desired behavior takes place; it is withheld if the behavior is not manifested. Historically, the preferred reward has been money and related benefits. In recent decades, the understanding has emerged that people are not motivated at work simply by money, and praise and other forms of recognition have come to be seen as powerful extrinsic rewards. Since the rewards are granted by other people, this approach is often referred to as shaping behavior through environmental manipulation.

The use of extrinsic rewards is based on B. F. Skinner's well-known selective reinforcement theory, which is commonly applied in compensation and incentive systems, such as bonus plans, management by objectives, and other performance reward systems. Much of the extensive literature deals with the use of rewards to reinforce existing modes of behavior and to attain greater efficiencies within them. In transformational change, however, the issue is the need to change the way behaviors are rewarded, as well as the need to determine which new behaviors to reward. In this chapter we attempt to show how this issue may be approached. We will define the issue, provide some examples of how some organizations are dealing with it, and suggest a general direction for others to follow.

The Role of Extrinsic Rewards in Transformational Change

In incremental change efforts, reinforcement is used to motivate people to do essentially what they are already doing but in a more efficient and productive way. The role of extrinsic rewards in transformational change is to support implementation of desired new behaviors; therefore, reward systems may need to be changed or modified to be consistent with the new paradigm being advocated. The same reinforcers may be used in either situation, but the outcomes being rewarded will vary, and the reinforcers and new behaviors may be linked differently in each case. For example, bonuses may be used either to reinforce individual performance or as group incentives, depending on how much independent or coordinated behavior is desired. Similarly, money may be used as a reward for productivity gains, or it may be related to flexibility in providing customer service. In these instances, traditional means may be used in the service of two kinds of performance that are associated with currently popular transformational behavior outcomes: self-managed teams and flexible customer service. However, new paradigms also call for consideration of other kinds of reinforcers. For example, two that are very appealing to knowledge workers are access to resources and the opportunity to learn and grow. However, these are hard to link to desired behaviors, or they are overlooked in favor of direct monetary rewards.

Thus, two issues need to be considered in using extrinsic rewards to support transformational change: the behaviors to be rewarded need to be identified, and these behaviors need to be linked with rewards that are important to the people involved. Transformational change calls for creating new structures and processes, for living with uncertainty and ambiguity, for giving up old ways that have become dysfunctional, for release of fresh and creative energy, for being more entrepreneurial, and for developing new skills that will make work more productive and enjoyable.

A great deal still needs to be learned about how to identify and reward these outcomes, but we can start by listing some of the questions to be considered:

- With regard to structural requirements:

  How can meaningful rewards be developed for working from a total system perspective as opposed to local optimization?

  How can extrinsic reward systems be developed for horizontally linked work groups such as cross-functional teams, networks, and alliances?

  How can work units and divisions be rewarded for making learning investments, that is, for investing in acquisition and utilization of new knowledge, independent of achieving short-term goals?

- With regard to learning and experimentation:

  How can experimentation be reinforced, rewarding the very act rather than the result?

  How can systems be developed for rewarding people who have begun to change their ways but have not yet fully achieved the desired new state?

  To what extent can individuals be rewarded who engage in skill development at work or in self-directed education?

- With regard to multiple realities:

  How can the fact that people respond differentially to various reinforcers be dealt with?

Are there particularly desirable extrinsic rewards for professional and knowledge workers, who tend to be strongly motivated by the challenge of their work per se?

If organizations are truly to transform themselves rather than merely to "strap wings on the caterpillar," these are the questions that need to be explored and answered during the second (Exploratory), third (Generative), and fourth (Internalization) phases of an organization's transformation (see Chapter Three). We offer these questions here not because we have all the answers but as a way to focus and frame the discussion that follows.

Behavior-Reward Relationships in Transformational Change

We turn now to a discussion of systems of behavior and reinforcement that are relevant to transformational change. How do these systems differ from reward systems designed to improve the efficiency of work processes that are already in place? How are they the same? If the objective is to produce significant change, how are behaviors that support this goal to be identified and rewarded?

We can begin to examine the identification of desired behaviors by looking at leading firms, especially those that have been successful in renewal or transformation efforts. In these cases, a number of targeted behaviors stand out, including flexibility; acceptance of continuous change; customer orientation; ability to work well in horizontal, interdependent relationships; managers acting as coaches rather than as controllers; and a focus on integrated, systemic solutions to problems. If change leaders want to be successful, these are the behaviors that need to be reinforced using appropriate rewards. Table 10.1 lists some of these behaviors and suggested rewards, contrasting them with those used when the goal is increased efficiency in current modes of operation or incremental change efforts.

Table 10.1. Behavior-Reward Relationships in Incremental and Transformational Change Efforts.

Change Objective	Desired Behaviors	Appropriate Rewards
Incremental (Old Reality)	Predictability of output; stability	Merit and longevity; salary increase; praise from work group manager
	Controlling behavior of others	Punishment systems
	Increased productivity	Increases related to units produced
	Limited work focus	Individual rewards; subunit profit center incentives
	Functional expertise	Educational opportunities such as conferences and schooling, related to specific skills
	Short-term targets	Grant reward soon after the behavior
Transformational (New Reality)	Flexibility; responsiveness	Reward process improvements; reward customer service activities
	Working under conditions of uncertainty, ambiguity, and transition	Reassurance re: job security
	Experimental behavior	Reward tryouts and pilot projects using various recognition awards
	Broader skill acquisition	Knowledge-based pay system; educational opportunities that stretch
	Responsibility; independent decision making	Involvement in target setting and in more challenging work
	Coordinated collaborative work effort	Group incentives; multiple unit profit center incentives; company-wide profit sharing
	Developing/coaching others	Incentive rewards related to the performance of others
	Long-term results	Reward knowledge-generating activities; rewards based on performance over time

The table reveals a sharp difference between the desired behaviors and appropriate rewards in the two types of change. Clearly, the behavior-reward contingencies of transformational change involve behavior that is much harder to measure than traditional behaviors; they put more emphasis on process improvements; and they assume that productivity gains will follow from this approach. The behaviors are also more directly linked to actions and attitudes that allow change to occur in a relatively noncontrolling way. By contrast, the behavior-reward contingencies of incremental change emphasize stability and control. The implication is that the fewer unpredictable or performance variations there are, the better.

There are challenges to handling each situation well, but leaders of transformational change are charting largely unexplored waters. For example, very few performance appraisal systems actually reward a manager for developing other people. A great deal of lip service is paid to this management approach, but there are few organizations in which support of such behavior is truly reflected in rewards. Similarly, reinforcement of tryouts and pilot projects is often lacking, or they are negatively rewarded by punishment for failure. Even knowledge-based pay is at present used by few firms, largely because it is difficult to measure its behavioral outcomes. Furthermore, in numerous instances in which attention is paid to appropriate, desired behaviors, inappropriate rewards are utilized.

Before looking at examples of effective use of extrinsic rewards, it may be useful to look at some ineffective applications, as an aid in understanding the effective applications.

Misapplication of Extrinsic Rewards

In March 1987, the information systems division of AT&T awarded $16 million in bonuses while in the midst of a major reduction in work force. The division lost $800 million in 1986, the year for which the bonuses were awarded. A spokesperson for AT&T said that managers were given the bonuses "on recognition that they had put in a long, tough year" (Sims, 1987, p. 42). Thus, some managers were rewarded for hard work rather than bottom-line results, and others were made redundant. This makes sense if those who were let go were clearly not hard workers. However, the message sent to these managers is that hard work is more important than effectiveness.

A second example deals with the very common practice in industrial settings of division or product managers preparing annual business plans and budgets that contain performance incentives based on the achievement of selected budget targets. The targets can be increases in market share, net earnings, gross margin percentage, and so forth. In one company in which we were involved for many years, the senior vice president in charge of the divisions presented an annual award called the "sandbagger of the year" to the division executives who beat their budgeted targets by the greatest amount. The implication was that this division had "lowballed" its budget numbers so that it would look very good when its actual results were made known. Of course, if executives did not exceed the targets by much, they could still say they had achieved their targets. The net effect of such a procedure is to reward game playing rather than honest reporting in business plans.

A third example is an electronics company in which for years it had been customary to develop annual business plans that contained performance bonus incentives for upper managers. Several years ago, one division had a highly profitable year, to the point that its managers received bonuses well in excess of those in any other division. This would appear to indicate that the system worked: the more the targets were exceeded, the greater were the rewards. However, the result produced jealousy and resentment in sister divisions and consternation on the part of the corporation's compensation committee. As a consequence, the division was given a new bonus formula for the following year so that its payouts would not be excessive or that far out of line with other divisions. (Paradoxically, this division's manager had won the company's "best general manager" award the year before the bonus formula was developed; in effect, he was punished for his earlier success.)

It may well be that the bonus formula for the corporation was inappropriate and needed revision. It seems to us, however, that this became a case of punishing people for their success. Would it not have made more sense for the corporation to hold this division up to the other divisions as an example of truly good performance and how it is rewarded?

A fourth example shows how misuse of extrinsic rewards in a transformational change effort, which was seen by the company as an important experiment in significantly reducing product development cycle time, resulted in punishment of the senior manager leading the change. In an action-research approach conducted with the assistance of the MIT Center for Organizational Learning, the most successful new product launch in the history of the company was achieved through innovative use of system dynamics. However, partly because traditional company norms were changed in the process, the leader of the project was removed from his job and subsequently fired. Whatever the reason for his dismissal, the "message" to the organization was that doing anything new and different can be a career-limiting act. It is very unlikely that other high-level managers in that company who are familiar with the case will take responsibility for trying out something that is at all risky.

Each of these cases shows the difficulty in using extrinsic rewards effectively. The AT&T example is a case of well-meaning use of rewards in which the timing and reason for granting the reward will please some people but also generate negative unintended consequences in the future. The second case illustrates the problem that can occur when a secondary reward is inadvertently made significant enough to overpower the basic reward system. The case of the electronics company shows the difficulty in capping rewards in a way that does not punish people who are successes under a prevailing arrangement. Finally, the fourth case shows how an intended transformational effort can be undermined by unintended consequences, largely of a political nature. Taken together, these cases show how difficult it is to develop and implement a successful system of extrinsic rewards.

To understand how problems can be minimized, it may help to take a brief look at the dynamics of selective reinforcement and the underlying theory that supports the use of extrinsic rewards.

The Dynamics of Selective Reinforcement

The offering by organizations of extrinsic rewards to individuals for appropriate behavior is based on exchange theory. In an exchange relationship, the employee "gives" something that the organization values, and in return he or she "gets" something that the organization can provide. Obviously, what the individual gives the organization gets, and what the organization gives the individual gets. Exchange theory has been a fundamental part of the world of work ever since people began to produce goods and services for use by those other than themselves. Yet, despite the historic role of exchange in the workplace, probably no other aspect of organizational life is more misunderstood, more incorrectly applied, and more likely to create bad feelings between employees and employers than the misuse of extrinsic rewards.

The theory of selective reinforcement provides the principles for an effective exchange relationship. Selective reinforcement means selecting the behaviors that one wants to encourage and rewarding them soon after they occur. The reward is given *only* when the desired behavior or result is achieved, and it is withheld if the goal is not attained. In this way, people learn to focus on organizationally desired targets. The process is known as the shaping of behavior. The acts that are rewarded grow to be more frequent, while nonrewarded acts tend to decrease in frequency.

Underlying Principles

Several underlying principles are critical to this approach:

1. *Behavior is viewed as a function of its consequences.* What happens after the behavior occurs—that is, a response from the environment—determines whether the behavior will be repeated. External actions and events are seen as the means for controlling behavior.

   Example: Pay someone after they have done the work, not before. Presumably, this will encourage people to work.

2. *Appropriate linkage of desired behavior and important reward is highly motivating.* The task of management is to be specific about the behavior, and to link it with a relevant reinforcer.

   Example: Double pay for working overtime hours is highly motivating if people want money more than other things, but not if they are seeking fewer work hours.

3. *Reinforcement must be contingent.* It is given only if the desired behavior occurs. If given when the desired behavior does not occur, it is not motivating. Conversely, without reinforcement, the desired behavior will become extinct.

   Example: An incentive bonus is given if the desired results are obtained, but is withheld if it is not attained. Presumably, repeated adherence to this sequence will increase the probability of people working to achieve the bonus.

Given the above conditions and principles, it is easy to see what the problem is in each of the cases cited earlier. In some cases, the principle of contingent reward was not followed. In one, there was a lack of clarity about what the desired behavior was, and how it was to be linked with the reward (or even if the award was an appropriate one). In another case, desirable but conflicting outcomes worked against each other.

In summary, reinforcement methods depend on appropriate selection of the relevant behaviors to be achieved. Thus, a bonus system based on increased market share has very different implications than one based on return on equity. Each system encourages managers to make different assumptions about investment and pricing. In addition, identification of meaningful rewards (for example, the reward is significant enough in size to make a difference) is critical. To provide a range of 3 to 6 percent annual salary increases may be nice, but the difference between receiving 3 percent and 6 percent is not really enough to produce new, highly motivated behavior.

Early Applications

One of the oldest applications of the method, other than simply granting wages for work performed, was the development of *piece-rate payment plans*. In these systems, workers are paid according to the amount they produce. Usually, these plans have been applied in settings where the tasks are relatively simple and able to be learned quickly by people with little education or experience. While there are some negative aspects to this approach, it has an advantage when the behavior to be reinforced is easy to identify and readily linked to a desirable goal. Yet, even with such an apparently important linkage, the incentive provided by piecework does not always produce increased performance. The legends of the labor and industrial relations movement are full of stories to this effect, and the problem of "rate busters" who work harder than their peers reveals that social context often determines the outcome.

The continued growth of the modern bureaucratic form of organization, as well as the influence of the organized labor movement, led to more impersonal reward systems in which equity was to be the guiding principle. The *merit pay raise* was employed as a major reinforcer. Judgments about the differential contributions of workers within a class of employees were to be the basis for a corresponding scale of rewards. This approach continues to be popular in many organizations, even though it is now generally assumed that the original intent has been subverted. While earlier times of lower wages may have allowed such raises to be significant, it is highly questionable whether they currently have any motivational effect, especially since increases generally fall within a narrow differential between lowest and highest possible increase.

Also, the fact that firms go to great lengths to keep salary data private does not help the situation. Public listing of salaries and raises might at least provide a picture of "model" employees and how they are rewarded. However, most human resource specialists say that to do so would create bad feelings among employees. What does this say about what is really being reinforced in such systems? Some have said that the reward is really for tenure, and that it would be better to call it that and find other incentives to promote increased productivity. Two of the companies we discuss in detail, Semco in Chapter Three and Oticon in Chapter Twelve, make salary and incentive bonus information public, and they believe that such open information has helped motivate people in a positive way. To deal with reward for tenure, Oticon gives employees shares in the company each year. In this way, incentives for tenure and for productivity are treated independently.

One other early application is worthy of mention: *the Scanlon Plan*. Named for Joseph Scanlon, a labor relations consultant working at MIT, the plan linked principles of participation with those of selective reinforcement. It was the first of the gainsharing systems that have been developed over the past fifty years. More a set of principles than a rigid system, the Scanlon Plan uses a bonus system based on participatively developed cost savings and increased labor productivity. A formula is used to calculate these awards, which are paid monthly or quarterly, in keeping with the principle that reinforcers should follow soon after the behavior they are rewarding. A brief introduction to the Scanlon Plan is contained in Ramquist (1982).

Although numerous firms have adopted the Scanlon Plan and similar gainsharing plans, it is interesting that this approach has never achieved the broad popularity that it seems to warrant. This appears to be largely due to the substantial work required to measure baseline "standard costs" accurately, and to a lack of faith that participative implementation will work. A notable exception is Herman Miller, the furniture company. Since 1950, Herman Miller has used the Scanlon Plan as a major management tool, starting with the manufacturing organization and expanding to the entire company in 1978. The Herman Miller program eliminates all piece rates and merit raises, substituting a monthly bonus that has ranged between 9 and 23 percent of base pay annually over thirty years and that has been negative only for an occasional month.

In the early 1970s, a number of successful applications at the incremental change level were reported. Extrinsic reward methods were applied to loggers (Weyerhaeuser), maintenance personnel in telephone companies (Michigan Bell), garbage collectors (the city of Detroit), and freight handlers (Emery Air Freight). These applications used money and praise or recognition as rewards, and all led to significant increases in productivity and/or cost reductions.

At higher levels of management, it has now become customary to engage in profit-sharing or bonuses as reward for achieving certain performance levels. This application has to do with the achievement of outcomes that involve numerous tasks and behaviors, usually on the part of a number of people and/or groups. It is designed to reward complex, integrative activity rather than specific tasks and behaviors. Those who are to be rewarded are expected to pull together whatever is required for the achievement of the selected targets, which are designed around the performance of larger units of the organization such as departments, divisions, or lines of business. The prototypical executive compensation program is based on this model.

A case in point is the incentive program at Tyco Laboratories (Kozlowski, 1993). This program focuses on stock price appreciation through earnings growth. Basically, the more the executives earn for the shareholders, the more they earn for themselves. Two hundred and fifty profit centers, constituting four major businesses, are organized to operate as independent entities, and rewards are a preestablished percentage of each entity's earnings. There is no reward for corporate-level results, as these are considered beyond the unit-level individual's control. Award opportunities are uncapped; the established bonus percentage applies to every dollar of profit-center earnings. L. Dennis Kozlowski, president of Tyco Laboratories, says: "We believe our incentive compensation program is at the heart of our company's success." He further indicates that "the quality of our budgeting process has substantially improved since we adopted this approach" (1993, p. 44).

Conflicting Views of the Value of Extrinsic Rewards

One reason that the skillful use of extrinsic rewards in transformational change is not more fully developed is that not all change practitioners believe in their importance as motivators. There are practitioners who have a firm belief that such rewards are essential for the creation of social reality, and that socialization of employees is impossible without them. This perspective is supported by a materialistic view of human nature and a focus on money as a reward. It rests on the premise that reward and punishment are important when people are asked to perform an action or behave in a way other than what they might prefer at a given time. The assumption is that some work behaviors are relatively undesirable and will be performed only if desirable external rewards are offered.

In the other camp, however, are those practitioners who believe that the theory of selective reinforcement is, at best, of limited value, and at worst, harmful. They see extrinsic rewards as being of minimal importance or as hindrances to the achievement of high-level performance, and they believe instead in the support of intrinsic motivation by setting conditions that bring out the best in people independent of externally controlled rewards. This argument advocates that work should be made more attractive so that people will want to carry it out without the promise of external rewards. In recent years, this view has been supported by numerous cases in which people who were offered extrinsic rewards for doing things actually lowered their performance.

A highly provocative book by Alfie Kohn (1993) has renewed the controversy surrounding the use of rewards as motivators. The book marshals a great deal of evidence to show the damaging effects of extrinsic rewards on performance. In responding to Kohn and to other critics, supporters of extrinsic rewards attempt to show that many criticisms of the approach derive from its faulty use or misapplication.

Despite the conflicting arguments, we believe that extrinsic reward methods are critical to the success of transformation efforts. It is asking too much of people to think that they can give up old ways and adopt new ones without an environment that rewards them and complements internal motivation. It is also naive to say that money is not a motivator. Rather, money has different meanings for different people and the multiple realities in which they live. The real issue is: can initiators of change give up their old-fashioned equations of behavior-reward contingencies? "What's in it for me?" is a reasonable attitude, but it needs to be seen in a broader context that includes intrinsic rewards such as interesting work and opportunities to be in on things—not, however, at the expense of eliminating extrinsic rewards. Thus, we assume that the use of extrinsic rewards is an effective strategy, and that new paradigms require new behaviors and payoffs that are in a new kind of relationship with each other.

External Rewards and Multiple Realities

Whatever the merits of each point of view about the value of extrinsic rewards, the use of this method raises again the issue of how reality is constructed, and of the possibility that there is more than one reality. Is it possible that both perspectives on extrinsic rewards are appropriate for describing and constructing reality, but that they each lead to different realities? What, if any, is the impact of the presence of different multiple realities on the determination of what should be rewarded and what the rewards should be? Such questions suggest that a sophisticated approach to reward systems should focus on differential behavior-reward sequences. Can organizational leadership accept the notion of pluralism? For example, incentive bonus systems will work well with organizational units that are highly independent of other units and that do not draw on technology from a common organizational knowledge pool. For units that are highly interdependent, a general profit-sharing plan may be much more effective.

Cultural differences play an important role in determining the impact of rewards. Most prevailing reward systems stem from the days of Taylorism—with its focus on narrow job specialization and its poor-immigrant labor pool—yet none of these systems has ever been perfect in its application.

An example is a well-known tale about a setting in which young female sewing machine operators were offered incentives to earn more money yet did not increase their output. It turned out that they came from traditional European families in which working children were required to give their earnings to their fathers. The more they earned, the more money their fathers received, and they did not get any more for themselves. There were three realities operating in this case: that of the workers, that of the employers, and that of the fathers. The incentive system was inadvertently designed to meet the needs of the fathers, but it did not meet the requirements of the other groups, as was its intention.

A totally different reality is suggested by the complex tasks and interdependent relationships that make up much of the current world of work, in which it is much harder to identify specific behaviors to reward and harder to determine how to allocate rewards among all the parties involved. Perhaps an even greater element of these relationships is that other motivating factors that exist at all levels of work become more critical as task complexity and environmental uncertainty increase. There is ample evidence that shows that people will work long, hard hours without paying attention to extrinsic rewards when they are deeply committed to what they are doing. An example of this is well described in Tracy Kidder's popular book *The Soul of a New Machine* (1981), in which an extremely dedicated group performed heroically, with little or no extra reward, to develop a new computer at Data General. Experiences such as these suggest that the opportunity to do challenging work may be very important as a reward for some groups, if not for all.

It is thus evident that the reinforcers used to reward behavior must be important in the mind of the recipient, not just in the mind of the manager of the programs. Some of the controversy over the utility of extrinsic rewards would dissolve if reward programs were customized to fit the situation better. There are some settings in which contingent monetary rewards are highly motivating and in which they can be used well. (There is widespread belief that this is true for individual commission salespeople and truly autonomous profit centers.) However, people for whom work is inherently exciting and motivating are not as likely to be motivated by the promise of bonuses, once they have achieved a reasonable standard of living. If they are already intrinsically well motivated, why not reward them by making their work more exciting rather than dangling monetary carrots in front of them?

Successful Use of Extrinsic Rewards in Transformational Change

With the preceding as background, we now look in a more detailed way at several examples of where the method of extrinsic rewards has been used effectively.

AT&T

This case is presented partly to contrast it with an earlier AT&T example of an ineffective use of extrinsic rewards. Although we address here only a major change in the compensation system, keep in mind that many other changes began at AT&T around the same time.

In 1986, AT&T decided to abandon its program of "fat salaries" and guaranteed raises and moved to a salary-plus-bonus system. Since its salaries were already much higher than those of its competitors, the company began to hold down base pay and it gradually increased bonuses to the point where, in 1990, AT&T salaries were below the average of its industry. However, by 1992, bonuses were between 11 to 15 percent of salary for middle managers and scientists.

In 1993, a new plan was established to reflect growing decentralization of the firm. The plan is related to Economic Value Analysis (EVA) and has three parts. One part is an annual payoff that rewards the performance of managers of small work teams. The formula is complicated; the payoff shrinks or grows in relation to the entire firm's EVA. The range of payoff is from nothing for poor performers to as much as 15 percent of salary for very good performers. The second part of the plan is for unit-level performance of more than 35 profit centers. Those who meet their targets receive a bonus; those who do not, receive nothing. The third aspect of the plan is based on total firm performance. If the company as a whole meets its EVA target, every manager (even those who do not get bonuses under the other two parts of the program) receives an extra 7.3 percent of salary and can make as much as 11 percent. In 1993, total bonuses ranged from 20 percent of salary to 30 percent for superior performers. AT&T states that it has emphasized all of these levels to make a point about the different performance required to achieve each level. The third bonus level, firmwide performance, is emphasized because the company wants its business units to work together and not to focus only on their own unit's results.

This case shows appropriate application of the method of extrinsic rewards. First, desired behavior is rewarded only if it is achieved. Second, the range of awards is wide enough to make reward differentials meaningful. Third, the shift is away from narrow unit rewards—usually found in incremental efficiency programs—and toward an additional focus on total system needs. The latter focus was one of the important goals of the changes initiated when the plan was established. The program shows a remarkable shift from the 1987 bonus award procedure discussed earlier in this chapter.

Firm X, a Large, Diversified Company

This example illustrates the use of extrinsic rewards to stimulate transformation, as opposed to using it in support of a change effort that is well under way. It is also a good example of coherence in relating desired behaviors and rewards. The case is discussed in a thoughtful paper by Crystal and Hurwich (1986) in which they argue that most executive compensation systems emphasize short-term objectives, whether based on unit performance or corporatewide results. They state that bonuses reinforce short-term performance and stock options reward long-term performance. Thus, a firm would do well to see which they want to emphasize and choose the reward appropriately. "Firm X" is an example of a company in which this was done.

Firm X is a company whose divisions are discrete businesses with no interchange of people, products, or technology. They developed an incentive plan based on results over five years, with a new plan starting each year. The formula was made up of return on equity, adjusted to reflect the true cost of capital. The resulting number was called "Additional Shareholder Value" (ASV). Rewards are based on the cumulative ASV for five years. Essentially, the message of this system is that the focus is to be on use of capital and that long-term return on capital is to be rewarded. Improving returns on current capital employed and/or reducing the capital required to achieve targeted levels of performance will earn the reward. There is no question that senior managers will make very different decisions if they are focusing on return on equity than if, for example, they are asked to focus on increased market share.

This approach would need to be modified if divisions were highly interdependent, but the principle of long-term rewards can still be maintained. While both incremental and transformational change endeavors can focus on either short-term or long-term performance, our sense is that most transformational change efforts are designed to encourage employees to take a more long-range point of view. Incentive systems that support this, particularly when initiated early in the change process, will make a strong contribution to the change.

Johnsonville Foods

This is the case of a small food manufacturer that transformed itself so that it could compete better with the giants of the industry. The CEO, who recognized that he was part of the problem as a result of his traditional style of management, led the development of a new vision in which the customer was seen as the "boss." In addition, a change in organizational structure required organizational members to take more responsibility, including responsibility for personnel matters. To reinforce this, the human resources department was abolished and people were referred to as "members" rather than as employees. In order to serve the customer better, the firm was reorganized into teams that were given responsibility for decision making at lower levels than had previously been the case.

Of particular interest is how the company drastically changed its performance review and incentive compensation systems. A major element of the new program was a structured peer review for salary increases based on competencies achieved. This included the payment of monthly bonuses in amounts determined by the members of the team in which each person works. Thus, there are rewards to the group, which then decides if there have been differential contributions by its members.

Another interesting feature is the use of "result blocks" derived from fifteen performance criteria, and knowledge-based salary increases are granted when earned. Whenever employees feel that they have acquired new skills, they request an appraisal by their "internal customer." When this development is verified, a salary increase is granted.

The interested reader is referred to a more detailed discussion of this case (Talbott, 1994). Suffice it to say, the company increased its sales from $15 million to $135 million in the period from 1982 to 1990, with substantial profitability growth.

Semco

This case has been discussed in detail in Chapter Three, and readers will be familiar with the transformation that occurred after leadership passed from the founding father to his son. As in the Johnsonville Foods example, Semco's transformation was driven by a leader who decided that he had to change himself first if he expected others to change. One of the ways he changed was to give up a complicated measurement and reward system that he controlled, in favor of a highly creative participatory approach to performance measurement and rewards. The company has since been seen as somewhat unorthodox, relative to traditional means of managing, but the result is a highly flexible firm that is able to do well in both the good and the bad economic times that are experienced in Brazil.

Several aspects of Semco's use of extrinsic rewards are noteworthy. Open information sharing is a key part of the approach. Salaries, which are self-set by a significant percentage of the organizational members, are public knowledge. At a time when business was bad, people decided to lower their salaries in return for a profit-sharing plan, so that they could make more money when times were good. Since then, salaries have been kept at modest levels, with employees involved in deciding the percentage of profits to be shared and the process for doing this. Typically, about 23 percent of the profits are given to each business unit, which divides them among the members of that unit. Semco is also interesting in that some employees have fixed salaries and some have variable salaries based on royalties or bonuses deriving from self-set project accomplishments.

Perhaps an even more dramatic use of extrinsic rewards at Semco is the process of helping employees to set up their own satellite firms, supported by Semco orders but able to solicit business from other companies. White-collar workers, tax accountants, computer programmers, and human resource people have availed themselves of this option. There are numerous ways in which compensation for service is provided to the satellites, depending on the level of entrepreneurial risk-gain relationships preferred by each firm. Fixed fees, hourly stipends, percentage of sales increases, honorariums, and retainers converted into royalty payments are available.

This case is illuminating in several respects. First, the transformation was aided by heavy use of participation and structural rearrangement. Second, all financial information, performance reviews, and salaries are available to everyone in the firm. Third, the reward system shifted away from individual rewards given for narrow accomplishments to one emphasizing group rewards and broader firm accomplishments. Fourth, multiple realities have been taken fully into account in the different compensation arrangements that are available. Finally, control by senior management was lessened significantly, yet the company prospered. It may not be possible to duplicate in other places what is being done at Semco, but it shows what can be attained when a direction is maintained until a firm finds what is right for itself.

Analysis of the Cases

While the examples just discussed are relatively few in number, they were chosen as a fairly representative sample of the use of extrinsic rewards. Analysis of these cases, and of many others that have been reported or summarized in professional and popular literature, yields several important observations about developing trends in transformational change. We contrast these with more traditional ways of using extrinsic rewards.

1.   *There has been a shift from individual incentives to group, team, unit, and corporate-level awards.* For many years, managers have pleaded for better teamwork and cooperation, while maintaining reward systems that favor reinforcement of individual achievement. Because of the individualistic nature of Western cultures, this lack of alignment has been hard to change. However, due to growing recognition of the interdependence of work, newer systems have at least a combination of individual and group-level incentives. In some cases, group or corporate-level awards have taken precedence over individual ones, as awareness of the importance of a total systems perspective has grown. AT&T, Semco, and Johnsonville Foods are clearly moving in this direction.

2.   *Participation in implementing systems has increased.* Years ago it would have been almost unthinkable to involve employees in designing and operating reward systems. In some sense, it may seem that to do this lessens the power of rewards to shape behavior. However, our examples show that at least in moderate-size organizations, employee ownership of the reward systems has served to enhance motivation. Apparently, allowing people to have a say in how they want to be rewarded does not "give away the store." If anything, doing so has made it easier to lower compensation levels when economic times at a firm are bad.

3.   *There is more focus on long-term objectives.* Although most organizations still favor short-term rewards (to some extent, this is a function of how capital is raised in money markets), more firms have moved to five-year cumulative plans. Some reward systems are designed to balance both objectives. In today's uncertain world, with many firms and industries fighting for survival, this may be the only realistic way to go. However, to give managers a message that their jobs will depend on how well they produce short-term results

means that the long term is very likely to be sacrificed unless substantial incentive exists to focus on the long-term issues.

4. *There is more focus on complex behaviors and on complex work relationships.* While selective reinforcement continues to be applied to specific behaviors at lower levels of the organization, there is much less interest in this use, and much more in rewarding aggregated behaviors. There are two reasons for this: the information age requires more sophisticated work routines, and managers are more aware of the price paid in rewarding suboptimization of effort at the micro level of work.

5. *More reward systems focus on monetary rewards.* Despite the other rewards that are available, almost all the cases we could find talked about monetary awards. If other incentives are used—such as access to resources, recognition, educational and other developmental opportunities, and being invited to participate in higher-level decision making—they are very seldom discussed in case reports. Monetary rewards are either offered without any contingency or they are not seen by senior management as effective rewards.

Using Extrinsic Rewards Effectively

Although it is clear that the use of extrinsic rewards has been and will continue to be an important method of influence, we believe that the full impact of its power is seldom seen in transformational change efforts. It often appears that the other methods are relied on more heavily, as though senior management uses extrinsic rewards to keep the firm on an even keel and uses other approaches to achieve significant change. Furthermore, reward systems are often designed with an eye on stockholder implications, or on how to please the investment community. However, such systems do not necessarily facilitate transformational change.

There are obstacles to taking more advantage of this method, but there are also opportunities. Let us examine some of these.

1.   *Eliminate or drastically revise merit raise plans.* As currently constituted, most merit raise plans reward good behavior or tenure, but not more than they reward ordinary contribution. In fact, the narrow range of most annual percentage increases is so small that they may actually serve as disincentives. Why would anyone be more than ordinarily motivated by an increase that is only two or three percentage points more than someone who just meets minimum standards? A more meaningful approach is to offer heavy rewards to those who earn them and incremental awards for tenure. Another approach, which is becoming much more common, is to keep baseline compensation steady but provide for profit sharing and other bonus awards based on a combination of individual, unit, and corporate achievements. This is illustrated by the earlier example of AT&T's new system.

2.   *Offer a variety of reward systems.* The Semco approach does an excellent job of taking into account differences among people. It allows for those with an entrepreneurial spirit to take more risk in the hope of greater rewards, which is exactly what is desired in transformational change. Those who are more conservative can select a more modest award system without interfering with the opportunities of the risk takers to choose their own systems. Where there is one system for all, it tends to be based on the lowest common denominator and therefore unnecessarily inhibits high levels of motivation.

3.   *Develop more flexible definitions of what constitutes a work group, how it is measured, and how its members are rewarded.* Most traditional work group plans are based on the model of a supervisor/manager who has a clearly identified work team, very specific targets, and an incentive plan based on how closely the group reaches the targets with the assigned human and monetary resources. This plan implies that the targets are readily and easily measured and that workable performance review systems exist and can be used by those making award decisions. However, in much of today's world this goal is almost impossible to achieve in an orderly

way. How accounting is done can influence performance measures (in fact, financial accounting may not help much if a desired behavior is increased customer satisfaction). Similarly, in these days of cross-firm alliances, responsibility for the numbers may not be located solely within the boundary of a single firm. In addition, many managers have little opportunity to make direct observations of their people, who often work in cross-functional, geographically far-flung teams and networks. Transformational change exacerbates this condition and requires much more flexibility in defining work units, work objectives, and behavior-reward contingencies.

4. *Direct more attention toward rewarding process improvements.* One of the aims of transformational change is to create a culture that accepts the notion of continuous improvement. To be consistent with this aim, reward systems need to take into account awards for actions that change the way things are done, as well as awards for the outcomes. This is not a new idea. Scanlon Plans and TQM systems attempt to do this, but there seems to be less application of the idea at the managerial level. For example, if managers show clear evidence of modifying their behavior away from a discrete-unit focus to an aggregated-unit focus (for example, network, related functional area, division, and so forth) there ought to be a way to reinforce this behavior—and we do not mean a monetary reward. Rather, we believe that these kinds of things are well handled by public recognition and related nonmonetary rewards. The latter have been overlooked in general, and provide some untapped opportunities.

5. *Pay more attention to combining extrinsic rewards with other influence methods.* All too often, the development of reward systems is dissociated from other influence approaches. Frequently, because of managerial attitudes that the subject is too controversial to be a public affair, the system is developed by a few people behind closed doors and then announced. Cases like Semco and Johnsonville Foods show how combining participation with extrinsic rewards adds considerably to transformation efforts, but other methods are also important. Structural rearrangement will not work well unless

the reward system is changed to be consistent with the new structure. Less obvious, but useful, is to concentrate on expectancy and
role modeling as supports. Expectancy conveys faith that people can
manage the new system, and role modeling provides a way to show
that people who have behaved in specifically desirable ways have
been successful in achieving certain reward levels. (While there are
arguments for not sharing incentive award information, there are
many more for so doing: it makes it harder for senior management
to indulge in favoritism, and it helps an organization highlight successful behaviors and appropriate role models.)

   6.   *Enhance rewards for "soft" objectives.* As noted earlier, there
is much talk about rewarding managers for such initiatives as developing their people, but there are few instances in which this
support has included some kind of incentive award. While it is true
that development of others is an essential task of managers, it is
frequently relegated to a subordinate priority position in the face of
great pressures for immediate results. To counteract this tendency,
it may be very helpful to find an incentive that would encourage
more concern for development of people. This reward need not
be monetary, and it might be customized to fit the desires of the
individual manager.

   7.   *Experimentation needs to be reinforced, even if it fails.* Lack of
rewards for what are often called "small failures" deprives organizational members of motivation to delve into untried things. For organizational learning to take place there needs to be a healthy
environment for pilot projects. Obviously, a tryout that loses money
cannot be rewarded with a monetary bonus, but there are other
ways of responding. Some Japanese firms periodically "celebrate"
failures: a day is given to honoring the attempt and to an analysis
of what was learned from it. While this may seem like an odd
way to respond to failure, it sends a clear message that learning and
risk taking are valued.

   8.   *Use changes in reward systems to initiate transformational
change.* Extrinsic rewards tend to be emphasized after the initial

steps in the transformation process. There will be some circumstances, however, in which examining the reward system may be the best way to engage people in transformation. The sequence in this case is to create a new reward system, perhaps with the involvement of employees, and then ask them to change the organization in whatever ways will help them attain the potential rewards. This probably will require some use of coercion to get the process off the ground, but hopefully this would be temporary until the new system is launched.

There are undoubtedly other implications to be derived from our argument and the cases we have presented, but we mention these in the hope of stimulating new ways of applying extrinsic rewards.

Summary

In this chapter we have discussed the role that extrinsic rewards can play in transformational change efforts. Our major point is that different behavior-reward contingencies are required than those used in day-to-day incremental changes. We have indicated what these different reward systems are and how some organizations have used them successfully. Although extrinsic rewards has been used for a long time, and experienced managers already know something about their use, this knowledge has not always been translated into successful reward systems. Conversely, because the concepts are not entirely new, there is much hope that initiators of transformational change can make changes in their use of reward systems. To do so will take a full commitment to being open to new ways of approaching a fundamental aspect of business management, but that is essentially what transformation is about, and those who give and those who receive incentive rewards can benefit substantially from the effort.

11

Coercion

Using It Legitimately

In a democratic society, the overt use of coercion can seem something of an anomaly. Yet wherever one looks—be it at social institutions, TV programs, playgrounds, or corporate organizations—coercion is ubiquitous. The use of coercion is, as the saying goes, a fact of life—so much so that in many cases it is hardly recognized as such any more. Most of us pay our taxes with little more than a grumble; we went to school despite a strong preference to be elsewhere; and we stop at red lights even when we are in a great hurry. In examples such as these, we have accepted the legitimacy of doing something we do not really want to do, as a necessary accommodation we must make in order to enjoy the benefits of living in a civilized society.

We are generally less accepting of other instances of the exercise of coercion that are nevertheless not altogether uncommon. Most of use do not condone fraternity hazings that put pledges in situations of real physical danger, nor do we generally applaud the idea of mobsters forcing shop owners to pay protection money or suffer the consequences. Bosses who take advantage of their legitimate power in order to satisfy personal, neurotic, or simply inconsiderate ends arouse our displeasure and dismay, as the following examples illustrate.

At the corporate headquarters of a large regional financial institution, the CEO often called impromptu executive meetings late in the afternoon on Fridays. When this occurred, the executives were required to call home and cancel dinner and/or social engagements. On several occasions, it had been made painfully clear that to say that one could not attend was simply not acceptable. On each occasion when one of the executives had demurred or had inquired as to the urgency of the issues to be discussed, the CEO had publicly and menacingly called into question the executive's priorities, loyalty, and ultimate suitability as part of the company's top team.

In this example, there was no compelling business reason for the CEO's behavior, which made that behavior exceedingly difficult for the executives to stomach. As the next two cases demonstrate, however, couching coercion in the context of a business plan or the urgency of a turnaround does not remove the sting.

Norman Lowell, the new CEO of the Baedeker Corporation, made things quite clear on his first day at work when he addressed his executive group. He outlined his program for change and told the assembled employees that if they disagreed with him they might just as well pick up their paycheck right now and leave. With hindsight, many wished that they had listened and taken him up on it. It would have saved them much agony later on. It didn't take long for the executive group to realize that he meant business. One senior executive who questioned the wisdom of one of his orders got a dressing down he had not had since he was in boot camp, and found himself fired. . . . [The CEO's] tongue-lashings made most executives tremble and what was worse was that Lowell seemed to get pleasure out of these scenes [Kets de Vries, 1989, pp. 57–58].

When young Tim Babcock was put in charge of a division of a large manufacturing company and told to "turn it around," he spent the first few weeks studying it from afar. He decided that the division was in disastrous shape and that he would need to take many large steps to change it. To be able to do that, he realized that he needed to quickly develop considerable power over the division's management and staff. He did the following:

- He gave the division's management two hours' notice of his arrival.

- He outlined briefly his assessment of the situation, his commitment to turn things around, and the basic direction in which he wanted to move.

- He then fired the four top managers in the room and told them they had to be out of the building in two hours.

- He then said he would personally dedicate himself to sabotaging the career of anyone who tried to block his efforts to save the division.

- He ended the sixty-minute meeting by announcing that his assistants would set up appointments for him with each of them starting at 7:00 A.M. the next morning.

Throughout the critical six-month period that followed, those who remained at the division generally cooperated energetically with Mr. Babcock (Kotter, 1979, pp. 131–132).

Drawbacks of Using Coercion

Embedded in the three cases just presented are a number of the issues that make the use of coercion problematic. First and foremost is the fact that *coercion can serve as a vehicle for the neurotic expression of narcissistic, histrionic, or paranoid behavior, and as a means of satisfying an individual's inappropriately aggressive needs for dominance.* Numerous books address the issue of dysfunctional leadership that shows itself in day-to-day behavior (see, for example, Levinson,

1972; Levinson and Rosenthal, 1984; Kets de Vries, 1989; Kets de Vries and Miller, 1984).

A second "problem" is that *as a method for getting people to do things they would not otherwise do, coercion works—at least in the short run*. The reasons for its short-term effectiveness are twofold. Supported by the full force of an organization's hierarchy and structure of authority, the use of coercion is generally perceived as *legitimate* by both parties to the interaction. Managers believe that "calling the shots" and "making the tough decisions" are what they are being paid to do, and employees traditionally have accepted this almost as the natural order of things. Historically, organizations have been designed to support these assumptions. Beginning with the notion of the divine right of kings, the knowledge required for effective decision making has until recently resided at the top, and lacking education, the people at the bottom have been almost entirely dependent on their "lords" for their survival. Thus, in some very real ways the effectiveness of coercion is based on the *mutual*, largely tacit acknowledgment on the part of both the user of coercion and the person or persons being coerced that the former has a right to coerce and the latter, for one reason or another, has *no choice* but to comply.

The reasons for this perceived lack of freedom may vary widely. The most common is fear: of losing a job, of letting others down, of being seen as a failure by oneself or one's peers, of appearing to be disloyal. The degree to which these assessments are based on verifiable data is almost irrelevant; at the moment of coercion, perception becomes reality. Those who use coercion often take advantage of this fact by doing whatever they can to reinforce not only this perceived lack of choice but also the possible *negative consequences* that would follow any exercise of free choice.

It is this dynamic that frequently fuels behaviors such as those described in the previous cases. Each case contains examples of the articulation of the dire consequences that would follow any and all instances of choosing to behave in a fashion other than that demanded by the coercing executive. In two of the cases, there appears to be a choice—do as I tell you, or leave, but neither option is one that the employee would freely choose. Thus, *real* freedom or the lack thereof is an important aspect of the issue of choice. Further, while in both cases forcing another person to exit the field is a possible consequence of the coercion, the person using their coercive power counts to a large extent on the recipients' *inability to leave the field* as a key factor in the effective use of coercion. In other words, if the person or persons coerced did choose to exit the field, to "vote with their feet," especially if it were a large number of people, or if the individual leaving possessed some key or critical skill, then in an important sense compliance would not have been achieved and the coercion would have failed. Finally, if leaving or not complying were realistically available to everyone at all times, coercion would not really be an option; the person giving the ultimatum would simply have failed to persuade the others to do as he or she wished. In general, then, a key factor in the successful use of coercion is the expectation by both parties that the coerced party cannot exit the scene.

The third issue that makes the use of coercion problematic is the implicit assumption that underlies the executive behaviors described in these three cases. While short-term gains were achieved, coerciveness of the sort depicted is not without serious cost to the organization. As described in Chapter One, the new business environment calls for organizations to be based on cooperation and collaboration, flatter flexible networks, leaders functioning as servants, multiple possible scenarios, systemic solutions, and continuous change. Few if any of these attributes could even exist, much less flourish, in an environment such as that created by the executives in the examples. The risk taking, experimentation, and fundamental interpersonal respect necessary to realize a successful organization in today's world simply could not survive the autocratic, egocentric, neurotic style of the executives described.

However, as the following case illustrates, even a less threatening, less public form of coercion would be inimical to the kind of open, free-flowing dialogue necessary for the development of real collaboration, multiple possible scenarios, and the role of leader as servant.

> In his classic study of decision making in the handling of the Cuban missile crisis during the presidency of John F. Kennedy, Allison (1971) describes how the president's cabinet members were told informally by Robert Kennedy that the president expected them to stand behind him on this issue. Many of them later reported that they were opposed to the invasion of Cuba but did not say this while the decision was being made for fear of being seen as uncooperative, weak on communism, or unsupportive of the president.

In response to Robert Kennedy's pressure, everyone went along with the decision, believing that failure to do so would somehow be letting the president down. Each person was unaware that others in the meeting had reservations similar to his own, because Robert Kennedy's coercive remarks had rendered them compliant and silent about their beliefs. Irving Janis (1972) has labeled this phenomenon "groupthink," a term that has been part of American English ever since. The dynamics of groupthink are similar to those described in the Abilene Paradox in Chapter Six.

Reasons to Use Coercion

Given this as background, is it possible to justify the use of coercion as a legitimate method of organizational transformation, and if it is, can situations such as those described earlier be avoided?

It is our belief that the answer to the first part of this question is yes. In arriving at this answer, we are acknowledging the extraordinary power of an existing organizational reality or culture to maintain itself in the face of even massive attempts to change it. This ability exists on two levels: the systemic and the individual.

At the systemic level, we find a web of behaviors, expectations, and prescribed roles and relationships, as well as a host of structures and infrastructures whose very purpose, as we discussed in Chapter Two, is to achieve and maintain stability. Everyone knows how hard it is to break even so obvious a habit as smoking. How much harder, then, must change be when the work habits that need to be changed are reinforced in a thousand subtle and invisible ways. Structures, processes, expectations, role models, extrinsic rewards! They all fit together like a Rubik's Cube. However, in industrial-age organizations there is also an inherent paradox: while all these structures and processes fit so neatly together, they also give participants a fragmented view of the world. Therefore, few individuals ever see enough of the overall picture to even begin to think about changing it. Furthermore, the subtle and sometimes not-so-subtle differences in language (for example, the languages of engineering, marketing, sales, and human resources) that make communication across organizational boundaries so difficult work against the collaborative action necessary for major change. The effect of this "tower of Babel" is to keep things as they are.

Fragmentation serves to preserve the status quo in another way. "Experts" from any given part of the system are not viewed as legitimate by other parts of the system. Repeatedly heard comments such as "Self-managed teams might work in a plant, but they would never work here" marginalize and dismiss any attempt to make significant change.

Another mechanism that preserves the status quo is labeling as deviant any behaviors that call into question the rightness of the existing system. Such a label stigmatizes the behavior in the eyes of others, and the deviants are treated in a way that serves as a warning. The case we described earlier in which a senior manager who had used innovative and creative methods to achieve a highly successful product launch was subsequently fired is one small example of how a system works to preserve itself.

Another way existing systems preserve themselves is by denying resources (money, time, people) to anything that is perceived as threatening. The keepers of the organizational resources are often those with the most to lose if the status quo were to fall. Frequently, the use of this mechanism is subtle: some resources will be approved, but never enough to really enable ultimate success.

Existing infrastructures are also powerful maintainers of the status quo, because they continue to perform their socializing and reinforcing functions day in and day out, rain or shine. At an individual level, powerful senior executives also continue to role model the old behaviors on a daily basis. They are also the ones who make the resource allocation decisions.

Given this scenario, coercion in some form is frequently the only way to quite literally break up the old organizational reality. It is no accident that a number of leaders have used revolutionary and war metaphors when talking about the need to transform—for a transformation can literally be a war between the old and the new. Furthermore, if coercion is used for its ability to break the ties to the past, it is also no accident that in all the transformations of which we are aware, it was the senior executive's use of coercion that, at least publicly, began the change.

To use coercion effectively in the service of transformation, without stepping over some invisible line, is not easy, however. In the remainder of this chapter we will explore the dynamics of its use, and provide examples of how it has been used successfully.

The Dynamics of Coercion

Thus far we have identified the use of coercion with its exercise by an individual. Before proceeding further, it is crucial that we also acknowledge the coercive aspects of many of the other methods of influence on which we have focused.

Both structural rearrangement and any system of extrinsic rewards contain within them certain coercive elements. Once work processes have been set and infrastructures put in place, people usually are not free to reject them. Those processes and structures possess the legitimacy of "the way things are supposed to be done," and leaving or doing the process differently somewhere else is seldom an option. Similarly, the use of extrinsic rewards in shaping behavior can be coercive in that it rewards only a narrow band of behaviors. In a sense, extrinsic reward programs are saying, "Do these behaviors at least reasonably well, or leave," in much the same fashion as did the executives in the cases presented at the beginning of this chapter.

Even participation can become coercive, if one is not given a choice about whether or not to participate. Role modeling and expectancy, too, can take on a coercive flavor if one is subjected to their influence whether one wants to be or not. In general, people are not free to pick their bosses, and although they may privately deplore the boss's behavior, it is difficult to remain entirely immune to its effect. To personally maintain behaviors that are not congruent with or explicitly sanctioned by those in higher positions is extremely difficult, and people often find themselves acting like their bosses, whether they like it or not. In much the same fashion, the expectations people have of one another can also feel coercive. Here, too, departing the scene is most often not an option, and people find themselves behaving according to the expectations of others, whether they want to or not.

A recognition of this coercive potential in almost all of our methods serves to underscore the fact that all social and organizational systems, by their very nature, are designed to channel behavior into certain acceptable paths. Recognizing that they do so in ways that are accepted as legitimate and virtually inescapable helps put the use of coercion as a specific method in a more useful context. The real issue thus becomes *how to take advantage of the pragmatic value of coercion while avoiding its potential to become oppressive and dysfunctional.*

In essence, then, coercion is any form of influence that plays on the fears of others at moments when their freedom to reject the influence is seen by them as being severely curtailed for one reason or another. More specifically, coercion is any instance of attempted influence that meets the following criteria:

- Control over the behavior of others

- Use of force, which may range from mild rules to legal or moral pressures to actual physical force

- Expectation by people that they may be punished if they do not conform, which would cause such feelings as guilt, fear of failure, rejection, and a sense of the loss of something valued

- Belief by those being coerced that they cannot exit the situation

Coercion of any form, then, takes advantage of that part of everyone's existence that restricts independence of movement. Thus, if one is afraid to leave a job in the belief that one cannot find another job, one is more susceptible to being coerced into performing behaviors not of one's own choosing. Schein, Schneier, and Barker's investigations (1961) are supportive of our perspective:

> We do not need to belabor the point, but it should be clear that the term "coercion" is applicable to the entire continuum of forces ranging from small constraints imposed by the very nature of the moral order governing interpersonal relationships to very sizable constraints which derive from combination of physical and social forces. . . . In other words, many more influence situations are really instances of coercive persuasion than might at first blush seem to be the case [p. 277].

In other words, coercion is everywhere, and in a very real sense, we could not live without it. At a societal level, any and every form of social organization must possess elements of coercion. At an individual level, when parents physically prevent a child from putting his or her hand on a hot stove or from running out into the middle of a busy highway, they are acting coercively toward that child. Few would argue that such coercion was inappropriate. In fact, many routine acts of coercion, as opposed to planned political suppression, are committed by people acting in good faith and on the assumption that what they are doing is good for all concerned.

That coercion is viewed as being useful in a variety of settings is illustrated by various therapies and self-help movements, particularly substance abuse programs. For example, Alcoholics Anonymous (AA) uses a form of coercion to induce people to feel badly if they cannot conform to certain rules and behaviors. AA members perceive that they cannot leave the program without being labeled a "loser" or a "cop-out." Such a fear can be as much a barrier as are walls or fences. As Schein, Schneier, and Barker (1961) note: "Certain organizations like Alcoholics Anonymous do not deliberately unfreeze an individual but refuse to take anyone under their care who is not already unfrozen. Thus, a person does not become eligible for care by AA unless he has really become desperate, is dissatisfied with himself and is prepared to turn his fate over to some greater power" (p. 272).

According to these authors, even in institutions that are entered voluntarily and from which the individual may withdraw voluntarily—such as AA, educational institutions, religious orders, psychoanalysis, revival meetings, and fraternities—the coercive power of social pressure is one of the legitimate methods used to elicit a set of desired behaviors. "In such institutions the social pressures which can be generated can be as coercive as the physical constraints previously described. Not only is voluntary withdrawal generally defined as failure but the act of entry into the institution may constitute a more or less irrevocable commitment in that the individual often cuts himself off from alternative paths when he makes his decision" (Schein, Schneier, and Barker, 1961, p. 275).

An example of the coercive power of group ridicule is found in the case of a young man who wished to resign from the armed forces during the probation period, a time when he was acting within his rights within the system. Accusations of not being a "real man" or of being a "wimp" because his friends could manage it and he could not were clear instances of attempted coercion.

Examples of this type of social pressure can be found even in companies in which transformational leadership is being embraced. In such instances, the repeated and forceful articulation of the expectation that everyone will adopt a new vision and become loyal missionaries has within it an identifiable kernel of coerciveness. Such exhortations play on the feeling that one will be hurting the company or letting down one's friends and associates if one does not jump on the transformation train.

Embedded in these and other examples is an issue that is central to the use of coercion in the creation of the new organizational reality: who gains as a result of its use? In the earlier example of the parent and child, the child benefited in a very real way from the coercion, which prevented harm. In most of the other examples we have given, it is, at least in the short run, the system or institution that benefits in that it has maintained itself in the face of behaviors that threaten its very existence. If everyone left the army or AA whenever they had to do something they did not want to do, the organizations would no longer be viable. The case can certainly be made that in the long run the individual also benefits from the coercion, but at the moment of coercion the user of coercion is usually putting the interests of the institution above the interests of the individual being coerced.

In fact, the essence of a manager's role in a hierarchical organization may be defined as that of putting the interests of the organization above the interests of the individual. The real issue, however, is the balancing of benefits. If either polarity (organization versus individual) is consistently chosen, the entire system will be unable to function effectively.

The Needs of the Organization

To function effectively, organizations require *reliability in organizational behavior*. Variety, uncertainty, and unpredictability need to be eliminated or kept to a minimum. The best way to accomplish this is to formulate a system of roles and responsibilities so that everyone knows with as much precision as possible what is expected of him or her. This system is promulgated and enforced through job descriptions and rules of conduct such as policies and procedures.

An organization also needs *legitimacy of authority*. This means that symbols and acts of authority are sanctioned by rules so that once decisions are made they are binding on employees, regardless of the employees' opinions or preferences.

Heretofore, the whole system has been based on *universal acceptance of the principle of hierarchy*. In other words, there has existed in organizations the unquestioned assumption that people will comply with authority as a matter of routine. This assumption has been shared by managers and employees alike, and both have traditionally experienced a need to maintain these hierarchical expectations.

There is a complementary dynamic, however, that is also fairly universal: *the desire of people to identify with their leaders and their organization*. This element involves the need to belong to something larger than oneself and to have leaders who can be admired and respected. The longer people have been in an organization, the greater is this identification, and hence the more difficult it is to think of leaving the organization.

In traditional organizations, *managers are accountable for the work of others*. Typically, managers get work done through others and are accountable for the performance of their work unit. In turn, they hold subordinates and others accountable for their expected contribution to the unit's performance. Elliott Jacques (1989) has referred to these relationships as "accountability hierarchies" (p. 1). Thus, in this system *managers are dependent on the performance of others*. For managers to meet their accountability targets, they must rely on others to meet their expected targets. The failure of their subordinates to perform makes the managers subject to criticism by their superiors, who in turn are dependent on them and accountable for that failure to their own superiors.

This dependence creates considerable *ambiguity and uncertainty in the managerial role*. In general, on a daily basis there is lack of clarity as to which problems will need management attention. The more ambiguous the environment, the greater is the likelihood that the manager will become anxious and experience stress.

On the basis of this overview, then, it is not difficult to construct a scenario in which managers act coercively and employees accept the legitimacy of that coercion. Managers seek to reduce the ambiguity in their roles by creating definable goals and predictable behavior. They are supported in this endeavor by their sense of accountability and by the authority they believe has been conferred on them as part of their managerial role. The more ambiguous the environment, the harder it is for them to accomplish their perceived mission, a situation that can lead to fear of failure and a general sense of anxiety that they typically do not share with others. And when others' performance produces uncertainty or unsatisfactory outputs, the managers' fears are compounded by the fact that they are dependent on that performance.

A normal response to a situation such as this is to become more controlling of those on whom one is dependent. One means of doing this is to coerce people into performing in a desired way. The coercion works because it is supported by the desire and need of those being controlled to maintain predictability, by their tendency to comply with legitimate authority, and by the strength of their identification with the company, an identification that frequently has been developed over a long period of time. In addition, feelings of fear, shame, and guilt may contribute to compliance. The complex dynamics of this sense of identification helps to explain why most people have difficulty leaving an organization in which they have invested themselves over time.

One of the striking things about this scenario is that it makes clear that the use of coercion is not always a matter of dysfunctional people exerting their power in order to dominate others. Rather, the use of coercion is almost an inevitable outcome of the systemic forces that surround traditional roles and relationships and that influence the way in which individuals try to live up to the demands of those roles and responsibilities under extremely difficult circumstances. In such a system, what coercion does is help an individual gain control over a threatening situation so that his or her accountabilities can be satisfied. In other words, the system and the situation have as much to do with engendering the use of coercion as does managerial style. At any given time, and under certain circumstances, all of us are capable of coercing others, and we do.

Recognition of the systemic forces that drive much of the use of coercion is significant in the context of organizational transformation for several reasons. First, if the organizational roles, relationships, accountabilities, and processes are changed fundamentally, the need for and uses of coercion will also change. What was legitimate within the old context is likely to be viewed as illegitimate within the transformed context. We do not mean to imply that coercion will no longer exist. We do want to suggest, however, that it will no doubt have a significantly different flavor.

Second, if the degree of alignment between organizational needs and individual needs that is necessary to internalize the new organizational behaviors has been achieved, then there should also be a noticeable decrease in the need to use overt forms of coercion. Striking a balance between the needs of the individual and those of the organization will become one of the prime leadership responsibilities, and the equation used to evaluate the "costs" of coercion will likely be different as well. We turn now to a further examination of those costs.

The Price of Using Coercion

As we have noted, coercion works because it counts on the inability of people to withdraw from the situation in which they find themselves. As such, it leads to what may be called "dependent change." Not surprisingly, many people resist being in a dependent relationship and as a result they usually find other ways to "leave" the situation. If they cannot leave physically, they frequently do so mentally. This "leaving" tends to manifest in avoidance of responsibility and the taking of a reactive rather than proactive posture toward their jobs, units, and the company as a whole.

Therefore, one of the real costs of coercion is the creation of or reinforcement of employee dependence. The use of any action that creates or reinforces dependence must be very carefully considered. Is it really necessary? Will no other method or combination of methods work? And finally, if there is no other way to move forward, what other methods need to be used simultaneously in order to minimize the potential for creating dependence?

A related cost of coercion is that its use creates an environment that is not conducive to real learning. Coercion may be an effective way of showing people *what* they need to learn, but it does not create the kind of open receptivity that is necessary for unlearning the old ways and internalizing the new. When in order to promote transformation we need people to learn to act in ways that are discontinuous with their previous behaviors, coercion creates rather than eliminates barriers to both learning and internalization.

The use of coercion can also drive resistance underground. Not everyone complies or leaves; they may give surface support, yet remain privately antagonistic, working to derail or sabotage the change effort behind the scenes. As noted in Chapter Four, the failure to acknowledge the existence of multiple realities can push resistance underground. The antidote to this potential is to acknowledge the existence of resistance, and to be willing to address the issue of multiple realities immediately after the use of coercion.

The problems we have just enumerated are all inherent in the use of coercion. However, there are two additional problems that are caused not by the use of coercion itself but by the nature of the climate or environment in which coercion is used. First, thirty years ago studies showed that people did what their bosses asked them to do because it was their job or their duty to do so. Today, the number of people who would react this way is much lower. People have become so independent, cynical, and mistrustful of organizations that it is far less likely that they will comply out of a sense of duty. Second, for some managers the use of participatory methods has become so close to being a moral imperative that they do not simply *prefer* not to use their coercive power—they go to great lengths to *avoid* using it.

Now that we have explored both the positive and negative elements of using coercion, we will examine the skills and conditions that are necessary for the constructive use of coercion in the context of creating and internalizing the new organizational reality.

Using Coercion Effectively

The best way to understand the conditions under which coercion may be employed is to think in terms of contingency management—in other words, under what circumstances is it a necessary method and under what circumstances is its use uncalled for? Table 11.1, based on the work of Dunphy and Stace (1988), presents one model that distinguishes between situations requiring incremental change and those requiring transformational change. The model develops four strategies, two of which call for collaborative or participatory approaches, and two of which call for coercion. In their discussion of the model, Dunphy and Stace make a case for the value of each of the four strategies in different situations.

Table 11.1. A Model for Choosing Between Collaborative and Coercive Strategies.

Collaborative Modes	Type 1 *Participative Evolution* Use when organization is in "fit" but needs minor adjustment, or is out of fit but time is available and key interest groups favor change	Type 2 *Charismatic Transformation* Use when organization is out of "fit," there is little time for extensive participation, but there is support for radical change within organization
Coercive Modes	Type 3 *Forced Evolution* Use when organization is in "fit," but needs minor adjustment, or is out of fit but time is available, but key interest groups oppose change	Type 4 *Dictatorial Transformation* Use when organization is "out of fit," there is no time for extensive participation and no support within the organization for radical change, but radical change is vital to organization and survival and fulfillment of basic mission

Source: Adapted from Dunphy and Stace (1988, p. 101). Used by permission.

This model is useful in making a distinction between situations in which collaboration is sufficient and those in which coercion is necessary. It is important to keep in mind, however, that Dunphy and Stace's definition of transformation does not explicitly consider issues related to resocialization or the need for it in creating and sustaining a new organizational reality.

There is no question in our minds that there are times when an organization is in crisis and something must be done right away, or that frequently only a few people in the organization initially see and understand the need for truly radical change. Yet, we wish to emphasize that when resocialization is part of the ultimate goal, the use of coercion in such situations, although fully justified, needs to be tempered with the use of other methods as quickly as possible.

In our experience and research there appears to be one aspect of transformational change for which coercion is not only the "drug of choice" but also the only drug available. In almost every case of transforming an organization from a traditional, authoritarian management structure and system to a more fluid, flexible, knowledge-based, collaborative structure and system, the process of transformation appears to have been initiated with some form of coercion. David Kearns of Xerox did not ask his management team to vote on "should we or shouldn't we." Lars Kolind of Oticon announced his intentions with, "I'm 100 percent sure we are going to try this" (LaBarre, 1994).

Use of coercion in this context serves to capture the attention of employees and to heighten their awareness of the problems and possible solutions. As transformation proceeds, however, people throughout the organization begin to develop an in-depth understanding of the "big picture." As they become more attuned to the organizational environment as a result of their involvement, the impetus for ongoing discontinuous change may emerge from multiple places within the organization as it struggles to stay "in fit" with its environment. It may be difficult to picture such a state of affairs from the vantage point of current managerial paradigms, but a great deal of the energy for change at Semco, for example, seems to now spring from throughout the organization. It is clear that at both Xerox and Oticon the objective of coercion was to energize the organization in service of the change effort, not to browbeat employees into submission. Using coercion to help generate a revised perspective in employees is therefore very different from using coercion to ram home implementation of an already designed action plan. In fact, Kearns and Kolind both moved very quickly into an extremely participative approach to the actual design and implementation of the transformation.

Thus, based on this discussion, it is possible to conclude that appropriate and effective use of coercion depends on the presence of several conditions:

- *It is one step in a process.* If the coercion is not disrespectful, and if methods other than coercion are clearly being used, people are far less likely to have a lasting negative reaction to any specific act of coercion. When Kolind told Oticon's work force that he was 100 percent sure the company was going to try to transform itself into a knowledge-based organization, he also said that individuals would have "enough time so that you can make your choice— whether you're going to try it with us . . . ," and in short order he began an inclusive process that "gave out chunks of this vision" to small groups throughout the organization (LaBarre, 1994, p. 24).

- *There is prior consideration of the consequences.* Since coercion can frequently leave a bad taste in the mouth, it is important to think through and prepare for the range of responses it can generate. This is especially important in the context of how the coercion will impact the process of resocialization. For example, while many organizations have been unable to avoid the reengineering of their business processes, a growing number of organizations have begun to focus significant attention on better ways to manage the process of change itself. Thus, they are ensuring that there is sufficient support in place as the process unfolds to help employees weather the storm.

- *Those who use coercion pay close attention to the reactions of others.* In a transformational context, listening to, taking in, and being willing to talk over the feelings and thoughts of those being coerced is key to successful use. This is one of the major ways in which leaders can demonstrate their respect for others. It also serves to surface the multiple realities, a process that in and of itself creates a beginning level of positive engagement.

- *It is used sparingly.* People can live with the occasional use of coercion without adverse reactions, especially when it is used in a way that draws attention to the seriousness of problems and the need for change. However, if it is used too frequently, it results in the creation of employee dependence, or in a situation in which anyone who can will leave the organization at the first decent opportunity.

- *Those who use it do so with a sense of humility.* By this we mean that the use of coercion on any given occasion is a "best choice," not a "correct decision."

Used according to these principles and to the criteria contained in the model presented in Table 11.1, coercion can be constructive rather than destructive. That this is so can be demonstrated by examining several cases of its successful use in the service of organizational transformation.

Successful Applications of Coercion

As indicated earlier, most change efforts, even those that involve all of the other change methods, do not start with a ground swell from the masses but rather with some decisive actions at the highest level. In Chapter Twelve we discuss several cases in which the seven methods of influence were combined to produce new organizational realities that could be sustained over time. In each of these cases, coercion was consciously used at the beginning of the change effort. We do not mean to imply that it was not also used during later stages; but it is worth noting the consistency of its use in the context of beginning the process.

We have already mentioned Kolind's use of coercion to begin the process of creating a new organizational reality at Oticon, and Kearns's use of this method at Xerox when he spoke of the absolute need to become a total quality company and to "overthrow" the old regime. At Balfour (see Chapters Seven and Twelve), the die makers were told that the company was going to use CAD-CAM in concert with the skills of the artisan; those who did not wish to be part of this endeavor were free to stay making tools the old way. However, this was the *only* chance one had to opt for this arrangement (Vassallo and Hohlmaier, 1988).

At Motorola, then CEO Robert Galvin conveyed his intentions in a somewhat oblique but no less coercive fashion by insisting that before senior managers could report performance results at the operations meetings, they would have to first present what they had done to improve their quality systems. In addition, Galvin's personal attendance as a "student" at the quality improvement courses made it virtually impossible for anyone to turn down the "request" to attend these programs.

While each of the acts just mentioned was clearly an act of coercion, in every case the senior executive was respectful in his application, and also clearly showed repeated and sincere interest in his employees' reactions to the coercion. Galvin, Kolind, and Kearns were all accessible to their people before, during, and after the use of coercion, and in each case virtually every other aspect of the transformation was handled in a highly participative, open, trusting, respectful, and honest manner.

Another example in which concern was combined with coercion is the Harwood-Weldon merger. Harwood acquired Weldon and attempted to bring its authoritarian culture more in line with Harwood's participatory culture. Its executives went to great lengths to assure Weldon's people that their operation would continue. They reorganized production operations so as to create a more efficient and satisfying work environment, and they helped the Weldon management to study and improve their investment in their human resources.

Though Harwood's management expected to make changes slowly and with concern for the impact of these changes on people, it soon became apparent that stronger, more broadly based interventions were necessary. Taking some advantage of the needs of Weldon employees to keep their jobs, they insisted that Weldon employees attend workshops and training sessions designed to break the old patterns of distrust, secrecy, and noncooperation that had existed in the company. The transformation that occurred over time is documented in detail in the book *Management by Participation* (Marrow, Bowers, and Seashore, 1967). Although participation and structural rearrangement were the major methods employed in this transformation, coercive power was also a useful tool. In fact, it is somewhat ironic that the pressure to become more participative resulted in the decision of some of the people in Weldon's Puerto Rican plant to leave the company because they preferred to have managers who were strong enough not to feel the need to consult with their employees.

Summary

Because of the manipulation involved, and because of the frequent negative responses to its use, there are those who say it is always wrong to use coercion. Many change practitioners feel that if coercion is required, it means that other, more appropriate change methods were not used in a timely fashion, or that the other methods were used poorly.

We believe that this is an inappropriate conclusion. The use of coercion as one of several "medications" for an ailing company seems to be entirely appropriate. There are times when its use may be the intervention of choice rather than a default when all else has failed. This is frequently the case in the management of a crisis situation. Even Abraham Maslow, one of the founders of humanistic psychology and a true believer in participatory democracy, made it clear that if he were on an oceangoing ship in the midst of a big storm, he would not like to have the ship's captain call a meeting to decide what to do. Thus, in situations in which time is of the essence, coercion becomes an important tool in ensuring the survival of the organization.

We have also explored its use as a catalyst for beginning the transformation process and for helping to focus people's attention on the need to change when that need is not apparent. We have explored the issues of legitimacy, lack of choice, and the inability to leave the field, as the interpersonal and organizational underpinnings that make the use of coercion possible. In this context we raised the issue of who benefits from the coercion, and we pointed out that organizational systems themselves frequently make coercion necessary. We then explored the limitations of the use of coercion, pointing out its potential for creating employee dependence, its lack of conduciveness to learning, and its real potential for driving resistance underground.

To balance this picture, we then examined the effective use of coercion and offered several examples of its successful use. None of these examples included the use of coercion as a standard means of bullying others, proving who is boss, or satisfying one's own ego needs. In concert with most responsible practitioners, we see such use as decidedly illegitimate and counterproductive.

Finally, then, from our perspective, coercion should be used only with a full understanding of its strengths, weaknesses, and pitfalls and a clear assessment of the conditions appropriate for its effective use.

12

Integrating the Strategies
for Maximum Impact

We began this book by reframing transformational change as the creation of a new organizational reality. We also noted that to sustain a new organizational reality, an organization must explicitly undertake the task of resocializing organizational members into that new reality so that the new reality becomes internalized as *the* reality. We then defined organizational resistance as the fruit of multiple realities, those coexisting, alternate constructions that derive from the experiences, worldviews, and consciousness of individuals, subgroups, and referent groups. In large measure, transformational change is about managing these differing realities to articulate and implement a new shared reality that has been allowed to emerge from seemingly disparate positions.

One of the greatest obstacles to the success of transformational change, however, is the tenacity with which the old system resists resocialization. Although previously successful organizational paradigms may have become less effective, by definition they enable a continuation of the old, even in the face of substantial forces for change. As we noted at the outset, paradigms endure for a number of inherent reasons. First, people become emotionally and communally invested in paradigms; and second, through a variety of mechanisms paradigms prevent people from seeing alternatives. Individual strands of reality may be cut, but the remaining threads tenaciously hold the overall sense of what is real firmly in place.

These paradigmatic forces that work to retain the status quo are operating every minute of every day; therefore, the only way a fragile, not yet fully formed alternative can hope to overcome the incumbent reality is to mount a systemic assault. Coercion and certain forms of persuasive communication may help to loosen the ties and crack the protective shell of the current reality, but several effective leaders of transformational change have connoted the intensity of the struggle by characterizing the transformation effort as a "war" or "revolution." Even a heavy dose of structural rearrangement is not enough on its own to bring the new organizational reality into being. Resocialization is a systemic process, and as such it requires a simultaneous approach from every possible angle. Concurrent use of all seven methods also allows attention to be paid to the many relevant organizational and individual realities, thereby providing multiple points of leverage for pushing transformation forward.

A further argument for the integrated use of all seven methods is that in combination the force of each method is substantially enhanced. For example, use of expectancy and persuasive communication together creates an intellectual and emotional vision that embodies the desired new performance levels. By adding the use of role modeling, however, the new behaviors are enabled to become more than aspirations; they become real, and therefore learnable. Implementing extrinsic rewards in order to focus and reinforce progress toward manifesting the new ways of acting and thinking adds one more force to the others pushing toward their attainment. If organizational structures and processes are also altered to support the new modes of activity, in essence a set of guides and coaches have been created that will provide day-to-day reminders of how people need to behave. Finally, the use of various forms of participation increases the impact of the other methods in two important ways. First, it provides multiple opportunities for leaders to personally share their expectations with and role model the new behaviors to a broad cross section of organizational members. Second, by increasing opportunities to tap into the creativity of those members and thereby enable their input into the new structures and processes, their commitment to act in accordance with the new is increased, as are their opportunities to begin to try out the new behaviors themselves.

In this chapter we will look at four cases of successful transformation, each of which has approached the process from an integrated, systemic perspective. After assessing the cases, we will examine them together to identify any patterns that will help to further understanding of the process of transformation.

Examples of Successful Transformation

Although there is still a lot to learn about transformational change, stories about successful transformational efforts have been told for some years now. There is a growing literature about organizations such as ABB, AT&T, Xerox, Oticon, Blue Cross–Blue Shield of Ohio, Semco, Motorola, the Wharton Business School, Johnsonville Foods, Whirlpool, British Airways, and other large and small firms that have found ways to meet the challenge of the discontinuous environment. In all of these cases, most or all of the seven methods of influence have been applied simultaneously to the task of resocialization. Also, whether because of the particular environmental pressures, the nature of the industry, or the culture of the firm, each organization went about the task differently. In some cases success was achieved with very limited use of role modeling; in others, role modeling became a major aspect of the program. In some instances use of extrinsic rewards was largely through participative means; in others, senior leadership controlled this aspect. Some changes started with coercive implementation of structural rearrangement; others restructured later in the change process.

The existence of variety in cases of transformational change indicates that more than a mere mechanical application of the methods is required. Just as socialization in the U.S. Marine Corps differs from socialization in the Israeli Air Force, the paths to resocialization will vary from one organizational culture to another.

We now present four cases to show how they utilized an integrated influence approach in different ways. In developing these cases, we draw upon numerous sources.

The Xerox Case

Much has been written about the revitalization of Xerox over the past fifteen years. By the late 1970s, Xerox recognized that the incremental changes it was making were insufficient to address the problems it was having. CEO David Kearns realized that Xerox was "fine-tuning a bad product, . . . our management system" (Kearns and Nadler, 1992, p. 124). The real task at hand was "trying to get a hundred thousand people to act and think differently toward the product, the customer, and each other every hour of the day" (p. 147), and it was simply not happening. The managers came to an understanding that there was no unity to the multiple change products and hence no cultural change.

To address these issues, Xerox decided that the company was faced with managing nothing less than an organizational and cultural transformation. Employees needed not simply to be trained in the use of TQM tools and the intensification of cost control measures but to change *their whole approach to work*. Significant attitudinal and behavioral change would be required. Kearns told his senior managers:

This is a revolution . . . and we have to overthrow the old regime. The quality transition team is the junta in place to run things on a temporary basis. The standards and measures equate to the law of the land. . . . The reward and recognition system is the gaining control of the banks. . . . The training is capturing control of the universities. Communication is seizing control of the press, and the senior management behavior is putting your own people in place to reflect the revolution. All of these elements are needed to change a culture . . . to one of a total quality program [Kearns and Nadler, 1992, p. 184].

The use of several methods is already evident. Foremost is persuasive communication, with the introduction of new language and the metaphor of revolution to capture people's attention. The reference to the rewards system and the putting of appropriate people into roles that are important to the success of the "revolution" indicate an intention to develop a new approach to extrinsic rewards and to use role modeling to show the behavior desired. Note also that the suggestion by the CEO that he was fomenting a revolution carries with it a not-so-hidden threat of the use of coercion.

As a result of this senior management meeting, a quality implementation team was identified, but many of the appointments to it proved to be problematic. Paradoxically, those who were able to give the effort the necessary status were those who had succeeded by behaving in what were now recognized as dysfunctional ways. This is an example of negative role modeling, which served to heighten the awareness that new models were required. With the addition of some new people, the team proceeded to lay out a five-year plan: 1983 was to be the start-up year, during which, through the use of persuasive communication, dissatisfaction with the existing culture would be created; the goal in 1984 would be to continue to build awareness, and four thousand managers would be trained in the use of quality tools; by 1986 all one hundred thousand employees would be trained, and the pursuit of total quality would be a way of life at Xerox—that is, resocialization would have been achieved. Implicit in the plan was the recognition that employee participation would be essential to the success of the effort. To obtain the required behavior change, every employee needed to embody the new way of doing things.

The training model was designed to overcome the common fate of many new methods. Typically, the old ways reassert themselves because the work environment is not designed to support the new tools and processes that are taught. To combat this tendency, Xerox decided to begin training at the top, and to have each level of management train the level below them. Intact teams would be trained so that peer support and peer pressure would hasten the use of the new methods. Prior to the actual training, everyone was involved in a quality awareness session based on a video that starkly depicted Xerox's ineptitude. These sessions are examples of the combined use of coercion and persuasive communication.

In addition, a new infrastructure was developed to support the new way of thinking. For example, to highlight the centrality of a customer focus, any work for whom there was no customer was immediately stopped. No meeting could be scheduled unless the meeting's "customer" was clearly identified and customer requirements were spelled out. Only active participants were allowed to attend these meetings, whereas previously meeting attendance had been something of a status symbol—a practice that resulted in meetings that were so large that no real work could be accomplished in them. This is an example of the use of structural rearrangement. Training was also focused on solving root causes of problems rather than just treating symptoms, and a set of interactive skills was introduced to support active listening and to develop the ability to build on new ideas rather than attacking and defending them. This is an example of skill development in support of participation and collaborative efforts.

Progress was widely communicated throughout the company and participative quality teams became the way work was accomplished. Teamwork days were instituted in which the best teams from each location came together to share their innovations—an example of the use of recognition as an extrinsic reward. Kearns soon realized, however, that he himself was not applying total quality processes and was still driving the organization to "get the numbers up," rather than to improve quality systems. There was "a lack of leadership and role modeling, as well as a dearth of inspection and management" (Kearns and Nadler, 1992, p. 231). Only in France were the results different. Upon investigation, it was found that top management there were effective role models who had also used every symbolic and actual means to reinforce the importance of the new behaviors.

Xerox also discovered that it was still rewarding and promoting people who did not embody the total quality approach. Being a role model for quality was added as a promotion criteria in performance reviews—an example of the addition of extrinsic rewards to role modeling. Kearns also began to place a much stronger emphasis on quality in his monthly operations reviews. Symbolically, he moved a review of quality progress from last on the agenda to the after-lunch period. It quickly became clear that if you expected to stay with the company you would have to take quality seriously. Note the integrated use of structural rearrangement, role modeling, and coercion at this stage of implementation.

By 1988, the results began to roll in. Customers were measurably more satisfied. Revenue and profits were on the rise, and the company had recaptured market share from Japanese companies. Morale was up. Virtually every department in the company was benchmarking against the best in other firms. On a daily basis, assembly line workers were receiving detailed information on defects, new products were being designed to be simple to operate and repair, and Xerox could now tell customers the exact date on which the product would arrive. The customer was being treated as "king," and Xerox was using quality methods at every level of the company. These results indicate that institutionalization of a new company culture stemming from the structural rearrangement was occurring.

Progress into the Generative Phase was further advanced when Xerox won the Baldrige Award in 1988, but both Kearns and his successor, Paul Allaire, recognized that the old culture had not yet been finally revised. As a way of preventing Xerox from repeating its mistakes, Allaire instituted a series of presidential reviews to focus on products and processes that had failed. Efforts to address the weak spots uncovered in the process of applying for the Baldrige Award continued as Xerox embarked on becoming "The Document Company" rather than being seen simply as a photocopier manufacturer. These efforts illustrate the use of structural rearrangement and persuasive communication in support of internalization of the new order; in other words, Xerox had moved into the Internalization Phase. That this revolution worked well is indicated by the fact that Xerox continues to be seen as a high-quality office solutions company more than a decade later.

This case needs little additional comment, other than to note that a period of eight years elapsed between the start of the transformation and the attainment of the Baldrige Award. Even with effective use of all seven methods, it is clear that transformation cannot be accomplished quickly.

The Oticon Case

This case is derived from articles by LaBarre (1994), Kolind (1994) and Savage (1994). We present a summary and synthesis of these reports.

Faced with the realization that further development in its industry would not come simply as a result of new technology but from the ability of all of its employees to "think the unthinkable," Oticon, a Danish manufacturer of hearing aids, decided to transform itself into a knowledge-based company. This meant finding a way to structure the company so that technologists, audiologists, psychologists, customers, and those who sell, fit, and fine-tune the hearing devices could all work together to improve the quality of life of Oticon's customers. According to Lars Kolind, CEO, nothing short of a revolution could transform a traditional company like Oticon into a knowledge-based organization. Note the use, again, of the term "revolution." As in the Xerox case, this is an example of persuasive communication that uses a powerful metaphor to project a new vision.

Over a fifteen-month period, roles and relationships were dramatically altered throughout the company. The restructuring also included a complete rethinking of the company's business, information, management, and human resource systems. An entirely new physical layout of the work space was also put into place. As we will show, heavy use was made of structural rearrangement.

To overcome the resistance to these dramatic changes, especially from managers who would lose some of their power base, Kolind told all employees at the outset that he was "100 percent sure that we will try this. There's enough time so that you can make your choice whether you are going to try it with us" (LaBarre, 1994, p. 24). Note the use of coercion early in the change process. Although perhaps stated in a subtle manner, Kolind left no doubt in anyone's mind as to their lack of real choice in the matter.

Symbolic of the change was a move to a new facility designed to encourage as much face-to-face interaction as possible. Gone were the private offices, including Kolind's. Everyone was given a movable file cabinet that could be rolled to any work station, depending on one's current project. Job titles, departments, and functions were eliminated and replaced by an intricate, self-defining and self-coordinating network of project teams. This is another example of the extensive use of structural rearrangement. In no small way, it was assumed that behavior would change if the environment were transformed. In addition, everyone was expected to work on at least two projects of their own choosing. One would be in an area of their major expertise and the other in an area in which they had some interest or in which they could add value. For example, Kolind himself finished working on a training manual, and an employee whose primary competence was in administrative work decided that her language skills would add value to a sales project focused on the Spanish-speaking market. This is an example of combining expectancy and role modeling. The implication is that people are to be treated as though they have the potential to do more than just satisfy a narrow definition of their job. Role modeling comes into play through the examples that are set by individuals (in other words, Kolind and others) who are seen to be behaving in new and interesting ways.

Kolind likens the organizational structure to a bowl of spaghetti. However, this seemingly chaotic tangle is given coherence by a set of relationships or patterns based on three dimensions: the project management dimension, the professional dimension, and the people dimension. In the project management dimension, there are project leaders (former managers) and project owners (members of a ten-person management team—the last vestige of hierarchy in the company). Project owners are responsible for supporting the projects' success; project leaders are part of the day-to-day working teams. The professional dimension consists of professional specialists coordinated by project management. In the people dimension, everyone is responsible for their own career development, but every employee chooses a mentor from the management group. The mentoring role includes coordinating annual salary adjustments in conjunction with the employee's project leaders and peers, as well as making sure that the employee is happy and productive. This is another example of the use of structural rearrangement, coupled with role modeling and reinforced by some influence over extrinsic rewards.

To support this network of ever-changing projects, Oticon's structural transformation included a remarkable paradox. The organization is supported by one of the most advanced office automation systems in existence. Every morning all mail is scanned into the computer and then shredded. To ensure that all employees would develop the necessary level of computer literacy, Oticon supplied each person with a duplicate workstation at home, with the understanding that they would take responsibility for becoming proficient. Here the explicit use of expectancy comes into play. To address this challenge, the employees formed a personal computer club on their own time to train and support each other in the learning process, demonstrating the effectiveness of creating positive expectations. Every piece of information (with only a handful of exceptions)—including the company's strategic plan—is available to everyone.

The paradox, however, is that the important communications take place face to face. "Watercooler talk" is considered important. To ensure that people connect, every floor has a long coffee bar in the center with plenty of room for people to meet and talk. In fact, such meetings are encouraged. Dialogue rooms with comfortable chairs and a table are available throughout the building, and the elevator is not used, to encourage people to stop and talk on the stairs. People are so well connected at Oticon that electronic communications, such as postings for the more than one hundred projects that are going on at any given time are seldom used. Obviously, great use is being made of structural rearrangement to support participation.

This example also illustrates the point made in Chapter Eleven, on coercion, that structural rearrangement may contain elements of coercion (for example, shredding incoming documents). Even participation can become coercive, and there is a clear message implicit in the emphasis on and support for participative approaches: participation is not only encouraged, supported, and expected; it is also hard to imagine how one could not participate and yet succeed for very long. Again, this illustrates our point that all social and organizational systems are coercive in that they are designed to elicit a specified set of behaviors.

Projects at Oticon are developed as personal interests, and assessment of short-term and long-term business opportunities evolve. While there is a strategic plan and a budget, these are used as very flexible guidelines. In two years, this flexibility has produced a number of innovations that are completely new to the industry. For example, elimination of functional boundaries led to the realization that the company had invented the fully automatic hearing aid some years earlier but because of poor communication between R&D and marketing and some minor technical problems, no one had even noticed this (Kolind, 1994, p. 6).

Energy and creativity that were released in this setting led Oticon to expand its vision. From a focus on helping people with hearing deficiencies the firm has moved into new products and services and they are now focused on improving the hearing of normal people in a variety of public settings in which background noise can interfere with the ability to hear. In 1993, the company's sales grew by 23 percent in a declining market, it experienced a 35 percent increase in volume, and it increased profits by 25 percent. Through use of its multifunctional project teams, it cut time to market by 50 percent, and the proportion of revenues stemming from new products increased from 20 percent in 1991 to 50 percent in 1993 (Kolind, 1994, p. 9).

It is worthy of note that Kolind sees himself not as the captain of the ship but rather as an architect who designs the ship. He believes that it is far more important to create the conditions for responsible and creative performance than it is to try to control everything (LaBarre, 1994). This view supports our premise that the role of an advocate of change is not to come up with and implement a detailed change plan but rather to take the lead in developing a vision that will release energy in people. Kolind attributes the success of Oticon to countless hours of interaction in which consensus was developed about the fundamental values and strategic direction of the company. Once again, this is an example of an extraordinary emphasis on participation, this time in the service of Internalization.

A few comments about this case may be helpful. Many organizations might not be able to do the kinds of things that were done at Oticon. After all, Oticon is a modestly sized firm and not a mammoth multinational corporation. Also, the approach they took is congruent with the Danish culture. Yet the case can still serve as a model of what is possible. As we have pointed out, there is no one way to transform a company. For us, the issues are akin to the struggle faced by the quality movement: nothing can be swallowed whole, whether it be across cultures or organizations; but principles, ideas, and concepts can and have been reshaped, modified, and adapted to fit environments very different from the ones that initially spawned them. People in a transformed organization will hopefully be able to reach the point where instead of saying, "That won't work because . . . ," they will say, "How intriguing. I wonder if . . ." or "I wonder how . . ."

The Balfour Case

This case has a somewhat different focus. It is an example of the transformation that can occur as a result of the introduction of new technology. While it may not seem as dramatic as the Xerox and Oticon cases, it makes some important points about resocialization. The case is drawn from Vassallo and Hohlmaier (1988).

Attleboro, Massachusetts, the "hub of the jewelry industry," was where L. G. Balfour founded the company that was to become the largest manufacturer of recognition items in the world. (Recognition items include such things as school and class rings and plaques and trophies used for awards.) In Attleboro, Balfour found a large supply of skilled toolmakers and die cutters, the backbone of manufacturing as it was done in 1913. Historically, the training of such artisans would take four to six years. Working on the inverse image of the desired end product, an artisan might do such delicate work as putting fur on an animal for use by an international brotherhood or preparing a complicated design for a fraternity pin or class ring.

In the early 1970s, Balfour, like so many other firms, was faced with a decline in the skilled work force. Older artisans were retiring and younger individuals had become unwilling to spend the years necessary to learn the toolmaking and die-cutting trades. Questions facing Balfour and similar firms included:

- Could parts of both the design and machining process be automated in order to replace the human processes?

- Could tools be placed in the hands of neophyte artisans that would shorten their training period?

- What is the combination of work that can be automated and work that needs to be done by human hands?

- Could older workers be induced to accept training to apply automation that would amplify their skills?

Balfour decided to go ahead with the introduction of CAD-CAM as a means of addressing the above questions. The introduction of automation of this magnitude required significant changes in the way business was conducted. The process began with a visit by a vice president and an engineer to a site where a vendor had installed a system close to what Balfour required. With the help of the vendor's people, the engineer produced five tools and took them back to Balfour to show others what was possible. A decision was made to purchase a system and to install it at a location away from the major plant. A team was put together and moved to the new location for training in using CAD-CAM. A new system leader was chosen by management and told to take charge. People were given an opportunity to join this experimental venture and were told that they could also remain as artisans if they wished. However, they were told that this was the *only* chance they would have to make this decision. This is an example of the use of structural rearrangement akin to what is done with start-up operations. While the invitation to join the team suggests use of participation, the time limit to the invitation added a coercive element, especially since the option was presented by a high-ranking manager.

An initial period of three weeks passed with not one tool being produced at the new location. The management-chosen leader blamed this on the team and asked for a new team. Recognizing their previous mistake, senior management responded by replacing the team leader with the engineer who had first championed CAD-CAM. The first issue the engineer addressed was the restoration of the team members' faith in themselves as competent craftsmen. To erase any negative thoughts, threats, and accusations, the employees were told by the engineer that they had years of valuable experience and that he was confident they were the right team for the task. To further help the employees achieve some small successes, the engineer worked along with the team. He abolished time cards and work rules. He put forth a challenge to produce ten usable tools within six weeks of taking over. The team achieved this within three weeks, and was then challenged to produce two hundred tools a week within three weeks. This goal was also accomplished. Here, a combination of expectancy, role modeling, and significant structural rearrangement was used. Of additional interest is the fact that the engineer had gone through the initial training with the team even though he was not its manager—a clear example of role modeling the new behaviors.

As the team worked together and expanded, it changed its hours of work to provide a flexible schedule. Though the rewards system did not change—the team leader averred that he did not believe much in patting people on the back—he spent a great deal of time with team members and was observed praising them quite often. Thus, he continued to expect a lot from them, but he also maintained steady encouragement that they had the ability to achieve difficult goals. He also encouraged give-and-take discussions in which he was free to state his views and judgments, and team members could also confront him with their opinions and concerns. When the case writer asked to interview him about this project, he insisted on a joint interview of himself and the team members. In this case, although there was no change in the formal extrinsic reward systems, there was a significant increase in encouragement beyond what had been previously offered. The leader used expectancy and role modeling through continuous involvement with his people.

The results of this change were dramatic. In 1978, Balfour produced 14,000 tools with a work force of 136 people. In 1988, 35,000 tools were produced with a work force of 104, an increase of 150 percent with 25 percent fewer employees. Normal attrition was the only form of employment reduction. Absenteeism became almost nil. The automated group was later comingled with those who continued to use manual methods, and the artisans and the CAD-CAM people work side by side.

Several things are of interest in this case. Once the changes were under way, there seemed to be minimal use of coercion and extrinsic reward. The opportunity for the team to create its own culture, supported by the expectancy and role modeling approach of the leader, kept the group from being overwhelmed by the old way of doing things. Moreover, by allowing for both manual and automated operations, people were allowed to participate in the decision about how they wanted to work. This also eliminated the need to transfer the new system to all employees, which would undoubtedly have created resistance in the form of "not invented here" attitudes. In a sense, management acted in appreciation of the multiple realities in the company, rather than attacking one in favor of another.

The Motorola Case

This book has emphasized cases in which generally successful organizations experienced serious difficulties requiring a major change in the way they conducted business. The focus has been on how to influence organization members to make discontinuous changes. These changes are referred to as revolution, revitalization, or in our framework, transformation. In our definition, part of transformation involves internalizing the ability to continue to transform as the need arises, to adapt creatively as the changing discontinuous environment requires. This ability, often referred to as renewal, can involve large-scale, discontinuous, periodic, and opportunistic shifts in response to anticipated environmental or technological changes. In these instances, major current problems may exist, but the culture of the firm has internalized the understanding that transformational change is not a one-time issue, and that significant changes will continue to be a fact of life. Xerox, Semco, and Motorola all appear to have internalized this concept.

Motorola is a firm in which the concept of renewal has existed since the days of its founder, Paul Galvin. We have referred to Motorola several times in conjunction with the use of some of our methods, but we would like to present a more detailed picture of the firm as an example of how use of the multiple methods of influence has helped to produce organizational effectiveness over an extended period. Many observers believe that Motorola is a model worth studying. It was one of the first recipients of the Baldrige Award in 1988, and in 1994 it moved into fourth place, out of approximately four hundred firms, on *Fortune* magazine's list of America's most admired companies (Jacob, 1995).

There is an extensive literature describing Motorola, including works by its own leaders (for example, Feder, 1993; Galvin, 1991; Henkoff, 1993; Katzenbach and Smith, 1993; Morone, 1993; Petrakis, 1965; Schmidt and Finnigan, 1992; Wiggenhorn, 1990). We make no attempt to cover all of this material, but we present sufficient detail to indicate how a culture evolved that embodies expectations of ongoing change.

Motorola was founded in 1928 by Paul Galvin. Its first products were a line of batteries for the growing automobile industry. This was followed by police radios, household radios, and military field radios such as the famous walkie-talkie of World War II. To this line of products was added TV sets, which were later abandoned in favor of other products, such as pagers. Though not a major force in the industry, they then began to make computers. A major change was made when the company decided to manufacture semiconductors in Phoenix, Arizona. Currently, the firm is working on a system for worldwide wireless communication using satellites (the Iridium

System). As mentioned earlier, one observer of this progression has referred to Motorola as "the company that likes to obsolete itself" (Slutsker, 1993). Throughout this history, the firm was able to exit businesses and enter new ones with much less difficulty than most firms have encountered. This does not mean that these changes were easy to make; it mainly indicates a culture and a leadership group that could anticipate opportunities and readily conceive of giving up cherished products for new ones.

The capacity for self-renewal at Motorola is attributed largely to the impact of its founder, Galvin. Having failed in two business ventures before starting the company, Galvin was almost obsessed with concern that complacency would lead his new company to failure. It was he who first promulgated the concept of renewal as a basic requirement of a successful business, and he influenced others to think this way. Among those influenced was his son, Robert, who became CEO and who has been responsible for many of the changes in the last thirty years. The use of the concept of renewal continues to this day; the term is used often by today's Motorola managers. Indeed, a plaque with Galvin's original statement about renewal hangs prominently in the entrance lobby of the executive offices in Schaumburg, Illinois!

Obviously, the notion of renewal as a vision is not sufficient in itself to produce a successful company. One of the ways it has been translated into action at Motorola is in the enormous effort put into the achievement of technological excellence. Another way is the development of forceful operations managers with a strong bottom-line orientation. Expectations for performance are high in the company although Motorola's reputation stresses that it provides developmental experiences for its people (for example, every employee receives at least a week of education annually, and the company spends almost 5 percent of its revenues on education of all kinds). There is a no-nonsense attitude about making the numbers, and senior operations managers are not above using coercion from time to time. In addition, expectations are well ingrained that Motorola people can perform at high levels.

Motorola stands out in several ways. First, senior managers have learned the importance of the language they use in communicating with others. A good deal of attention is paid to how things are labeled, including how change efforts are named and what metaphors are used. In addition to "renewal," the term "Six Sigma" symbolizes the level of quality expected. The effective use of persuasive communication has become part of Motorola's culture.

The second Motorola distinction is the accessibility of its senior management, which has provided powerful role models with which people can identify. Role modeling is reflected even more strongly in the way managers responsible for change efforts develop and use a large number of role models early in their programs. We have noted this use in more detail in Chapter Eight, on role modeling. There is also a long history of attention to the use of extrinsic rewards, and the company was an early adopter of the Scanlon Plan in many of its plants. More recently, as Total Quality Management has become a way of life, programs using recognition awards for quality teams have become a regular feature, including a program in which three thousand quality teams develop improvement plans for which awards are granted at a large annual meeting of quality teams. The use of teams reflects a growing trend at the company to maximize teamwork, a clear indication that use of participation has become part of the organizational reality.

The main lesson to be learned from a study of Motorola is not that it is a paragon of virtue—there are several areas in which it could do better, such as integrating different parts of the company through use of a stronger system perspective, and perhaps being less product-oriented and more service-oriented. It might also do better in balancing its emphasis on engineering with development of a similar level of competence in the marketing area. The major lesson is that the company has been able to add to effective strategic thinking and an effective technological competence *continual attention to change*. While change does not take place at Motorola without significant difficulty and hard work, at least there is a broad understanding that the firm will engage in transformational change on a continuous basis. People have been socialized to expect change.

Implications

Mapping our cases according to the matrix shown in Table 12.1 revealed a number of key patterns in the use of the seven methods during the four phases of transformation. While there are clearly important differences between these case examples, some of the similarities are striking. Five cases are analyzed, the four discussed in this chapter and Semco, discussed earlier, particularly in Chapter Three.

Of particular note is the pairing of persuasive communication with coercion during the Traditional Phase. Each of the companies used persuasive communication as the prime means of informing the organization of the reasons why significant change was necessary; as a way to begin to create a common language and set of pictures and symbols to help delineate the general dimensions of the change; and to focus attention on the critical variables. To ensure that these messages received the attention they deserved, and to help break up the old mental models, the messages were almost uniformly delivered in ways that left no doubt in anyone's mind that participation in the unfolding of the changes was not optional. However, according to all the information we have been able to gather, this use of coercion was never heavy handed. Use of the other methods during this phase was minimal, possibly because the old approaches to change still prevailed. The single exception to this was Balfour, which kicked off its change with the use of structural rearrangement.

Both Semco and Xerox tried a number of less radical approaches before they recognized the need for transformation; Motorola seems

Table 12.1. Integrated Use of Methods in Five Cases of
Transformational Change.

Resocialization Strategy	Phases of Transformational Change			
Influence Method	Traditional	Exploratory	Generative	Internalization
Persuasive communication	M XX O B S	M XX OO B SS	M X O S	
Participation		MM XX OOO SS	MMM XX OOO B SSS	MM XX OO SS
Expectancy		M BB O S X	M O BB SS XX	M O S X
Role modeling		XX B OO SSS MM	XX OO BB SS MM	X O S M
Structural rearrangement	BB	MM XX OO B SS	MM XX OOO B SSS	MM XX O SS
Extrinsic rewards		X S O	M XX SS	S
Coercion	M X O B S			

Legend:

X = Xerox	1 letter = More than minimal use
O = Oticon	2 letters = Significant use
B = Balfour	3 letters = Heavy use
S = Semco	
M = Motorola	

to have spent less time in this early phase, perhaps because renewal has long been part of its organizational culture; and Oticon, based on available data, seems to have moved through this phase more rapidly than the other companies. This may be explained in part by the fact that Xerox and Semco recognized the need for transformation a number of years before Oticon, and because they were pioneers, fewer role models were available to them; hence, their longer start-up phases.

Each of the cases illustrate that as the companies moved into the Exploratory Phase, persuasive communication continued to play an important role, coercion was used less frequently, and participation, role modeling, structural rearrangement, and expectancy were all employed in significant ways. The use of extrinsic rewards played some part at Semco and Xerox, but there is little evidence that this method was used with any frequency during this phase in the other companies.

As the companies progressed into the Generative Phase, the need to persuade the employees of the need for change through the use of rational or emotional argument decreased significantly, while the use of participation and structural rearrangement reached even higher levels of use. During the Generative Phase, expectancy and role modeling continued to be important methods, and there was some increase in the use of extrinsic rewards, although use of this method seems to have been in the context of bringing the extrinsic reward systems into alignment with the new structures and processes.

By the time the companies reached the Internalization Phase, the need for persuasive communication had disappeared (although we hasten to point out that this in no way means that communication decreased. In fact, in almost all of the companies, free and open flows of information became a cornerstone of the organization's transformation). During internalization, participation and structural rearrangement continued to be important, in part because both these methods had become integral to the new ways of behaving.

Explicit use of expectancy and role modeling, however, decreased, as the new behaviors became standard operating procedure—an indication that the behaviors had been internalized and were therefore no longer new. Finally, only Semco seems to have continued to experiment with the use of extrinsic rewards as it broadened its use of "self-set" and "risk" salaries.

Most of the cases also make it clear that transformational change is both time consuming and painful. There were repeated instances of intense frustration at how difficult the process was, how painful it was to tear one's self away from the habits of a lifetime, and how wrenching it was to have to downsize, or to take action when it was clear that someone could not make the change. But on the whole, there was also a remarkable degree of faith on the part of the leaders that almost everyone could make it, given half a chance.

In almost all of the examples, progress unfolded over multiple years, and by the time the Internalization Phase had been reached, it was clear to most people in these organizations that they would never be "done." One organization articulated this as recognizing that there is no "there" there, and implicit in such an insight is the understanding that the future is in many ways unmappable. In fact, there is no evidence that anyone in any of the organizations we looked at had any idea at the outset how things would turn out. Rather, as we stated in our opening chapter, the future turned out to be a nonlinear combination of vision and emerging possibility.

A final comment concerning the leadership of the organizations we examined seems in order. Almost all of them went through some form of personal transformation, and in a variety of ways became, in the words of Oticon's Kolind, designers rather than captains. Whether we look at Kolind, Semler, Galvin or Kearns, we see men whose personal sense of mission and vision made them powerful guides to their organizations, but not at the expense of the organizations' being able to develop identities in which the whole reflects more than the sum of the parts. In the language of Peter Block (1993), they were able to become stewards and servants, without in any way abdicating the tough decisions. Their expectations of themselves were high, and their expectations of others were high, and they repeatedly and consistently acted in ways that transformed their expectations into reality.

Of course, only time will tell how things will continue to unfold, and we hope that as organizations move forward along this path, a great deal more will be learned about the process of transformation, both as means and as end. What we hope we have demonstrated thus far, however, is that if organizations want butterflies to emerge from the chrysalis, rather than caterpillars with wings strapped on their backs, they must continue to shift attention away from the strictly rational and tangible parts and pieces of the organization to include the observation and orchestration of the invisible—by which we mean the acknowledgment of the importance of addressing issues on the emotional as well as intellectual level, of making better and more purposive use of expectations, role models, and changing patterns of relationships, and of focusing on learning more about the ways in which complex sets of variables interact with and affect one another. As did the physicists in the quantum world of subatomic particles, we must learn to see what may be invisible to the naked eye but not to the inquiring mind and heart.

Finally, few things are more complex and difficult than the management of transformational change. We have offered a particular view of the subject and have proposed a model and strategy that we hope will stimulate the reader to explore new avenues of thought and practice. We also hope that we have been provocative enough to engage an ever-widening circle of people to add their intelligence and energy to the growing understanding of the problems and potential solutions involved in the complex undertaking that is organizational transformation.

References

Allison, G. *Essence of Decision*. Boston: Little, Brown, 1971.

Bartlett, C., and Ghoshal, S. "Beyond the M-Form: Toward a Managerial Theory of the Firm." *Strategic Management Journal*, 1993, *14*, 23–46.

Bass, B. *Leadership and Performance Beyond Expectations*. New York: Free Press, 1985.

Beckhard, R. "The Confrontation Meeting." *Harvard Business Review*, Apr.-May 1967.

Beckhard, R., and Pritchard, W. *Changing the Essence: The Art of Creating and Leading Fundamental Change in Organizations*. San Francisco: Jossey-Bass, 1992.

Beer, M., Eisenstat, R. A., and Spector, B. *The Critical Path to Corporate Renewal*. Boston: Harvard Business School Press, 1990.

Beer, M., Eisenstat, R. A., and Spector, B. "Why Change Programs Don't Produce Change." *Harvard Business Review*, Nov.-Dec. 1990, pp. 158–166.

Bennis, W., and Nanus, B. *Leaders: The Strategies for Taking Charge*. New York: HarperCollins, 1985.

Berger, P., and Luckman, T. *The Social Construction of Reality*. New York: Anchor Books, 1966.

Block, P. *Stewardship*. San Francisco: Berrett-Koehler, 1993.

Burns, J. M. *Leadership*. New York: HarperCollins, 1978.

Conger, J. A., and Kanungo, R. N. "The Empowerment Process: Integrating Theory and Practice." *Academy of Management Review*, 1988, *13* (3), 472–473.

Crystal, G. S., and Hurwich, M. R. "The Case for Divisional Long-Term Incentives." *California Management Review*, 1986, *29* (1), 60–74.

Dunphy, D., and Stace, D. A. "Transformational and Coercive Strategies for Planned Organizational Change: Beyond the OD Model." *Organization Studies,* 1988, 9 (3), 85–104.

Eden, D. *Pygmalion in Management: Productivity as a Self-Fulfilling Prophecy.* Lexington, Mass.: Lexington Books, 1990.

Feder, B. L. "At Motorola, Quality Is a Team Sport." *New York Times,* Jan. 21, 1993, pp. C1, C6.

Flax, S. "Can Chrysler Keep Rolling Along?" *Fortune,* Jan. 7, 1985, pp. 34–39.

Foy, N., and Gadon, H. "Worker Participation: Contrasts in Three Countries." *Harvard Business Review,* May-June 1976, pp. 71–83.

Fragos, S. J. *Team Zebra: How 1500 Partners Revitalized Eastman Kodak's Black and White Film-Making Flow.* Essex Junction, Vt.: Oliver Wight, 1993.

Galvin, R. W. *The Idea of Ideas.* Schaumburg, Ill.: Motorola University Press, 1991.

Hartley, R. F. *Management Mistakes and Successes.* New York: Wiley, 1991.

Harvey, J. "The Abilene Paradox: The Management of Agreement." *Organization Dynamics,* 1988, *17* (1), 16–43.

Henkoff, R. "Companies That Train Best." *Fortune,* Mar. 22, 1993, pp. 62–75.

Hennig, M., and Jardim, A. *The Managerial Woman.* New York: Simon & Schuster, 1977.

Jacob, R. "Corporate Reputations." *Fortune,* Mar. 6, 1995, pp. 54–64.

Jacobs, R. W. *An Open Letter to Managers.* Ann Arbor, Mich.: Dannemiller Tyson Associates, 1990.

Jacobs, R. W. *Real Time Strategic Change.* San Francisco: Berrett-Koehler, 1994.

Jacques, E. *A Requisite Organization.* Arlington, Va.: Cason Hall, 1989.

Janis, I. *Victims of Groupthink.* Boston: Houghton Mifflin, 1972.

Johnson, J. Interview. *Parade Magazine,* Aug. 30, 1993, p. 6.

Kanter, R. M. *Community and Commitment.* Cambridge, Mass.: Harvard University Press, 1972.

Katzenbach, J. R., and Smith, D. K. *The Wisdom of Teams.* Boston: Harvard Business School Press, 1993.

Kearns, D. T., and Nadler, D. A. *Prophets in the Dark: How Xerox Reinvented Itself and Beat Back the Japanese.* New York: Harper Business Books, 1992.

Kets de Vries, M. F. *Prisoners of Leadership.* New York: Wiley, 1989.

Kets de Vries, M. F. "Making a Giant Dance." *Across the Board,* 1994, *31* (9), 27–32.

Kets de Vries, M. F., and Miller, D. *The Neurotic Organization: Diagnosing and Changing Counterproductive Styles of Management.* San Francisco: Jossey-Bass, 1984.

Kidder, T. *The Soul of a New Machine*. New York: Avon, 1981.

Kilmann, R. H. "A Completely Integrated Program for Organizational Change." In A. J. Mohrman, Jr., and Associates, *Large-Scale Organizational Change*. San Francisco: Jossey-Bass, 1989.

Klein, D. "Some Notes on the Dynamics of Resistance to Change: The Defender Role." In W. Bennis and others, *The Planning of Change*. (3rd ed.), 1976.

Knowles, R. N., and Brown, R. H. "The Leverage Is Within Ourselves." Third Annual Association for Quality and Participation Symposium on Work Redesign, Jacksonville, Fla., Jan. 1992.

Kohn, A. *Punished by Rewards*. Boston: Houghton Mifflin, 1993.

Kolind, L. "Thinking the Unthinkable." *Focus on Change Management*, Apr. 1994, pp. 4–9.

Kotter, J. "Power, Dependence, and Effective Management." *Harvard Business Review*, July–Aug. 1979, pp. 125–136.

Kotter, J. "Leading Change: Why Transformation Efforts Fail." *Harvard Business Review*, Mar.-Apr. 1995, pp. 59–71.

Kotter, J., and Heskett, J. P. *Corporate Culture and Performance*. New York: Free Press, 1992.

Kozlowski, L. D. "Rethinking Rewards" (letter in Special Perspectives section). *Harvard Business Review*, Nov.-Dec. 1993, pp. 37–49.

Kuhn, T. *The Structure of Scientific Revolutions*. Chicago: University of Chicago Press, 1970.

LaBarre, P. "The Dis-organization of Oticon." *Industry Week*, July 18, 1994, pp. 23–28.

Lancourt, J. "Human Resource Leadership in Re-engineering the Organizational Culture and Infrastructure." *Compensation and Benefits Management*, 1994, *10* (4), 58–70.

Lancourt, J., McGowan, P., Stroh, P., and Holland, B. Unpublished report, Digital Equipment Corp., 1993.

LeShan, L. *Alternate Realities*. New York: Ballantine Books, 1976.

Levine, D. I. "Participation, Productivity, and the Firm's Environment." *California Management Review*, Summer 1990, pp. 86–100.

Levinson, H. "Problems That Worry Executives." In A. J. Marrow (ed.), *The Failure of Success*. New York: AMACOM, 1976.

Levinson, H., and Rosenthal, S. *CEO: Corporate Leadership in Action*. New York: Basic Books, 1984.

Lewin, K. *Field Theory in Social Science*. New York: HarperCollins, 1951.

Livingston, J. S. "Pygmalion in Management." *Harvard Business Review*, Sept.-Oct. 1988. (Originally published 1969)

McGregor, D. *The Human Side of Enterprise*. New York: McGraw-Hill, 1960.

Marmor, J. "Common Operational Factors in Diverse Approaches to Behavior Change." In A. Burton (ed.), *What Makes Behavior Change Possible*. New York: Brunner-Mazel, 1976.

Marrow, A. J., Bowers, X. X., and Seashore, S. *Management by Participation*. New York: HarperCollins, 1967.

Merton, R. *Social Theory and Social Structure*. (rev. ed.) New York: Free Press, 1957.

Morone, J. G. *Winning in High-Tech Markets*. Boston: Harvard Business School Press, 1993.

Nadler, D. A., Shaw, R. B., Walton, A. E., and Associates. *Discontinuous Change: Leading Organizational Transformation*. San Francisco: Jossey-Bass, 1995.

Nevis, E. C. *Organizational Consulting: A Gestalt Perspective*. Cleveland, Ohio: Gestalt Institute of Cleveland Press, 1987.

Nevis, E., DiBella, A., and Gould, J. M. *Organizations as Learning Systems*. Research Report No. 93–01. Lexington, Mass.: International Consortium of Executive Development Research, 1993.

Nevis, E., DiBella, A., and Gould, J. M. "Understanding Organizations as Learning Systems." *Sloan Management Review*, 1995, 36 (2).

Nicolas, J. M. "The Comparative Impact of Organization Development Interventions on Hard Criteria Measures." *Academy of Management Review*, 1982, 7 (4), 531–542.

Perloff, R. M. *The Dynamics of Persuasion*. Hillsdale, N.J.: Erlbaum, 1993.

Persico, J., and McLean, G. N. "The Evolving Merger of Socio-Technical Systems and Quality Improvement Theories." *Human Systems Management*, 1994, 13, 11–18.

Petrakis, H. M. *The Founder's Touch: The Life of Paul Galvin of Motorola*. Chicago: Motorola University Press/J. G. Ferguson Publishing, 1965.

Pffeifer, J. *Managing with Power*. Boston: Harvard Business School Press, 1992.

Porras, J. I., and others. "Modeling-Based Organizational Development: A Longitudinal Assessment." *Journal of Applied Behavioral Science*, 1982, 18, 433–446.

Ramquist, J. "Labor-Management Cooperation: The Scanlon Plan at Work." *Sloan Management Review*, Spring 1982, pp. 49–55.

Savage, C. "The Future of Human Resources: Does It Have a Future?" Paper presented at the Ernst & Young Center for Business Innovation, Boston, Nov. 1994.

Schein, E. H., "The Role of the Founder in Creating Organizational Culture." *Organizational Dynamics*, Summer 1983, pp. 13–28.

Schein, E. H., Schneier, I., and Barker, E. *Coercive Persuasion*. New York: Norton, 1961.

Schmidt, W. H., and Finnigan, J. P. *The Race Without a Finish Line: America's Quest for Total Quality*. San Francisco: Jossey-Bass, 1992.

Schutz, A. *Collective Papers I: The Problem of Social Reality*. (2nd ed.) The Hague: Nijhoff, 1967.

Semler, R. *Maverick*. New York: Warner Books, 1993.

Semler, R. "Why My Former Employees Still Work for Me." *Harvard Business Review*, Jan.-Feb. 1994, pp. 64–74.

Senge, P. *The Fifth Discipline*. New York: Doubleday, 1990.

Sheridan, J. N. "Aligning Structure with Strategy." *Industry Week*, May 15, 1989, pp. 15–23.

Shipper, F., and Manz, C. C. "Employee Self-Management Without Formally Designated Teams: An Alternative Road to Empowerment." *Organization Dynamics*, 1992, 20 (3), 48–61.

Sims, C. "AT&T Unit to Give Bonuses Despite Loss." *New York Times*, Mar. 9, 1987, p. 42.

Slutsker, G. "The Company That Likes to Obsolete Itself." *Forbes*, Sept. 13, 1993, pp. 139–144.

Smircich, L., and Morgan, G. "Leadership: The Management of Meaning." *Journal of Applied Behavioral Science*, 1982, 18 (3), 257–273.

Smith, S. J. *Blue Cross–Blue Shield of Ohio: A Profile in Change*. Boston: Ernst & Young Center for Business Innovation, 1994.

Strupp, H. "The Nature of the Therapeutic Influence and Its Basic Ingredients." In A. Burton (ed.), *What Makes Behavior Change Possible*. New York: Brunner-Mazel, 1976.

Talbott, S. P. "Peer Review Drives Compensation at Johnsonville." *Personnel Journal*, 1994, 73 (10), 126–132.

Troxel, J. P. (ed.). *Participation Works*. Alexandria, Va.: Miles River Press, 1993.

Tuecke, P. "Transforming a Defense Research Organization: Can It Happen Fast Enough to Survive?" In J. P. Troxel (ed.), *Participation Works*. Alexandria, Va.: Miles River Press, 1993.

"Unlikely Team Captures Chess Title." *New York Times*, May 10, 1983, p. 28.

Vassallo, H. G., and Hohlmaier, K. "The Successful Integration of Artisans and Automation: A Case Study." Paper presented at the Institute of Industrial Engineering Integrated Systems Conference, St. Louis, Mo., 1988.

Weick, K. *The Social Psychology of Organizing*. Reading, Mass.: Addison-Wesley, 1979.

Weick, K. "The Management of Eloquence." *Executive*, Summer 1980, pp. 18–21.

Weisbord, M. R. *Productive Workplaces: Organizing and Managing for Dignity, Meaning, and Community.* San Francisco: Jossey-Bass, 1987.

Weisbord, M. R., and others. *Discovering Common Ground.* San Francisco: Berrett-Koehler, 1992.

Wheatley, F. R. "The Eye of the Needle: Cultural and Personal Transformation in a Traditional Organization." *Human Relations,* 1990, 43 (3), 273–293.

Wheatley, M. J. *Leadership and the New Science.* San Francisco: Berrett-Koehler, 1992.

Wheatley, M. J. "Can the U.S. Army Become a Learning Organization?" *Journal for Quality and Participation,* Mar. 1994, p. 52.

Whiteside, T. "A Countervailing Force: Profile of Ralph Nader," Part 2. *New Yorker,* Oct. 15, 1973, pp. 53–54.

Wiggenhorn, W. "Motorola U.: When Training Becomes an Education." *Harvard Business Review,* July-Aug. 1990.

Zeleny, M., Cornet, R., and Stoner, J. "Moving from the Age of Specialization to the Era of Integration." *Human Systems Management,* 1990, 9, 153–171.

Index

Printed in the United States
144420LV00005B/13/A